W9-ABI-597

HESITANT FIRE

Hesitant Fire

◆

SELECTED PROSE

OF

Max Jacob

◆

TRANSLATED AND

EDITED BY

MOISHE BLACK AND

MARIA GREEN

◆

University of Nebraska Press

Lincoln & London

Copyright information on the French-language
versions of the pieces collected here may be found on
pages v–vi, which constitute an extension
of the copyright page.

Copyright © 1991 by the University of Nebraska Press
All rights reserved
Manufactured in the United States of America

The paper in this book meets the minimum
requirements of American National Standard for
Information Sciences – Permanence of Paper
for Printed Library Materials, ANSI z39.48-1984.

Library of Congress Cataloging in
Publication Data
Jacob, Max, 1876-1944.
Hesitant Fire: selected prose of
Max Jacob / translated and edited by
Moishe Black and Maria Green.
p. cm. – (French modernist library)
ISBN 0-8032-2574-1 (cl.)
1. Jacob, Max, 1876-1944 –
Translations into English.
I. Title. II. Series.
PQ2619.A17A225 1992
841'.912–dc20
91-17612 CIP

Grateful acknowledgment is made to Éditions Gallimard, Mme Sylvia Lorant, and M. Didier Gompel for permission to publish in translation the selections in this book from the following sources:

The Story of King Kabul the First and Gawain the Kitchen-Boy from *Histoire du roi Kaboul 1ᵉʳ et du marmiton Gauwain*, © Éditions Gallimard 1971.

"The Sailor's Homecoming" and "The Man Who Forced Girls" from *La Côte* (Paris: chez l'auteur, 1911), © Sylvia Lorant.

"The Twelve Species of Common Adultery" and "Advanced Degeneracy" from *Le Phanérogame*, © Éditions Gallimard 1918.

"The Revelation," "Visitation," "Vision," "Meanings," and "Exhortation" from *La Défense de Tartufe*, © Éditions Gallimard 1964.

The Artist Introduces Himself from *Présentation de l'auteur par lui-même*, © Sylvia Lorant.

"The Girl Who Found a Husband," "The Lawyer Who Meant to Have Two Wives Instead of One," "The Man Who Had Never Traveled First Class on the Train Before," and "The Unmarried Teacher at the High School in Cherbourg" from *Cinématoma*, © Éditions Gallimard 1929.

Don't Hang Up, Miss! from *Ne Coupez pas Mademoiselle, ou Les Erreurs des P.T.T.* (Paris: Galerie Simon, 1921), © Sylvia Lorant.

"Surprised and Delighted," "Cousin Joseph," "Another Night—'Understanding with Your Eyes Shut,'" "Daytime—'The Tale of the Handsome Arab,'" "Night to Remember, better known as Medical Walpurgisnacht," "Cockcrow," and "It's Still Only Daybreak" from *Le Roi de Béotie*, © Éditions Gallimard 1971.

"All Honor to the Sardana and the Tenora" from *Le Laboratoire central*, © Éditions Gallimard 1960.

"Another Letter Written While in Hospital," "Letter to Mrs. Goldencalf," "Letter from a Working Girl to Her Employer's Son," "They Sat in the Bar and Laughed Over It," and "Advice to a Young Doctor from an Established Practitioner" from *Le Cabinet noir*, © Éditions Gallimard 1928.

I said to him, "Suppose you had to describe that fire there, what would you say?"

The man thought deeply: "*Hesitant* fire!" It was exactly the word that fitted. I advised him always to write like that, to put down on paper only what had been deeply thought and felt.

MAX JACOB
letter to Marcel Béalu

CONTENTS

*The titles enclosed in brackets were supplied by the editors.

ACKNOWLEDGMENTS

In the preparation of this volume, Moishe Black has been chiefly responsible for the translations, Maria Green for the notes and introductions. They are indebted to

Gerry Black for suggesting improvements in style;

Didier Gompel for permission to consult rare editions of Jacob and to copy an unpublished manuscript;

Hélène Henry for elucidating certain obscure references in Jacob's text;

then dean Art Knight for support and advice in dealing with practical problems;

Kathleen Swann for typing the manuscript including revisions, and for manuscript layout;

Pascale Valyi for a clearer understanding of specific word groups in Jacob's French text;

the University of Saskatchewan for sabbatical leaves during which much of the work was done;

and Christine Van Rogger-Andreucci for a fuller grasp of Jacob's religious symbolism.

I have written elsewhere that "Max Jacob does not have just one style; he has dozens."[1] His great contribution to prose fiction is the way he gets totally inside one of his characters and, as he himself said, puts into the character's mouth "only words . . . which that particular mouth is bound to utter." Sex, social class, occupation, determine the "style" in which each personage expresses a reaction to events, or a desire for dignity and recognition. The personages are often narrators; when they are not, the nameless narrator is again a personage with a style. To choose the words that can reflect this diversity in another tongue, the translator must often draw on his own experience of people.

Further variations in style arise from Jacob's imitations of great authors whose works he knew well, imitations ranging from unconscious following in footsteps to deliberate pastiche: "Now, then, O Muse of La Bruyère," exclaims Miss Tripier, "inspire me." Here the translator's concern is to avoid aping La Bruyère, Pascal, and others, and to remember that what must be translated is Max Jacob —or one of his characters—aping La Bruyère, Pascal, and so on.

Jacob was a compulsive punster. Out of an irritating social habit he made wordplay into a fecund source of unexpected, often surreal visions of reality. One of his characters refers to an "untranslatable play on words," and indeed puns have always been the translator's nightmare: he must induce in himself a trancelike state from which, with luck, he will emerge an hour later clutching not a translation but an English equivalent.

The connotations of words change with time. "We hear an old expression from the previous generation," Jacob wrote, "and we become aware that words don't have the same meaning any more

1. M. Black, "Traduire en anglais la prose de Max Jacob . . ." (*Centre de Recherches Max Jacob*, Univ. de Saint-Etienne, 1985, p. 43).

and that today we wouldn't understand our grandfather or even our father." One can palliate this difficulty by consulting the dictionaries of one's father or even one's grandfather; by the same token the translator can give preference to French–English dictionaries published in Britain rather than in North America, since words often have pan-European meanings.

There remains the problem of being tempted to "help" the reader, by making a sentence clearer than the original, or by saying that the traveler with a Chaix in his pocket had a Chaix railway-timetable in his pocket. Sometimes the translator resists temptation, sometimes (deliberately) not.

My own attitude to these matters is twofold. First, once the meaning has been deciphered, translation ceases to be an intellectual exercise: the translator steeps himself in Max Jacob's text and then, as best he can, says the same thing in the other language. Second, again assuming the meaning has been correctly deciphered, a successful translator is one of whose presence the reader is unaware. The pieces in this book are by Max Jacob.

MOISHE BLACK

Introduction

Max Jacob (1876–1944) is best known for his poems, which prefigure Surrealist poetry. In recent years, however, there has been a renewal of interest in his considerable and varied prose writings; thus in 1982 the *Histoire littéraire de la France* stated (our transl.): "As for Max Jacob the novelist and storyteller, that part of his work still remains to be really rediscovered and given its rightful place, which will unquestionably be alongside the very best and most original writings of the period between the two world wars."

French readers can still find a number of Jacob's prose works in bookstores, but for those who read English there is almost nothing.[1] The present anthology offers a broad sampling, including satirical sketches in the classical tradition, pieces dramatizing the plight of the downtrodden, religious meditations, whimsical fantasies, letters of advice to an aspiring poet, and the "children's" story of King Kabul.

A few dates, place-names, and facts; then we can turn to the more absorbing topic of who Max Jacob was.

1876–94: Quimper

Quimper is the town in Brittany where Max Jacob was born into a freethinking middle-class Jewish family and where he went to school. Throughout his later life he returned regularly to his much-loved Quimper.

1. In Contrast, *The Dice Cup*, which is poetry, has been translated repeatedly in part or in full, most recently by Judith Morgenroth Schneider in Sidney Lévy's *The Play of the Text: Max Jacob's "Le Cornet à dés"* (Wisconsin Univ. Press, 1981).

1894–1921: Paris

Jacob made several false starts in Paris. He attended the Ecole Coloniale for overseas civil servants, but gave that up after two years. He completed a law degree but never practiced. He began his military service but was soon discharged as unsuited. Civil servants, lawyers, and army officers would people his prose fiction. He even made a false start in love, living several months with a certain "Cécile."

He decided to be a painter and as his family would not support him in this, he knew years of extreme poverty, holding low-paying jobs: Jacob was everything from department store clerk to nursemaid! His prose writing shines with an understanding of poverty, the poor, and the downtrodden.

He met Picasso; and then they both met the poet Guillaume Apollinaire. A three-way friendship was born which would last for decades, though there were to be jealousies and betrayals. In printed word and public utterance, the three were in the early years great promoters of one another's talents; together, they stand at the head of modern poetry and art in France.

Picasso for a time shared Max's bare but ample room on the boulevard Voltaire. Picasso later moved to the Bateau-Lavoir (the "floating washhouse," so dubbed because of the building's odd shape), which became a landmark as the haunt of new artists: Picasso, Juan Gris, Braque, and others; and new poets such as Jacob, Apollinaire, Pierre Mac Orlan.

One other acquaintance is singled out here: less prestigious, but stauncher and lifelong, would be the friendship bestowed on Max by poet André Salmon.

Jacob began to write, but for some years refused to publish, jealously guarding his poems in an old trunk, occasionally taking a few out and reading them to friends. He also had a brief career as an art critic.

A permanent fascination with hidden significances emerged. Max devised his own classification, based on astrology, of human beings into thirty-six categories; he accumulated files of details about real people who fitted each category, and drew on these to create fictional characters.

There were moments of relative affluence, as when art patron

Jacques Doucet bought the manuscripts of works by Jacob, or when Jacob's gouaches were suddenly in demand. But poverty was the norm.

The years in Paris included two pivotal moments for Max Jacob the man and the writer: his conversion to Christianity in 1909, following what he took to be the apparition of Christ on the wall of his room, and the publication in 1917 of *The Dice Cup*, a collection of prose poems prefiguring Surrealism and which remains his most famous work.

1921–28: Saint-Benoît-sur-Loire

Max withdrew to Saint-Benoît-sur-Loire, a town near Orleans, known for its basilica. "Withdrew," because Paris offered temptations he wanted to escape: worldly success as writer and painter, easy access to homosexual—hence in his own eyes sinful—loves. In Saint-Benoît he gave much time to his spiritual life, praying and meditating in the basilica, and living for some time in a cell of the abandoned monastery, where he could also write and paint.

The Paris he had left now came to him: he received visits from publisher Gaston Gallimard, writers André Malraux and Paul Claudel, and a host of other poets, artists, and theater people.

There were more signs of recognition, such as publication of his major novel *The Bouchaballe Property* (in 1923), or a commission to write the libretto for an operetta. And there was an immense disappointment: poets led by André Breton launched the "Surrealist" movement, and nowhere in their manifestoes did they mention Max Jacob.

1928–36: Paris again

Painting was now a greater source of income for Jacob than writing, and poetry took more of his creative time than prose. He continued, however, to write personal letters and religious meditations: volumes of both continued to be edited in the 1970s, 1980s, and 1990s.

There was further official recognition: special issues of the reviews *Le Mail* and the *Année poétique* were devoted to Max Jacob, and he even was made a member of the Legion of Honor.

1936–44: Saint-Benoît again

Max participated in Saint-Benoît parish life, and made new literary friends whom he tried to convert to active Catholicism. He corresponded with many people, and was invited to lecture in various French cities and abroad.

He wrote his *Advice to a Young Poet* (published posthumously, 1945), stating his ideas on poetry. Jacob was given a last honor when a special issue of the review *Aquedal* appeared with tributes by André Gide, Paul Claudel, Jean Cocteau, Gertrude Stein, and others.

World War II came. Not drafted, Jacob sent meditations and parcels to anonymous soldiers at the front; the fighting drew closer and he saw bombardments.

The Germans occupied Saint-Benoît, identified Max as a Jew, and made him wear the yellow star. Members of Max's family were arrested one by one in Quimper and Paris and deported. Finally in 1944 it was his turn, except that he never reached the death camps but died of bronchial pneumonia in a transit prison at Drancy near Paris. His friends had tried to save him: Jean Cocteau drafted a letter appealing to the German authorities, and they all signed it, except Picasso who refused.

In 1949 Jacob's remains were moved to Saint-Benoît, which has become something of a place of pilgrimage for the Association of Friends of Max Jacob.

Other details of his life emerge from the notes to passages of this anthology. There is a comprehensive biography in French by Pierre Andreu, *Vie et mort de Max Jacob* (Table Ronde, 1982), to which we are in part indebted here. In English, A. S. Huffington's biography of Picasso (Simon and Schuster, 1988) has innumerable detailed references to Jacob.

But who was he? What was he? He was a man of many selves, shifting constantly from one to the other. "Protean," wrote a critic; "kaleidoscopic," said a friend. With the many faces went many writing styles, changing "chameleon-like" (Max's phrase) to blend with character and circumstance. There appears to be no recurrent style one can call Jacobian. Indeed he did not wish to be always the same; he defined consistent personality as persistent error. What can be done here is to identify several of the selves—some may

seem contradictory; each is to some extent the real Max Jacob—
and to mention passages of this anthology that reflect each self.

Max Jacob was a poet

He lived for poetry. Disloyally left unmentioned when poets he
had helped establish and who imitated him burst upon the literary
world with what they called Surrealism, he is today regaining his
place, so that the Larousse Encyclopedia boldly places him alongside Apollinaire as "one of the masters of modernism in poetry,"
while a French National Library exhibition in 1990, displaying
handwritten originals of important French books down through
the centuries, included the manuscript of *The Dice Cup*. Our collection is prose-based, but poetry is present everywhere: in the de-
scription of his native town (see "Sunday in Guichen"), in the fever-
ridden images of "Medical Walpurgisnacht," in the Salvador Dali
flashes of "Vision" and "Exhortation" from *Defense of Tartufe*. Max
Jacob also claimed to have invented—we would more modestly say
reinvented—the French prose poem.

Max was a buffoon

At gatherings with his literary and artistic friends he danced on
tabletops, did imitations, played with words—like the Englishman
in "Cousin Joseph." His reputation for clowning retarded his literary reputation: he was the one who kept things stirred up, just part
of the scene, not to be taken seriously.

But foolery was a path to truth and understanding. The whimsy
of *Don't Hang Up, Miss!* produces a new and unexpected vision of
the world; the list in "The Twelve Species of Common Adultery" is
at first glance simply zany, at second reading a succinct, profound
analysis of marital infidelity.

Always with Max there is what Jean Rousselot calls the secret
smile; you are left unsure whether the author is simply describing
the Catalonian dance in "All Honor to the Sardana," mocking its
rusticity, mocking his own enjoyment of it, or . . . mocking you for
not being sure.

In the tradition of great comic writers, Max found his own
wellspring of human comedy: misguided earnestness. In farce,
stupidly earnest people are merely funny; in good comedy they

leave us close to tears because they try so hard, and they make us pensive when we realize the harm they can do. Such are Anna Bourdin of "They Sat in the Bar and Laughed," and Cousin Joseph.

Jacob was a Christian

His supreme religious experience, what he took to be a vision of Christ, is here in the five pieces from the *Defense of Tartufe;* his mystic side, and the endless hours spent trying to understand his faith more fully, are represented in the *Four Meditations;* his search for the way others have expressed their Christianity is evoked by the art works he singled out in *A Traveler's Notebook;* his linking of literary creation with religious suffering emerges from the first of the *Letters to Marcel Béalu.*

But he was a Jew

A Jew endlessly if humbly questioning authority in his search for justice here, now: Is it right for God to punish girls who have babies? ("The Girl Who Found a Husband") Do hospitals have to be inhumane? ("It's Still Only Daybreak"). A Jew with that self-deprecatory Jewish sense of humor (*The Artist Introduces Himself*); a Jew keenly interested in symbols and hidden meanings; finally a Jew to be killed for the crime of being a Jew (see the last few *Letters to Marcel Béalu*).

Max Jacob was a Breton

His love for his native Brittany is sly and pokes fun, as with "Sunday in Guichen"; spurious in its expression as with the literary hoax of *The Coast;* sentimental as with the many Breton landscapes he painted; linguistic as with "The Girl Who Found a Husband," but very real. Breton novelist Per Jakez Hélias describes Max Jacob's efforts to master Breton, a Celtic tongue; in fact what the poet mastered even more was the special way that Bretons speak French.

Max was a homosexual

No particular extract in this book represents that face of the writer because, like his contemporary Somerset Maugham, Max did not advertise his proclivity in writing. Yet some specialists will think they detect it precisely in the "many selves" listed here, or in the sympathy for the underprivileged women of "The Maid," "Letter from a Working-Girl," and "The Social Welfare Bureau," or again, in the failure ever to describe a happy couple or marriage ("Letter to Mrs. Goldencalf"), or in the author's ability to enter totally into a character and speak with the voice and viewpoint of that character, for example the down-and-outer of "Another Letter Written While in Hospital," the general practitioner of "Advice to a Young Doctor," and the insouciant young man of "Surprised and Delighted." This ability of the writer to be "many," which may have harmed his reputation in a world where literary greatness is associated with being outstandingly one thing, is—whether related to his homosexuality or not—Max's contribution to prose fiction.

Jacob was an artist, and a recognized one
His specialties were watercolors, gouaches, and line drawings. He would sell pieces of his art, or books in which he had done drawings, to support himself. He dreamed of having a studio and heaps of friends. "I never got the studio but I did have heaps of friends," he wrote, reminding us of Cousin Joseph.

The Artist Introduces Himself is a thumbnail sketch by Jacob of his own artistic career, and the *Letters to Marcel Béalu* contain references to art work in progress.

Jacob was also the friend of major painters: Picasso, Derain, Modigliani, Braque, Juan Gris. He was the subject of art: there are portraits of him by Picasso, Cocteau, Modigliani, Louis Marcoussis, C. Van Dongen (caricature), Marie Laurencin, Man Ray (photo), Chagall (caricature). And early editions of Jacob's books were illustrated by Derain, Juan Gris, and especially Picasso.

He was a renegade bourgeois
He hated the values of the social class from which he sprang, its hypocrisy, its pretensions, above all its steely hard, vicious, servant-abusing matrons ("Letter to Mrs. Goldencalf").

Jacob was a friend and critic
Writers past counting—Malraux, Louis Aragon, René Guy Cadou, Michel Manoll, Béalu—took him or sent him their work. "I bring luck to all my friends," he would say when it was noticed that an astonishing number of his young protégés were achieving success. Or, less modestly: "I'm a born teacher."

He gave of his time: biographer Pierre Andreu recalls himself and other writers sending up poems with one of their group, while the rest waited outside fearfully. In the event, they spent the whole day with Jacob.

To those in need he gave the bit of cash that he had.

Especially he gave encouragement, advice, and firm criticism. When the criticism took written form, it produced Jacobian writing at its most impressive, with basic ideas on distancing in art, on suffering and the creative process, and on being one's own distinct self as a poet. The counsel and theories are represented here in the *Letters to Marcel Béalu*.

Finally, Max Jacob was a writer of prose

Prose was the touchstone. To write good poetry, he told would-be poets, first learn to write prose. A longer prose work must be "meditated and premeditated." The words uttered by fictional characters should be chosen with care, for "the most revealing thing about a person is his vocabulary." He also said: "I attach very great importance to style, I always try to make mine clear and human." And after twelve hours at his writing table, lunch forgotten, "I go to bed like a satisfied workman" (from *Comment ils écrivent,* in which several authors describe their work methods [Aubier-Montaigne, 1932]).

All these aspects of the writer's craft, and the ability to breathe life into them, are already present in Jacob's first published work, *The Story of King Kabul,* which opens this anthology. The plot with its two countries and two groups of characters is complex but crystal clear. There are no loose ends: watertowers, innocuously planted as a landmark at the start, are there when needed for the action at the end. Chapters are kept rigorously short so the tale moves swiftly. And there is a king who swears like a king upon his royal word, while a kitchen-lad, remaining a kitchen-lad in the presence of his lord, nervously mangles his chef's hat.

This self of Max Jacob, that of the gifted artisan in prose, synthesizing and serving as a vehicle for all the other selves, is what the present volume hopes to offer.

HESITANT FIRE

The Story
of King Kabul the First and
Gawain the Kitchen-Boy

For my dear little cousin, Thérèse Gompel

[In 1903, Max Jacob had developed sufficient confidence in himself to at-tempt to earn a living by pen and paint. *Accordingly he made arrangements with a baker to have bread delivered daily; and in six weeks, working in an unheated room, wearing all his clothes including all his socks, he completed his first story,* Histoire du roi Kaboul 1 er et du marmiton Gauwain, *originally published in 1904.*

On the face of it, the story is for children, but unlike cautionary tales such as Wilhelm Busch's Struwel Peter, *which attempt to frighten children into conformity, Kabul, like the Ugly Duckling, is based on the view that adult appraisals of worth can be wrong. Jacob, however, goes far beyond ques-tioning the justice of a particular appraisal. He questions the whole set of bourgeois values on which appraisals of merit and choice of goals are based.*

Gawain, his hero, who is a "Balibridgian Napoleon," a composite of both Louis Napoleon and Napoleon Bonaparte, is not satisfied with a world in which hard work is rewarded once a year at a sumptuous banquet, but wishes rather to marry into the class that can offer such banquets. In other words he is a typical fairy-tale hero who wants to marry a princess, but those he lives among are typical bourgeois: they explain to the lad that for class reasons it is quite impossible for him even to meet a princess and King Kabul himself explains that not even heroic deeds or king's promises can change matters—for heroic deeds one gets money, not princesses. Gawain, however, by dint of hard work and some Machiavellian maneuvering, does manage to gain the hand of the princess, who, it seems, prefers a hard-working bourgeois to idle princes. The story ends with the abdication of the happy pair and the institution of a bourgeois democracy.

Such a plot makes a strong appeal to those who are utterly prosaic, the kind of people who think Cinderella is unsuitably romantic for someone who wants to make his or her way in the world, for it is as close as anyone has ever come to creating the diametric opposite of the Cinderella plot. Indeed it is not very surprising that Jacob had little difficulty selling the story to a publisher who wanted to promote it as a book-prize for industrious pupils in the strictly secular schools and it is no surprise at all that the publisher felt that eliminating all references to the Church was in keeping with this object.

Jacob could have effected the required changes without drawing attention to the fact that there were changes, but he has made them so obvious that one cannot help feeling they are part of an overall satiric purpose. The setting is surely not a fairyland when people seek sanctuary at City Hall and ring schoolbells as tocsins; rather, this is a satiric presentation of bourgeois reality. Jacob would seem to have fallen in readily with the publisher's demands, not for the sake of the miserable sum he was paid—just enough to pay his baker, buy a new lamp, and purchase one meal of the kind described in the story—but because it fitted his purpose so well. Jacob's Kabul, *like Lewis Carroll's* Alice in Wonderland, *is really aimed at those who will read the story to children rather than the children themselves; it questions the standards of these grown-up readers by representing them as part of a social order that only a very naïve child could accept. For this reason* Kabul *deserves greater critical attention than it has hitherto received.*]

◆

Chapter One
The Official Banquet for the Best Pupils

In the land of the Balibridgians lived a king named Kabul the First, who, every year on his birthday, held a banquet for needy children. It was a habit he had got into. The head cook from the royal kitchens would make his way into the playground of the primary school a month ahead of time, paper and pencil in hand, and have a talk with the teacher.

"I have come to ask you," he would say, "for the names of the best pupils in the class; the ones who have earned the most merit points will be invited to dine with the King." [1]

The teacher would say: "Well, there's that child over there and that one and that one." No more than thirty were ever chosen. At four o'clock on the day of the banquet, five golden carriages waited for the top pupils and took them to the palace.

The palace is still there today and there is no finer one in all the world. It is on a hill outside the town, at the place where the big tanks stand with their supply of pure water for the townsfolk. The chambers of the palace are so high that plants as tall as houses can be kept in them, and so broad that they contain groves of trees, and columns too and aquariums full of golden fish, and fountains; the gardens are so big that a great many terraces have been built into them, with palm-trees and orange-trees growing out from the marble paving, amid carpets, paintings, and ornamental ponds.

At the banquet given by the King, there was a servant to stand behind each of the children and present the various courses. These consisted mainly of desserts: puff pastries with almonds, vanilla, and cream; flowers rolled in sugar; a choice of cherry-juice, raspberry, maraschino, or tutti-frutti sherbet; crumbled Peruvian chestnuts; candied, glazed, and fresh tropical fruit served in meringues or flavored extracts, in liqueur sauces or rum syrup, or else in transparent pastry-shells that had been painted, decorated, and shaped so they would delight the eye while they pleased the palate

The children from the primary school had never eaten anything half so good.

◆

Chapter Two
Pupil Francis Gawain Has Big Ideas

On a certain evening, after one of these banquets, a little boy named Francis Gawain came home from the King's palace, and he was very sad.

1. This is ironic as the *Story of King Kabul* itself was used as a school book-prize. All the existing copies having been distributed, the book was unavailable until 1951 when Madeleine Follain, wife of the poet Jean Follain, found a copy she had won as a child. The Association of Friends of Max Jacob republished it that year.

"Why are you sad, Francis?" asked his father, who was a black-smith. "What's troubling you?"

"Nothing, Father."

"Oh, now, Francis, you've got something on your mind and you aren't telling me what it is."

His mother too wanted to know why he was sad, and when he was in bed she came as usual to tuck in his blanket. Then, as she kissed him goodnight, she asked him why he was sad. Francis put his arm around his mother's neck and whispered:

"Mother, I would like to become a page-boy in the King's palace!"

"But child, to be a page-boy you have to have rich parents and we are just a poor family of blacksmiths."

"I would like to be a page-boy in the King's palace, Mother."

"Child, you're half asleep! Tomorrow you'll have forgotten all about it."

"Mother, suppose I went as a servant? Couldn't I be a servant in the King's palace?"

"You a servant, child! A blacksmith's son! No, Francis, you will not go and work in someone else's home."

"I would like very much to be a cook."

Gawain Senior, who was reading in the kitchen while he finished his glass of wine, came into the bedroom with his newspaper still in his hand.

"Why not?" he said. "Every trade is as good as the next! A man can never dishonor himself by working! It just so happens that I know a coachman who drives the royal horses. If you like, he can get you in to see the chief cook; it's easily done. But you have to start off as a kitchen-boy and, believe me, it's hard work!"

"Did you hear that, Mother? Did you hear what Dad said?"

"Child, child, it hurts me to hear you talk this way."

The next day, Francis was taken on as a kitchen-boy, thanks to the coachman who drove the royal horses and was a friend of Mr. Gawain. He was taken to the room where the servants' clothing was kept and there they tried hats and jackets on him for size.

The chief cook said to him:

"You'll sleep in the dormitory with the others and, mind you, no quarreling! No pillow-fights! We don't like that sort of thing! We get up at five and you're to help me make the King's break-fast! Then I chair the meeting of the Grand Menu Council. Menus are made up for the two meals of the day—the royal snack, and supper—and you're the one who takes them to the King, and he stamps them himself with his royal stamp: 'Read and approved.' But the other kitchen-lads will explain it all. Now, to work with you, young Sir."

◆

Chapter Three
The Ambition of Gawain the Kitchen-Boy

When the courtiers, chamberlains, officials, magistrates, page-boys, and guests left the ceremonial dining-hall to go and have coffee out in the garden, it was the servants' turn to eat, and as they ate they would chat about everything that was being said or done in the palace. Francis listened, and listening, he learned. He learned, for instance, that the King had three daughters, and that having seen her two older sisters married to princes who were rich but also idle and extravagant, the third daughter had sworn that she would marry none but a young man with job training, lots of drive, and great ability, so disgusted with idlers had she become from observing her brothers-in-law. Finally one day Francis said:

"I would like to marry the King's daughter, the young one!"

Naturally, everyone around the table burst out laughing; they all thought he was joking, for a kitchen-boy does not marry a princess—it just isn't done.

The chief cook laughed first and all the others followed his example. He laughed so hard that his wine went down the wrong way and he coughed for twelve minutes; a servant-girl dropped the leg of guinea-fowl she was gnawing at so she could enjoy her laugh without choking; one kitchen-boy swallowed a salmon bone, and another, who just at that moment was trying to fish foie gras out of a meat pasty the size of a barrel, fell headfirst through the outer crust. They hauled him up out of the pasty, all covered with the chopped meat and jellied gravy.

Francis was pink with embarrassment because people were looking at him. All around the table people were wiping their mouths and starting to eat again. Gawain, meanwhile, was thinking:

"I shall marry the King's daughter!"

◆

Chapter Four
Dialogue between a Food-Loving King and
an Inventive Kitchen-Boy, in Which
the Interests of the Kingdom Are Placed
before the Claims of the Heart

From that day on, Gawain worked and worked. So much and so hard did he work, so hard and so much, that he came to know all the recipes by heart, and even invented several others, so that he became the world's best cook.

Now, it happened that one fine Thursday the Supreme Head Cook of the Royal Kitchens had to go off to his sister's wedding. He came to leave his instructions with his second-in-command. To the kitchen-boys he said:

"Most important of all, no one is to tamper with the dessert; it is to simmer over a slow flame until the time comes to serve it, and only then will it be brought to the King, hot in its juice."

It was an almond plum-pudding!

Francis, who was sixteen years old and had been spending all his evenings studying the chemistry and botany of food, had combined aniseed, sugar, orange, piquant flavorings, and wild Hungarian thyme to produce a white powder which would impart a delicious taste to dessert dishes. Now he was anxious to see how well it worked.

That Thursday he was on duty in the kitchen and all the other kitchen-lads were outside playing ball, so he went over to the pot that held the royal desserts, lifted the lid and dropped in his flavoring powder.

That evening, the King said:

"Let the Master of the King's Meals be sent for! I want to know who made this almond plum-pudding. I have never eaten anything like it. Astonishing, upon my word as a king, quite astonishing!"

The Master of the King's Meals appeared, bowed to the right, bowed to the left, kissed the King's shoe and said:

"It must have been the Supreme Head Cook of the Royal Kitchens." But near the table was a very respectable elderly person, the

8

nurse to the Princesses Royal, and she interrupted the Master of the King's Meals:

"Have I permission to speak, O King? I have something to say."

"Speak, Nurse."

"The Supreme Head Cook is at his sister's wedding."

"Then who cooked this pudding?"

"It must have been the Supreme Assistant Head Cook."

The Supreme Assistant Head Cook appeared and boasted that he, indeed, was the one who had made the pudding.

"Very well," said the King, "then give me the recipe."

The second-in-command was not taken aback. He recited the usual recipe for puddings of that sort.

"You are deceiving me, you wretch! This plum-pudding smells of aniseed, piquant flavorings, and wild Hungarian thyme."

"Your Majesty has a sensitive nose."

"Take heed lest you get yours cut off for having tried to deceive your king. I order an immediate inquiry."

And so it was discovered that Gawain had put his seasoning powder into the pudding.

Francis was received in the great hall and congratulated, and one of the guests tried to hire Francis to be his personal chef.

"I shall never leave my king," said the kitchen-boy.

"Well said." Thus spoke the King. "What reward do you want?"

"A favorable hearing, Sire."

The courtiers thought to themselves: "There speaks a shrewd lad!" The King persisted:

"You are the one who did it, my young friend! And so I must reward you!"

"Your Majesty is most gracious."

"H'm. We must be fair, and you have done a good job. Well, now, what can I do for you? Speak up! What do you want?"

"Your Majesty holds the lives of his subjects in his hands; we owe our existence to Your Majesty and if we are useful to you, we are merely doing our duty."

"You speak not too badly for a kitchen-lad. You have afforded my palate one of the most satisfying moments a man can hope to have—"

"Oh, Sire!"

"—and I want to reward you . . ."

"Sire, you will never agree to satisfy my ambitions, so high do I aspire . . ."

"Well, let me see . . . let's see . . . we'll see about that!"

"Sire, let not your wrath fall upon me!"

"Have no fear, my boy. I am curious to know what desires may be hatching in that young mind of yours."

"It concerns the most beautiful girl in your entire kingdom, Sire: I should like to take her in marriage."

"And may we be told the name of the happy bride?"

"Her name is Julia!"

"The same name as that of my youngest daughter."

The kitchen-boy blushed.

"Can it be that you have dared to cast your eyes upon the Royal Princess?"

The kitchen-boy's gaze was fixed upon the white chef's hat he held in his hands.

"I find you extraordinarily audacious, my low-born fellow. . . . All the same, it's a surprising quality to find in a person of your order and not, when you stop to think of it, an entirely displeasing one. Well, now! Since it appears, young Master Turnspit, that you are not a fool, you must surely understand that a king is not free to give his daughter to the first man who comes along. He has the nation to consider, and his sons-in-law, and all that sort of thing."

"I do understand, Sire!"

"That's fortunate."

"No doubt I must strive to deserve Julia through some heroic deed?"

"Oh, my, my! See how he talks of shooting for the moon! Come now, there's a good lad; by all means go and accomplish your heroic deed, and we'll see what it amounts to. But meanwhile, the chief cashier will drop by to see you down there in your kitchens."

Intimidated, the kitchen-boy backed out of the hall, bowing and turning his white hat round and round in his hands.

◆

Chapter Five
In Which It Will Be Seen That a Kitchen-Boy
May Be a Great Warrior

Two years went by.

One evening when the King had received some magnificent caribou from a prince in Canada as a birthday present, Francis was walking up and down in the yard behind the buildings that housed the servants, trying to think how best to find suitable shelter for the royal gift. He was smoking a cigarette and taking the air: a refreshing thing to do, when you've been around ovens all day.

The caribou is an animal with flesh like a chicken's; it can be made into white meat dishes, which you cook in ass's milk.

Francis was musing: it was dark out; not a window was showing a light, except for the dormer windows where the kitchen-lads slept, on the eighth floor.

"That's odd," said Gawain, "I hear a noise somewhere nearby. It's a sort of clanking sound coming from under the ground! And yet at this hour no one is in the cellar. The wine stewards have left; could it be thieves?"

In the land of the Balibridgians, as in several other countries, air is supplied to cellar rooms by way of openings located at the top of basement walls, at ground level, and in some countries these openings are called ventilators and in others, basement windows. There were three such in the yard where Francis was.

Francis peered into one of the ventilators. The moon appeared and lit up the outside wall. Francis recoiled in horror: in the cellar he had seen—men!

"It's our enemies! They're back! The Bouloulabassians are back! They must have dug an underground tunnel, as they did once before."

Francis ran to the guard-room, but no one answered his calls: all the guards had been poisoned by a traitor disguised as a vendor of licorice-water. What was he to do? The King and his retinue were in the city at a theater, and the servants do not stay long in a palace when no one is there to give them orders. And yet the kingdom had

11

to be saved. Francis remembered that his fellow kitchen-boys were near at hand, and a moment later was knocking at the door of the room where they slept.

"Inez! Leon! Arthur! Merdwig! The enemy! The enemy! The enemy is inside the castle!"

The kitchen-boys were playing lotto under the lamplight.

"Who is it?"

"The enemy!"

"Don't hammer on the door like that! We're coming, Francis! Where are they?"

"In the cellar! Here's what we've got to do! Each of us will go to the stable and get some straw and wet it under the pump, and then we'll set fire to it and plug up the ventilators. Wet straw gives off thick smoke when it burns!"

◆

Chapter Six
Disaster Strikes the Bouloulabassians

Muffled blows could be heard coming from below the ground. The Bouloulabassians had five doors to shatter before they could come up to the ground floor; they had broken through only one of them when the smoke started coming in by way of the stopped-up ventilators.

"We're doomed!" they cried out in Bouloulabassian.

If the cellars had not had such high ceilings, they might have been able to clear the air-vents, but all they could do was shoot arrows up at the vents, and the arrows simply stuck in the straw and did no good. The smoke was black, the torches were no longer giving any light, and when the Bouloulabassians tried to get back to the passageway by which they had come, they kept bumping into the walls. Their feet became entangled in the iron racks that held the bottles of wine, and the noise of glass shattering mingled with the wretched moans of the wounded. Those who could manage to keep on walking trampled underfoot the bodies of those who could not.

Meanwhile, the kitchen-boys were shouting to attract attention. Countryfolk and passersby came hurrying; lackeys who had been asleep under the eaves of the palace were now arriving, rubbing their eyes to wake up; the barracks had been alerted; the princes were returning from the theater with their link-boys lighting the way; drums were heard along the road that leads to the castle; and from the grand outer staircase the trumpet was summoning everyone to arms. The schoolbell sounded the alarm and the whole population of the city poured out into the streets and hastened to the King's palace.

Merchants in fur-lined caps, happy to have an excuse for entering the King's palace, countrywomen in hastily donned dressing-gowns, rich young men, ladies still dressed for dancing, workmen, vagabonds, officials, constables, policemen, all were waving their hands, giving advice and orders, and when it was learned that the Bouloulabassians were locked up in the cellars and dying, all these folk vied with one another to be the first to throw a stone, fling a handful of mud, or shoot an arrow at them. The chief of police had to organize his men to keep the situation under control.

◆

Chapter Seven
Second Dialogue between a Valiant Kitchen-Boy and a Sarcastic King, in Which the Claims of the Heart Give Way to the Interests of the State

Later fireworks were set off and an outdoor dance was organized. The King appeared at the window, hastily donning his ermine cloak. The whole castle was lit up inside and a buffet set up for those of the guests who thought it advisable, after all that excitement, to calm their nerves by filling their stomachs.

Gawain was found and borne in triumph to the King, who kissed him with his very own lips, calling him:

"The young savior of my kingdom!"

And on the morrow, all day long, as visits of congratulation followed one upon another in the state reception hall, Gawain was kissed again at least sixty-three times by counts and countesses, barons and viscountesses, and by superiors of convents.

At last, when every bow had been made and every hand

squeezed, kissed, or shaken, the whole assembled company departed and Francis came and knelt before the King's slipper which was of pink felt embroidered with green chenille (a ceremonial slipper), and clasping it in his arms he said:

"I beg you to hear me speak, Sire."

"Speak, child, and I shall hear you favorably."

"Oh Sire, I beg you to remember the almond plum-pudding."

"Harrumph," said the King, taking a pinch of snuff.

"Does Your Majesty recall that after tasting the pudding you asked me certain questions? . . . You did me the signal honor of questioning me about my future plans."

"Well, and what of that, child?"

"You allowed me to hope that some day, when a heroic deed had brought your humble servant forth from the shadow of the kitchens, I might take my place among the suitors who are contending with one another for the rank of son-in-law to the greatest of kings!"

"But surely you jest, child. Ask me for something sensible; don't ask the impossible. The son of a blacksmith does not wed the daughter of a king!"

"You promised, Sire!"

"You lie, scamp! I make no promise that I cannot keep. Besides, just go ahead and ask her! Go and ask her for her hand! Go ahead and see what sort of reception you get! Go ahead; I'll sign a pass for you, otherwise her Nubian guards and serving-women would never let a churl of your sort through to my Julia's apartments. It just goes to show you, coddle these rascals the least little bit and it goes straight to their heads . . . this one's gone stark raving mad, upon my royal word! I'll send him to see a good alienist. Here is your pass, young rascal, and let me see no more of you! These little savages are all the same; let them kiss the tip of your finger and they think it would be nice to swallow your whole arm. But just you wait a bit, my fine fellow! . . ."

◆

Chapter Eight
The Kitchen-Boy and the Princess;
or, Valor Rewarded

Gawain walked up fifty steps of white marble between two walls of green marble. Princess Julia's servants, who were all from distant lands of Africa or Asia, bowed when he appeared, because he showed them the King's signature: *Kabul the First, King of the Balibridgians, Emperor of the Green Isles.*

A Nubian woman led him past flowering plants into a chamber hung with silver lamé chiffon, where, upon a bed that looked like a cloud in the sky just before the setting of the sun, slept one more beauteous even than that heavenly body, the daughter of Kabul the First.

Wherever you looked, curtains were held open by azaleas, daisies, and daffodils; wherever you gazed, furniture seemed to rise out of the flowers; wherever you cast your eyes, delicate mists wafted upward from incense-burners: it was like being in the Seventh Heaven. Gawain went down on one knee, so much did he marvel at his surroundings.

"Rise, Gawain," said a gentle voice. "That is no posture for a hero!"

"Alas," said he, "Daughter of Kings, would I were indeed a hero and so deserved your hand!"

"Take it, Gawain," said Julia, "and be a prince. Indeed who better than the conqueror of the Bouloulabassians will know how to keep my kingdom safe; who better than you will succeed in enlarging that kingdom? I can read courage in your eyes and I can read kindness in them as well. You will be feared by your enemies and loved by the people. Rise, Gawain, and help me to rise also."

Julia leaped out of bed; she was wearing a tulle skirt embroidered with garlands of roses; her tiny feet were like the feet of a doll; a hidden orchestra was playing ancient melodies. Gawain gallantly took the hand of his betrothed, as though to lead her onto the ballroom floor.

15

◆

Chapter Nine
The Tarpeian Rock Is near the Capitol

Past statues which seemed to be asleep, through gardens filled with silence and shade, he led her to King Kabul the First.

"To prison! To prison with you, unnatural daughter, who would choose your husband against a father's wishes! To prison, heartless girl! You ingrate! You wretched worm, you owe me your very existence, but you never think of that except when you want to take unfair advantage of my tender love! To prison with you, I say! Brainless puppet! O woman unfit to live, away with you to prison!"

"Father, Father, hear us! I cast myself at your feet!"

"To prison! Off—to—*prison!*"[2]

For the first time in all her life, Julia felt tears flowing down her cheeks.

"I shall never have any other husband than Gawain, Father!"

"May your poor mother not hear your horrible words as she lies there in her grave!"

"Would that she were at your side to beg you to have mercy upon me!"

"Guard, seize my daughter and take her to the palace prison! Here's a little note for the warden! As for you, you scoundrel, go back to your kitchen, and if you dare to come out I shall test the cutting edge of my saber on your neck!"

So spake the King, but as he was making his way to his private apartments a hand reached out and stopped him.

"Stay, Sire! That saber, which you think to try out upon my throat, may one day serve *my* purpose."

"What's that he says?"

"I say that I will avenge myself for this affront."

"Does the kitchen-boy forget that he is in the presence of his King?"

"Sire, I am leaving this kingdom, but not for good. I shall come

2. Jacob loved to imitate the platitudes of authority figures, mostly bourgeois and bureaucrats, by chopping up their words. According to his friends, he indulged with Shakespearean gusto in mimicking such personages to entertain his guests.

back here as a conqueror; then your throne will be my throne, and this palace, if such be my pleasure, will be destroyed so utterly that no trace of it remains!"

At these words, and without the King having given any sign, five soldiers marched over to Gawain and seized him.

"That's right," said the fat King, "let him go and cool off in a dungeon cell. It will do him good."

◆

Chapter Ten
There Is No Dungeon Cell
Whose Doors Do Not Open

The cell was in a dank tower, where, around a pool of water, scorpions, spiders, frogs, white worms, rats, mice, and bats scuttled to and fro. It was always dark there, and the straw that served the prisoners as a bed had not been changed for a hundred years, so that it was crumbling and rotted. The prisoners ate stale crusts and listened to the dismal creaking of a pulley lifting water from a well for them to drink.

Gawain, who was still very young for so much suffering, cried a great deal; he cried so much that he fainted.

When he opened his eyes daylight was coming in through the door and a tulle skirt embroidered with garlands of roses met his wondering gaze, as when we see the moon in the fullness of the night.

"Gawain," said a voice, "I am Julia, the princess; get up and be gone!"

"O My Benefactress, I shall find a way to show you my gratitude."

"Here, take this box of chocolate, my dearest; you must be hungry, for surely you haven't touched those mud-soaked crusts!"

It was three o'clock in the morning. When he came out of the tower, Gawain saw broad fields where as yet no one was working; the roosters were crowing and a few farmyard doors were ajar as countrywomen pushed them open with big bowls in their hands, taking the chickens and ducks their breakfast.

Gawain walked along, and people looked at this kitchen-boy

17

who had such a nice white uniform with lace cuffs and who was carrying a kitchen knife. He walked from morning till evening, and as he walked he found neither mulberries nor wild fruit nor plants with edible roots such as radishes, celery, beets, turnips, and so on. . . .

"Well," he thought, "the proverb teaches us that for the hungry man, to sleep is to dine. Let's stretch out under this palm-tree and have a rest."

He fell asleep.

◆

Chapter Eleven
A Modest Essay on the Cookery and Customs of the Bouloulabassians

Gawain awoke in a bed, and it was a bed such as he had never seen before: it was hung from the ceiling, so that you could put yourself to sleep in it by swinging, and this was considered to be enjoyable.

"Where am I?" said Gawain.

An old woman, who stood looking at him with her hands on her hips, heard his words and tried to understand him, but they didn't speak the same language.

"I'm in a foreign country," thought Gawain, "I must have walked a long way yesterday."

The old woman kept talking; she was holding her arms up and looked as though she felt sorry for him.

"She's a kind person, but she ought to give me something to eat."

And he pointed to his mouth and his stomach, which made the old woman laugh. She disappeared and came back carrying three dishes heaped with food. Was there in all the world a style of cooking that our kitchen-boy was unacquainted with? No, indeed. The moment he had tasted the meat and the gravy, he declared:

"That's Bouloulabassian cooking, that's what that is! I'm in the land of the Bouloulabassians. A good thing to know."

The old woman was using a stairway whose steps were arranged like the paddles on a mill-wheel. Remaining horizontal, the steps took people down to the main floor or brought them back up, depending whether you got onto them upstairs or downstairs. This stairway also had the advantage of being a giant fan, for as they revolved like paddlewheels, the steps stirred the air in the room and cooled it off; and since the land of the Bouloulabassians is tropical, this was very handy.

The main floor was as high as a town hall; the stove, table, and chairs were of stone, but the cooking-pots were made of wood. This is not a disadvantage, for no one in that part of the world ever lights a fire: they're quite hot enough without that, thank you! They heat their food by dropping alchemic substances into water, and as these substances dissolve they make the water boil.

◆

Chapter Twelve
A Kitchen-Boy in Exile Is Never at a Loss

Gawain inspected the inn and the outbuildings and, as a distraction, began to exercise his craft. Though there were many spices he could not obtain and though he was rather unaccustomed to wooden cooking-pots, still, when they got up from the table, the inn's regular customers gave Gawain to understand that they were both surprised and satisfied with the meal they had eaten. As for Gawain, he was thinking, as he rode back up on the stairway with a rose-colored candle in his hand:

"I'm going to stay right here. I have a plan!"

Next day he went to the garden and got some herbs, then he went to the barn and killed some chickens (the inn was also a farm), and he cooked a veritable feast without it costing the innkeeper anything. The day after that he repeated the process, and so on, every day.

For the merchants who travel the highways, for the furniture movers, the wagon drivers, he prepared such meals as dukes might eat. People heard about it; it was a topic of conversation in the houses of not-so-simple city folk; and the rich, curious to see this cook and taste his culinary creations, came to the inn for special dinners.

Then the money clinked in the cash-drawers: the inn became a hotel; hunters stopped there, and Gawain learned the Bouloulabassian language so he could converse with all these fine people.

Horses pawed the ground in front of the door; carriages waited under the trees in the orchard; entire hunting packs could be heard yapping and leaping about; and at night, city dwellers lingering over their supper at the inn could be heard exchanging jokes as they sat surrounded by their bottles of costly wines.

One day, a noble lord said to Gawain:

"Master Hotel-keeper, I am marrying off my daughter seven months from now, and as my son-in-law and I are both very fond of driving out into the country, it occurred to us to have the wedding festivities in your establishment. Will you take on the entire affair? I will pay whatever you ask and even more, if I am satisfied; but I want a wedding feast of the very finest. My son-in-law is a difficult man to please. I want him to be impressed; do you understand?"

"We understand one another, My Lord!"

The noble lord was called El Petrusco Ramiro della Barras, which translates into English as "the handsomest woodpigeon in the forest."

His titles were "First Chamberlain, First Banker, First Privy Councillor, First Chief Gentleman-in-Waiting, First High Favorite, First Huntsman, Second in the Kingdom."

◆

Chapter Thirteen
A Rustic Wedding in the Land
of the Bouloulabassians

Night and day did Gawain work to prepare the feast. High above the orchard he had placed striped awnings. Below on trestle tables he had set piles of fruit, and cooked fowl, and shining crystal.

Up in the trees he had suspended leafy balconies on which orchestras were to play, their strains muted through being heard at a distance. Tame birds, red, yellow, and blue, were to flit from branch to branch.

On the table, amid laces of all kinds, amid pieces of glassware and wonders of delicate metalwork, lay Egyptian mangoes and yams from Brazil, encased in icing that was lit from within.

Melanesian dolphins, brought at great expense from distant seas, disported themselves in the fishponds, among the flowering lotus-trees, and blew columns of fine mist out through their nostrils.

Needless to say, the noble lord had paid some money in advance, for three ordinary fortunes would not have sufficed to settle the bills from the food suppliers and the decorators who sent their workmen to set things up.

When the wedding procession arrived in carriages, actors from Paris, Milan, and Saint Petersburg presented dramatic tableaux and ballets; and villagers shouted: "Three cheers for the bride!" The bands all played the Bouloulabassian national anthem; and a daytime fireworks display, such as only the Chinese know how to contrive, suddenly filled the sky.

"What a pity that my lord the King can't see this!" said Ramiro.

"I must tell my close friend the Queen about this splendid show," said the bride.

"Not bad, I must admit, for a rustic feast," said the son-in-law.

They ate, then they danced; and the noble lord paid for the feast with a quantity of silver it would take twelve horses to pull if you were to load it onto wagons. Then the innkeeper shut down his inn, and Gawain, having put into his purse enough florins and crowns to live thereafter without having to work, followed Ramiro to the court where dwelt the King of the Bouloulabassians.

◆

Chapter Fourteen
In Which It Will Be Seen That a Skilled Kitchen-Boy May Be a Highly Successful Diplomat . . .

Gawain was a shrewd lad: he contrived to conduct himself correctly and the noble lord was well pleased with him. Protected by this powerful personage, Gawain assumed rank and dignities at the court. The King himself deigned to receive Gawain at his royal table whenever Ramiro came to dine at the palace, and one day he tweaked the ear of the sometime kitchen-boy and called him "my young friend!"

On a fall morning the King said to Gawain:

"Do come and have a chat with me after we're back from the hunt!"

This is what had happened:

Gawain, who, ever since the time when he had established himself at the inn, had always been acting with a single idea in view, told his story to Ramiro and took care to hide nothing from him. Ramiro reported the story in full to King Helforlether XXIV, as Gawain had foreseen he would:

"The man who could suffocate my army in a cellar can certainly bring my army glory on a battlefield!" exclaimed the King after a moment's silence.

When this utterance, which has since become historic, was repeated to Gawain, he turned pink with pleasure. The King thought himself very clever, because he imagined he was using the Balibridgian cook: he thought he had found in Gawain an instrument against Kabul the First; he wanted to make his enemy's former subject into his own devoted servant and turn to his own advantage the resentment felt by this unlucky aspirant to the hand of Princess Julia.

Poor King! He was arming his own executioner, working to ensure his own downfall. But who could have guessed at Gawain's ambition? The kitchen-boy had set his sights on two empires at once and crowned heads were his pawns. This silent youth was a Balibridgian Napoleon!

What was said that day, after they were back from the hunt? What words were uttered in the royal study? What secret was confided to the future leader of the troops? No one ever knew.

In the Bouloulabassian Annals, it is recorded that Gawain came out of the palace wearing a general's uniform, but absolutely no particulars of the interview are given:

"Gawain (Francis), former cook and Balibridgian by birth, took command and led his army against the man on whose table he once had waited."

That is how the Annals refer to the Bouloulabassian-Balibridgian war.

A man who was close to Helforlether XXIV, and who wrote a history of that king, has been generous with the details that came his way. He tells us all about the number of horses, the weight of the armor, how the supplies were organized, and the weary labors of the infantry.

Let us sum up in a few pages the stirring volumes that the chronicler devotes to the recital of this last struggle between two brother nations! We shall be brief since we are constrained to be so. It cannot be denied that the work contains many a useful statistic, many original strategic plans, many interesting observations, but only that which concerns Gawain the kitchen-boy can be given a place in our short narrative. Let us deem ourselves fortunate that this war should have had its chronicler just as the French-English War, which we call the Hundred-Years' War, had its Froissart, for thanks to him we know the dramatic events that shook two once-flourishing states to their very foundations.

◆

Chapter Fifteen
. . . But a Hopelessly Inept General!

A man may be a good cook and a bad general!

Gawain did not prosper! Atop a hill in a grassy region where there were no trees, Gawain, with seven bright young officers for an escort, gazed down upon the battle.

He saw half his army driven back to the banks of the Bouloula-bassian national river; he saw his horsemen falling into the water one after another; he saw his artillery fleeing out of sight over the horizon and his infantry abandoning rifles and crossbows in the grass; he saw the bonfires lit by the winning general; he heard the trumpets sounding forth the victory: but his disastrous defeat dismayed him not.

He pressed his horse's flanks with his legs to urge him into a gallop and said to his faithful followers:

"Gentlemen, the time has come to act: show the white flag which means we wish to negotiate!"

Then the seven officers became aware that Gawain had donned a mask.

In his tent, Kabul the First was getting up from the table when he was informed that the negotiators had come. Normally Kabul the First was friendly toward ambassadors, so he smiled, flicked the crumbs off his shirt-frill and his stomach, and waited.

Gawain appeared. Who would ever have recognized the one-time scullery-lad beneath this masked Bouloulabassian wearing a plumed cocked hat?

In any case, King Kabul was never distrustful when he had just had a good supper. He behaved in a friendly way, talking about the battle and telling the Bouloulabassians that it wasn't their fault they had been beaten, that they had been very courageous, and that it would be their turn to be victorious another time.

He invited them to have coffee, and chatted about his late wife and his daughter; he plied the gentlemen with questions. Deep down, he did not have great confidence in himself despite his good fortune, and when Francis, still wearing his cardboard mask, suggested signing a peace treaty, he at once replied:

"Why . . . just as you wish . . . my dear Sir!"

◆

Chapter Sixteen
A Voice from the Past, a Voice from the Heart

That same evening, everyone started off for the city of the Balibridgians. Gawain's seven officers rode standing up on the carriage-springs.

A victory celebration was in progress and the capital was lit up. At the palace gilded noblemen crowded the dining-hall where a cold supper had been prepared.

"You must be warm with that thing on your face!" said Kabul to Gawain as he passed his guest the dainties.

"It's something a person gets used to," said Gawain, taking a sip from his glass of wine. "I never take it off. On diplomatic missions such as this, I really recommend that you try wearing a mask. They're quite indispensable and not at all in the way!"

Drink up, Francis, for your voice is shaking! . . . Oh how poignant, how sweetly poignant are those far-off days of the past! How many, many memories this hall brings back! Memories of a castle built all of marble and of flowers! Oh, the charméd ghosts of childhood! Oh, the fair, sweet childhood of Francis, with its innocence, its candor, its purity of soul in those first fair days of youth! What mortal man but is pleased to dream of thee, O gentle past! What eyes are not bedewed when they gaze anew upon scenes of former days! . . . Gawain, now they're playing the national anthem! Proud heads are bowed. How sweet is this music to the heart of the exile! . . . O innocent wee kitchen-boy, huddled in a dungeon cell! Wee, innocent kitchen-boy in the dawn of empty fields! Remember, kitchen-boy, remember, young lad in love with Julia! . . .

But Gawain had no time for dreaming. For there stood Julia beside her father the King! The palace prison had not held her for long. But Gawain would not let himself be moved. Gawain was a man, and his mind was as much on royal purple, on authority, on vengeance, as it was on his former love.

"The time has come!" thought Gawain.

◆

Chapter Seventeen
In Which Everyone Gets a Stomachache

The next day they all went in procession to see the Museum, the School Complex, and the City Hall. In each building someone recited a courteous speech to the Bouloulabassian ambassadors; but Gawain did not answer these speeches with other speeches; he had a cold, he said.

Now, this was untrue; he did not have a cold, but he had just now committed a crime: he had just poisoned his fellow countrymen.

All along the road from the palace to Gawain's native city are the tanks containing the drinking water that is distributed to the residents of the town by a system of pipes. And into these tanks the cunning cook had thrown poison; a number of people were already writhing in agony during the public speeches.

Already mothers were dying without having time to bewail the lot of their children! Already fathers burying their sons were interrupted in their task by unbearable pains in their innards. The city was one unbroken moan of pain. The deputy mayor suddenly left the procession, clutching his belly! All the house-fronts were daubed with horse-droppings, the usual symbol of mourning in those lands.

Only the inhabitants of the castle, who drank nothing but mineral water, and Gawain's parents, who had been forewarned, were alive and well.

Following upon this public calamity, there were many events in a single day. To the King's great astonishment, Gawain's seven officers departed without saying where they were going, and Gawain himself disappeared. In that land, a town hall is a place where no one has the right to arrest another person. Gawain, fearful that the man responsible for all these deaths might be identified, went up into the bell-tower of the town hall; he also wanted to inspect the surrounding countryside from up there and wait for the right moment to show himself publicly.

As for the seven officers, they were to rally the soldiers of the Bouloulabassian army and, taking advantage of the grief-stricken Balibridgians, they were to come right back.

◆

Chapter Eighteen
Flourishes of Trumpets and Shouts of Triumph

Before the sun had set, Francis espied the regiments marching along the road.

They got bigger as they got closer, and now here they were! You could see the trumpets and the harnesses on the horses; already they were storming the very ramparts of the palace, whose occupants could not figure out what was happening.

Too late now, for already they had crossed the drawbridges!

Too late now to defend your king, you men of the guards! Three corpses lying in the courtyard! Axes hacking through the doors to the palace precincts! Maddened horses fleeing from the braying of the trumpets! Night was falling; fire lit the sky! They hunted Kabul from room to room, and now they had found him, they were clutching him, terrified, by the throat, while the squadron commanders ordered the artillery pieces surrounding the courtyard to fire victory salvos.

Of a sudden, from far away there came a shout, and this shout was like the noise of the tempest over the sea, a long melodious shout coming from the starry sky, a shout that filled the countryside right to the horizon, brought by the river and carried by the wind, striking against the walls of the palace as the battering ram, that antique instrument of war, was used to strike against the ramparts of cities and smash them, a great hurrah that filled the courtiers with fear, brought the King bolt upright where he sat pinned by his captors, and made the skeletons of the Balibridgian dynasty shake as they lay beneath the flagstones.

Suddenly, heralded by a tremendous cannon-blast, Gawain was in their midst. Off came the cardboard mask as he uttered these words:

"I am Francis Gawain!"

Then King Kabul fell into a swoon, and Julia gave her hand to the conqueror to show him she had not forgotten him. At the same time news of Gawain's coming spread far and wide; bands of men somehow appeared bearing sickles and staves. King Kabul the First was removed from his throne by his own subjects and Francis became emperor in the same city where once he had played at marbles.

◆

Chapter Nineteen
Everyone Comes Back to Life with Much Hugging and Kissing

Francis, first of that name, married young Julia. Somewhat to everyone's surprise, the entire capital city was present at the ceremony: the fact is that the poison had lost some of its potency in the water; the townspeople had not died, they had lost consciousness; and the commotion of the cannonade had restored their wits and their senses.

The house-fronts, cleansed of their funereal excrement, were purified, and the citizens came to present their greetings and com-

pliments to Francis, and were pleased to discover a former pupil of
the school.

The deputy mayor could not speak for the lump in his throat.
The schoolteacher, who had put on his frock coat, was weeping and
repeating:

"I always suspected . . . I always suspected . . . that this would
happen . . . he was so alert, so alert, as a youngster!"

Francis and Julia did not have many children, but they were
happy all the same. Helforlether was forced to hand over his kingdom to Gawain on account of public opinion. Although at first considerably put out, he got over it and ended up coming to live with
Kabul in a house that is still pointed out to tourists to this very day.

Finally, when peace was securely reestablished between the two
erstwhile enemy nations, Francis Gawain, the one-time schoolchild,
the one-time young kitchen-boy, remembered his humble origins
and renounced his throne with its absolute power, placing this
in the hands of his fellow citizens. And thenceforth and forever,
happiness reigned over those lands, which are shown in modern
atlases under the name "United Balibridgian and Bouloulabassian
Republic."

From *The Coast*

[*In the course of his career, Max Jacob produced two volumes of poetry inspired by Brittany. He claimed that his native land haunted him, possessed his eyes, his heart, and even his very fingers. With* La Côte, *he had a triple aim. First, in the tradition of James MacPherson's Ossian and other literary hoaxes, he wished to play a joke on his readers; second, he wanted to make fun of the so-called Bretonizing Bretons, who insisted on keeping up their own language; and third and most important, he wrote to create a masterpiece.*

The hoax consisted of claiming that what he wrote in French was a translation of old Breton poems and that he was now publishing his translations side by side with the "original" Breton text. Nobody was taken in by this pretense and in the middle of the volume, Jacob himself gave up using the inferior translations into Breton that were being done by an acquaintance of his. However, the picturesque Breton legends, which are genuine, fired his imagination, and the result bore his particular stamp: artfully produced simplicity suffused with the gentle irony and emotion of a poet in intimate communion with his beloved Brittany and his created world.

The first edition of The Coast, *illustrated by Picasso, was printed at the author's expense in 1911 in a limited edition. Jacob sold the copies himself in the cafés, at high society dinner parties, and through subscriptions. The proceeds saved him and his friends from starvation for a while. A second edition, a luxury one with the author's charming Breton gouaches, came out in 1927.*]

◆

The Sailor's Homecoming

I recognized the voice of the parrot I gave you, the one that used to repeat the first line of our love-song.

I recognized the leaves of the trees, and the branches bent in a hoop.

I recognized the braiding on your Breton dress, at the window.

But you're singing a *jabadao* that I don't recognize.[1]

You're minding how you sing the song, though, taking care to keep the rhythm! Are you sure your voice isn't tired, forgetful woman?

I keep hidden and you don't sense my presence, for you do not see with the eye of love.

But you do fulfill the duties of hospitality, from what I can observe, for there is a man in the house! A man is kissing you and you're letting him! So farewell!

And I'll hear the parrot! When I'm out at sea I'll hear the parrot saying the first line of our love-song over and over.

◆

The Man Who Forced Girls

The young baron thought to himself, as he walked in the garden: "That Jean Lelorit is a good-looking girl!"

Alas! To his sorrow and to the sorrow of the Lelorits, the young baron came to the house where the Lelorits lived.

"Good morrow and joy to this whole household. I want to see Jean; where is she?" "Jean has gone to take a young calf to Morlaix."

Along the road, Jean is tugging a little calf! She doesn't know what's in store for her. It's heartbreaking to tell.

Jean courteously greeted His Lordship. He said, "Let's see your

1. "Much could be said about the *jabadao*: it's a dance sung in double time, if I'm not mistaken, and the dancers know the words to it, though they may not always sing them as they dance" (note by Max Jacob).

calf, Jean Lelorit! There's no point your going all the way to Morlaix; I'll buy it from you."

"There's no point your standing in the road, My Lord. This animal isn't meant for you. I'm going to do what my father and mother told me to do and take him to the fair."

And so saying, she said good day to His Lordship and started to walk toward the town where the fair is held. "Jean, I shall have you whether you will or no. Whether you will or no, you shall come with me out onto the moors."

He dragged her off by force behind the gorse-bushes. What a heartbreak for Jean and what a grievous thing for her parents!

She came back home with a pouch of money in her right hand and dust upon her woolen skirt.

"What happened to you, Jean?" "I met the baron and he forced me, out there on the moors!"

"The young lord! I'll kill him with my sickle or my axe, for stealing my daughter's virtue."

A man from the Morlaix district, who was taking his cattle home because the sun had set, said to Jean Lelorit's father: "What are you waiting for, standing there beside the road?"

"I'm waiting for the young man who stole my daughter's virtue, so I can kill him to punish him for what he did."

As he walked up the steps between the posts,[1] Jean Lelorit's father said: "The hangman will get me, but first I got that man who forced girls."

1. "Presumably the gallows-posts" (note by Max Jacob).

From *The Flowering Plant*

[*Written in dialogue and monologue interspersed with a few poems and songs,* The Flowering Plant *is a "novel," according to its author. The modern reader might recognize in this work one of the first ancestors of the Theater of the Absurd.* Le Phanérogame *is filled to the brim with the "intellectual gymnastics and acrobatics" the author subjected himself to while writing it. He would walk for hours on an empty stomach, being too poor to eat, and make himself come up with an original idea while going from one lamppost to the next. There he would stay motionless till a new idea struck him. Likewise, he trained himself to stare at a postcard, displayed in a window, until he found a suitable way to describe it. Slowly he filled up his notebooks with the resulting ideas, finishing the "novel" in 1905, and publishing it at his own expense in 1918. Of the sixteen numbered copies on Japanese paper, illustrated by Picasso, one was auctioned in 1973 for 22,000 Swiss francs.*

Among other things, this "novel" is a parody on the wishful thinking of the kind of bourgeois who would like to see all nonconformists locked up. The punitive measures encompass all forms of punishment to which deviants have been subjected throughout the centuries, from the torture chambers of the Inquisition to the concentration camps and mental asylums of dictatorships. The author expresses the somber theme with the fireworks of his unbridled imagination. In 1918, he saw in The Flowering Plant *the gaiety of his first youth, "the golden age of art," and in 1940, he compared the work to a Modigliani painting, with "elongated necks and lots of wit, a real grain of serious folly."*]

◆

The Twelve Species of Common Adultery
[from "Chapter on Adultery in Adults or Adulterated Adultery"]

MR. OVERGROWNGLADIOLUS:
> I have identified twelve species of common adultery.

THE FLOWERING PLANT:
> Holy mackerel, as we say in the States!

MR. OVERGROWNGLADIOLUS:

1st	adultery resulting from disappointment or misplaced admiration
2nd	adultery resulting from excessive sociability
3rd	from a need to deceive
4th	from spontaneous flammability in one of the spouses
5th	from fear, weakness, or covetousness
6th	from deliberate choice or individualism
7th	from deadening of the moral sense, or grossness of character
8th	from genuine sensuality
9th	from a need for cosmic nourishment
10th	from a need to reach out emotionally or to possess the soul of another
11th	from one's official position
12th	from a need for trouble and strife.

◆

Advanced Degeneracy

Article III. The following categories of person shall be charged with Advanced Degeneracy: all persons bringing to their job or trade an undue degree of care and attention deemed prejudicial to the interests of the municipality, evidence of such undue care to include: particularly noticeable grimaces or nervous twitches, habitual nail biting, walking hurriedly, absent-mindedness, and so on and so forth . . . ; all persons who regularly ingest substances—such as fish, alcohol, hydrous ether commonly known as sulfuric ether,[1] shellfish, arsenic, honey, mustard, milk products, opium, henbane, hashish, orange, and lemon—intended to stimulate an unwarranted level of brain development, since excessive brain development constitutes unfair competition; all persons who do not sleep very much or eat very much or who show signs of reverence and respect for God; all persons having a liking for the arts or who themselves produce works of art; any person who in the course of his or her life has had an original idea, and so forth and so on. . . . Individual cases to be dealt with by the local municipal council.

Article IV. Incarceration of an Advanced Degenerate shall be immediate rather than delayed, on three accounts. The first is that a clear warning must be issued to the masses; the second, that it is important to avert rapid contagion among people who are prone to nervous disorders; and the third (we freely admit that we do not understand this third reason), because *error left to itself begets error (?)*

Article V. Since a number of patients have resisted bromide, the prescribed treatments shall be: (1) beatings; (2) baths in boiling water; (3) massage with stinging nettle; (4) the Rack; (5) the Boot; (6) water torture; (7) solitary confinement with absolutely no talking permitted. Those patients who refuse to get better shall, as punishment, be put in dark dungeon-cells, denied food, and condemned to eat their own excrement.

Article VI. Care and assistance for Advanced Degenerates are necessary requirements in a well-regulated society.

and so forth and so on . . .

Article XIX. The authorities of the Board of Review and Health are enjoined to avoid confusing Advanced Degenerates with Common Degenerates such as idiots, cretins, insane persons of either sex, and hydrophobics. Persons presently holding or likely hereafter to hold membership in any of the various academies, as well as priests of whatever denomination, shall not be eligible for admission to state asylums for Advanced Degeneracy, nor shall members of the teaching profession.

and so forth . . .

1. During his bohemian days in Montmartre from 1910 on, Max Jacob occasionally took ether to obtain unusual effects in his poetry, just as a later genera-

Five consecutive pieces from
In Defense of Tartufe

[*The key to understanding Max Jacob as a person is* In Defense of Tartufe, *which deals with the experience that revolutionized his life and led to his conversion. Written in 1910 (after his first vision of Christ the previous year), and published in 1919,* La Défense de Tartufe *reveals the poet's mystical and aesthetic preoccupations and their fusion.*

The Defense *is a self-accusation as much as a plea for sincerity. While "Tartufe" refers to one of Molière's characters, whose name is now a common term used to denote a religious hypocrite, it also refers to the* persona *of the poet. Jacob had already defended Tartufe in* The Flowering Plant, *claiming that he could have been pious while being in love with his benefactor's wife. Tartufe was tempted, but are not all saints tempted? Moreover, Tartufe must be in Paradise by now, whereas the Sun King who arrested him is probably not.*

As the title implies, Jacob was deeply concerned with the dual nature of Christians and by the yawning gulf between their aspirations and behavior. He sums up this eternal conflict in a letter written in 1941 to the late Michel Manoll: "I'm the greatest Tartufe of them all, sincere, but a Tartufe." The Defense *is a mixture of poems in prose and verse, diary excerpts, self-examinations, meditations, and prayers.*

The five consecutive pieces of the "Revelation" cycle are at the very heart of the work. The first piece has often been compared to Pascal's famous rendering of his mystical experience. However, Jacob typically mingles the familiar with the mystical levels of speech to heighten the effect and also to

---

tion of Beat artists took hashish or LSD for the same purpose. In his *Meditations*, he violently repudiated this "base trick" of his earlier years.

reveal the miraculous in the everyday. After expressing the beatific moment of enlightenment through a series of ecstatic exclamations, the poet engages with the Lord in a dialogue culminating in his pledge of total and lifelong dedication. In the last three pieces, poetic invention, pictorial imagination, apocalyptic visions, and the variegated symbolism of the Jewish Kabala follow one another in vertiginous succession.]

◆

The Revelation

I came back from the National Library; I put down my briefcase; I hunted around for my slippers and when I looked up, there was someone on the wall; there was someone there! There was someone on the red wallpaper. My flesh fell away! I was stripped naked by a lightning-bolt![1] Imperishable moment! Truth, oh, truth! Truth with its tears and its joy! Never-to-be-forgotten truth! The Divine Body is on the wall of a shabby room. Why, Lord? Forgive me! He's in a landscape, a landscape I drew a long time ago, but how beautiful *He* is! How graceful and gentle! The way He bears himself, the way He walks! He wears a yellow silk robe and blue facings. He turns around and I can see that peaceful, radiant countenance. Six monks now come into the room carrying a dead body. Near me is a woman with snakes around her arms and hair.

THE ANGEL: Innocent fool! You have seen God! You do not realize how fortunate you are.

ME: Let me weep; oh, let me weep! I am just a poor human creature.

THE ANGEL: The Evil Spirit has gone. He will be back.

ME: The Evil Spirit! Yes, I see!

THE ANGEL: Understanding.

ME: You don't know what a comfort it is to have you near me.

THE ANGEL: We love you, man of no account. Think upon it.

ME: Oh, rapture! I understand, Lord; oh, yes, I understand!

1. In a letter to his friend René Villard, Jacob again compares his conversion to a "lightning-bolt": "a single glance, and I died and was born again." He refers several times to what he calls a "mental death," and explains that two beings stir in the bosom of a man who wants to perfect himself: the old one cedes his place to the new one, but does not disappear. The image of the dead body being carried away expresses the poet's deepest longing to rid himself of his past.

◆

Visitation

My room is at the far end of a courtyard and behind some shops,
at number 7 Ravignan Street. Room, house, you will always be the
chapel of my undying remembrance! I lay there thinking, stretched
out on the box-spring held up by four bricks; and the landlord
made an opening in the zinc roof to let in more light. Who's knocking at my door so early in the morning? —Open up! Open the door!
Don't get dressed! —It's you, Lord! —The cross is heavy: I want to
set it down. —The door is very narrow; how will it get in? —It can
come in through the window. —Warm yourself in here, Lord! It's
so cold out! —Look at the cross! —My whole life long, Lord!

◆

Vision

A golden ray rolls itself up to form a crown. There are people
around my bed, but no one except me will see. Beneath the horse
lies the sea, a crumpled cloth. Above the sea rises a woman, in a
halo, and at the piano a poet asks God for inspiration. In the distance fires are lit. And what am I but a kneeling slave, a slave who
looks at me and whom I do not know?

◆

Meanings

The timorous monk (me) is praying by the stained-glass window
in Saint Eustache![2] He turns very pale and talks to himself as he
walks through the streets gesticulating. Christ bends his knee—
the knee is earth, repentance, and prayer—and enables the monk
to understand His misunderstood Body.[3] The purple darkness of

2. The church of Saint Eustache in Paris is named for a Roman general who,
like Max, became a convert after he saw a vision. Its stained-glass windows are
based on sketches by the seventeenth-century artist Philippe de Champaigne.
3. See "religious anatomy" in *Meditations*, "Blessings of God," note 7.

the stained-glass window makes the crude Body of the statue easy to understand and replaces it with delicate carving. The breast understands things better than the head: that is the meaning of the wound in the heart![4] Each separate finger speaks! Is it better to understand than to pray, or better to pray than to understand?

◆

Exhortation

The Breton (me!) is sitting surrounded by the flags of the world. The crescent moon cradles a star. The Breton is studying surrounded by the flags of the world and an angel has come down to him. "Cease your reading if God decides to visit you again." You know my sufferings, God! What have you written near your arm, oh angel with woman's arm? Three Hebrew letters which I cannot read. When the Holy Spirit comes to me, will he give me the gift of tongues?

My stupidity makes the angel furious.

4. The author was convinced that intellectual, abstract ideas are useless unless they are changed into strongly felt emotions, convictions that reside in the breast and come down into one's very bowels. In his *Advice to a Young Poet* he writes: "The spear which passed through the breast of Our Lord is the directional arrow showing the road ideas must take if they are to become valid.

Moreover, the Blood and water which came out of the Heart reflect the union of the Spirit with matter which is the only valid *understanding*.

I think you grasp my meaning. *Force it down in*."

The Artist Introduces Himself

[*The 1931* Dictionnaire biographique des artistes contemporains, *in a four-page entry including six reproductions, rates the attainments of* "Jacob (Max-Cyprien)" *in this order:* "Peintre, poète et littérateur." Littérateur, *while it can mean* "man of letters," *is most often pejorative, something akin to* "literary hack." *The present volume, without diminishing the reputation of the man as an artist, may serve as a suitable corrective to the casual dismissal of Jacob's attainments in the writing of prose.*

In The Artist Introduces Himself, *though discussing his artistic career, Jacob shows he has the writer's as well as the painter's eye for the characteristic detail that captures an individual's essence. He also displays a rare, because sincere, humility about his own worth.*

Présentation de l'auteur par lui-même was written as a préface for an exhibition of Jacob's art work in 1920, at the Bernheim-Jeune Gallery.[1]]

◆

I know something about dancing, singing and piano, and madrigals. I know the respect that is due to old men, learned men, and whitened sepulchers, and I know joy, love, hunger, loneliness, and success. I have university qualifications (Studied at . . .). I believe that only in suffering does man recognize himself as man, only in suffering does he come to know and recognize other men.[2] I am forty-three, I have but few hairs on my head, almost no teeth, and

---

1. It is a measure of Jacob's talent in a field other than writing that he should have been exhibited by the Bernheim-Jeunes, a distinguished family of art dealers from the early nineteenth century to the present, associated with the careers of Delacroix, Corot, Van Gogh, and others.

2. The concept of suffering is the very pivot of Jacob's life and work. He expressed it in prose and poetry, in the symbolic interpretation of the Scripture,

I'm writing this in a bright, pleasant hospital where they're treating this pneumonia of mine.[3]

Here is a story that I sometimes tell because I do a rather good imitation of an American accent. An American, at loose ends in Paris, wanders into an art academy so he can see naked girls (I'm sorry to say); embarrassed by the mocking glances cast in his direction, he pretends to be drawing, then, all of a sudden, he starts to draw in earnest, then finds that the gentleman in charge has come over to criticize. He is stunned to hear the man compliment him on his work: "Uh-oh! I'm a painter!" Genius chooses its instruments in unexpected ways. In the story of my painting, I'm afraid, there is neither genius, nor naked girls, nor compliments; that kind of thing is absolutely lacking. What there is, is a great deal of timidity, a vast love for earth and sky; that's all I can tell you in this introduction. For a fuller confession, I refer you to "In Defense of Tartufe, by Max Jacob, at La Société Littéraire, 10 rue de l'Odéon, City."

In high school, when the teacher's old beard and glasses happened to pause behind my drawing-paper, there would emerge from inside him a burst of mirthless, bitter laughter addressed to humanity at large; he would pick up the sheet of paper tweezer-fashion with the tips of his fingers and tap the paper with his other hand, raising a cloud of dust from my drawing-charcoal: "Little idiot! Young scamp! Turn the paper over . . . dabbler!" He rolled his *r*'s. Although he was from Brittany, daddy Villard pronounced his words Alsatian-style, I think out of distaste. He was a great artist, but they'd set him to teaching, and he was a bad teacher. When I had become a student and a free artist, he met me one day in the Gothic streets of my native town, carrying a sketchbook; for the first time he spoke to me in a calm, level manner.

---

in his meditations, and in his vast correspondence with young poets, writers, painters, musicians, and other friends. According to him, suffering is the way in which God points out the road leading to Himself. The concept of suffering is based on the analysis of Original Sin which, in the Jacobian interpretation, is not punishment but a gift of God to help humankind to make progress. Both suffering and active work lead the individual to God. Jacob does not consider suffering in terms of passive endurance, but as a real effort imposed by man upon himself to perfect himself.

3. See the introduction to "Another Night: Understanding with Your Eyes Shut."

The linear fantasies I produced as a child caused no one any astonishment. Since I had always looked like a solid middle-class sort of chap, great was the surprise when at the age of twenty-three I announced that I would be a painter. As I was a studious lad, there was considerable distress, distress which looking back I can sympathize with. At the time, I was hard, dogmatic, filled with a sense of moral obligations, quite inflexible. Dear me, how I have changed! A female relative said to me: "Well! No one in our family has ever suggested doing anything like that before!" From a cousin in Paris, however, I got a rather different reception: "Well, now," said she, "I hope we'll be seeing a Fine Arts scholarship winner before very long." At the Julian Academy I was not made to feel at all welcome.[4] An elegant young man asked me whether I was selling pencils; the gentleman was wasting his wit and his time: I was so overcome with shyness that I didn't understand this piece of insolence until long afterward when I thought about it. Mr. J.-P. Laurens looked me up and down with raised eyebrow and that painstaking little gaze of his, took my pencil and lovingly altered the line of a leg I had drawn, slanting it upward to make it right.[5] And that was all I ever saw of Mr. J.-P. Laurens. Mr. Benjamin Constant talked through his nose and uttered blue-gray poetry.[6] As he looked no more like a painter than I did, he may have felt some sympathy for me but if so he didn't show it. I was sad and I was poor. They advised me to try being a critic in order to earn my living. I have a genuine aptitude for criticism, as it turned out.[7] So of course it was pointed

4. The minor genre painter and portraitist Rodolphe Julian (1839–1907) made a fortune and achieved a worldwide reputation by establishing an academy staffed by the most celebrated painters and sculptors.

5. Jean-Paul Laurens (1838–1921) was a successful painter of scenes from French history at a time when this genre already was considered outdated. He participated in the decoration of the Hôtel de Ville and the Panthéon and played an important role in teaching at the Academy of Toulouse and the Julian Academy.

6. Benjamin Constant (1845–1902) started his career with the painting *Hamlet and the King*, but after his stay in Morocco he turned to oriental subjects. Toward the end of his life he participated in the decoration of the Hôtel de Ville, the Sorbonne, and the Opéra Comique and also became a very fashionable portraitist. He painted Queen Victoria and Queen Alexandra and was the most sought-after portraitist in English high society.

7. Jacob was a very sensitive art critic and wrote articles under the pseudonym of Léon David.

out to me that I knew nothing about writing.[8] Learning to write! Learning to paint! Oh, the jobs I took in order to foot the bill for all that learning: shop sweeper, law clerk, nursemaid (seriously!), and secretary; first, last, and always, a secretary! "You're like a little kid who wants an orange!" a department manager said to me one day. In point of fact I wanted two oranges and I didn't clearly realize this was so. One day I was dubbed a poet by some friends who were poets, poets of some distinction.[9] Later I was dubbed a painter by the best painters of our time, men who are just barely younger than I am.[10] More recently, an art dealer, who is extremely cultivated as well as being a very discerning art lover, has introduced me to the public. Never in my whole life had I dreamed of such an honor.

8. When his cousin, a famous Orientalist, criticized his style, Jacob gave up his new profession and decided to learn to write.

9. Apollinaire predicted in a public lecture that fame would soon catch up with Max Jacob in his meager abode on Ravignan Street.

10. Picasso, for instance, highly praised Max Jacob's early drawings.

From *Film-Flam*

[Film-Flam, *(Cinématoma) published in 1920, is a study of characters. Jacob, who was basically a moralist (in the French tradition: a writer who observes human nature), wanted to revive the outdated "portrait," a rapid but detailed character sketch of a person, real or hypothetical. There was a genuine craze for this in the seventeenth century, both as a literary genre and as a popular form of witty conversation in aristocratic salons. Jacob's unique contribution to the genre is that he lets his protagonists introduce and reveal themselves with their own words. Jacob used his "scientific" method, based on astrology and the ancient theory of the four elements. He kept the letters of his correspondents in thirty-six files, according to their birthdates, creating an ever-growing selection of their distinctive vocabulary. He was convinced that every word we use reveals us completely in accordance with our astral signs and our element: water is gliding, earth weighty, fire brilliant, air gentle. He perfected this technique with his own comments as a "field observer" of human behavior. Fernande Olivier, Picasso's first mistress, describes how Jacob loved to listen to the concierge, followed housewives engaged in their shopping on the Montmartre streets, and eagerly jotted down both the idle chatter of gossips and notes on the accompanying gestures and facial expressions.*

The diaries and letters of Film-Flam *ring true because the author does not base the characters on himself, but transposes himself onto them to become each of his protagonists in turn. He has put into the mouth of each character only what could possibly come out, with all the verbal tics, redundancies, and digressions of colloquial speech. The caricaturized and sometimes grotesque protagonists reveal their social status, the degree of their intelligence and sensibility, their professional idiosyncrasies, the different varieties of their hypocrisy, their lack of self-awareness, their secrets, all in the uncontrolled gush of chatter. Even if we consider the technical devices, the direct observations, Jacob's passion for words, his systematic study of every dictionary that came his way, his gift for discerning intuitively how a particular individual's mind works, or guessing the exact birthdate of a person at the very first encounter, we still would not encompass the magic of this work. The secret lies in Max Jacob's invention and irony; these are the qualities that enable him to endow his caricatural protagonists with such vitality.*]

◆

The Girl Who Found a Husband

Author's note: The country folk of Lower Brittany who know the French language adapt it to their own use, incorrectly but picturesquely. We have tried to follow them in their jargon, which, it seemed to us, had not as yet been faithfully recorded.[1]

A rowdy I am not.—MARIE LEBOLLOCH

Saint-Oâ (Finistère)

Monday. Corentin! Now the guy goes running away as fast as his legs will carry him. Oh, the Sister surely did say to me: "Marie Lebolloch, my child, there's nothing good to be gained from running around with boys!" And I said to Corentin, I said: "Corentin, look at the belly I got from being with you!" In the doorways of houses, that's right, when I'm down at the end of the street! Just you wait, you scoundrel, I'll find a way to catch you, boy oh boy! Oh my goodness, my mother hasn't seen yet. It was my own sister what I was scared of, my sister from Paris. Oh, she's a mean one, yes, indeed! So I was afraid, you know? I was afraid she might have noticed my belly but she didn't see. No, she hasn't seen yet!

"Look at this girl! Just look at this girl! The belly on her, sweet Jesus! How can people come to church with bellies like that! Oh my goodness!" That was Marie-Jeanne Gloaguen, the grocer's wife, over on du Pont Street! And what would I have said? So there I was at home back again! And my father was there; like a madman he was! "Oh my goodness," says I, "it was Simon who told him, Simon must have told! What a dirty thing to do, boy oh boy!" At the fur-

1. Translator's note: I, in turn, have transposed Max Jacob's Bretonized French into nonstandard English.

nace they are, the two of them, at the furnace in the paper-mill. My father was plenty mad, but he didn't know about me; he was mad 'cause he didn't want for us to have gone dancing in the public square, and my mother the same. And anyway he'd been drinking. When a man's been drinking, you know?

October. At four o'clock this morning! Oh, it hurts, let me tell you! Out to the dunghill in the yard I'd thought of going, but then I thought they'd see from the Gloaguens'. They stay up late there to make the bread. They're always breathing down my neck, those people. Way back, when I used to go to the Sisters' (at school I was), well, we used to throw stones at the windows. I'd forgotten all about it, naturally, but at the Gloaguens' they still be saying I'm a rowdy. A rowdy I am not, that's for sure! So, hurting the way I was, worse than I dunno what, I been and went to the Dry Well. Oh sweet Jesus, does it ever hurt, you know? At first I thought I would have left him at the Dry Well. But after I thought about it, "My goodness," says I, "this child here will be better off in the ground in the cemetery," says I. Off I go with the baby in my apron, straight to the cemetery, so then. "Hey!" says I, "Grandfather Mathiesse's grave! It won't be very hard, because it's not even a month since he went in there." Who would ever have taken a notion to go looking for him, poor little creature? "Corentin! You know, it's on account of you that a misfortune has happened!" says I to him. But Corentin didn't say anything. Oh, it's the truth: there's nothing good to be gained from running around with men!

November first. Risen God! Holy Virgin, Queen of Angels, patron of those in distress, patron of those named Marie! Saint Anne, Mother of mothers! Good, kind Saint Ronan! Saint Yves, lawyer most holy! A poor girl is in prison, in the prison where they put thieves; a poor girl who didn't believe she would have done wrong with Corentin Leborgne! The Lebolloch girl is in jail with all the bare-headed women and all the Marie Strappens.[2] Look at me, Holy Virgin; Holy Virgin, please just look! You'll get a candle as thick as my arm, if you look over in this direction. My father came here, my mother the same.

"Why didn't you say something, Marie?" says she. "For sure I

2. "This is the name used for women of dissolute morals. It corresponds to the French word 'une traînée,' a streetwalker" (note by Max Jacob).

wouldn't have let you fret yourself, now would I? I never heard of such a thing!"

The sexton was the first to notice: "Hey!" he says to the shoe-maker, "Don't tell me we're starting to get flies around the graves! That's a funny thing."

So then they both started scraping the earth away with a shovel and of course the little creature was there in the apron! Oh risen God, can things like that happen? Holy Virgin! Come on now . . . it's no use crying; will you be any better off after? . . .

"Well, look at this!" says the sexton. "It looks just like Marie Lebolloch's apron. . . . Mrs. Lebolloch, isn't this here apron one that belongs to your oldest daughter?"

"Yes," says my mother, "that's her apron!"

Then later the police came.

"Mrs. Lebolloch, Marie isn't home, is she?" says the police.

"No, Marie is not!"

Poor Marie, she was running around out there, worse than a ter-rier. Just wait, now; no, the police are not going to catch me, that's for sure! Five long days I was, running around through the fields; raw carrots I ate, and raw potatoes. Finally the police caught me.

"Hey, is that you, Marie Lebolloch?" says the jailer at the prison. "You've grown since I saw you, and nicely, too. You're a really fine looking girl, for sure! But what have you gone and done, to be brought in here? Your father and mother have come to see you; your mother's brought butter and eggs!"

Butter and eggs my mother had brought.

Then another time it was Corentin who came.

"Marie Lebolloch," says he, "I'll tell them it was my fault. Don't say no; I will, I'll tell them . . ."

"Corentin," says I, "don't go saying it was your fault. One person suffering is enough. You'll certainly find another girl in Saint-Oâ so you can get married."

"Marie Lebolloch, you're the one I'm going to get married to, if they don't convict you in this place."

"As for convicted, that I will not be, Corentin. Girls who have good references aren't convicted in this place; my lawyer said I have good references; the Sister said she'll give good references the same. A black cross she gave me as a present."

In the dirty prison in this place! Two months I've been in the dirty prison in this place, hanging around with beggars and bare-headed women.

March. "Oh, let me be, Mister Lawyer, Sir!" "It's the court of law for you, my girl, seeing that the little creature is dead." "Oh dear Jesus, it wasn't me as killed him! Tell them that, Sir! It wasn't me as killed him. Sentenced to hard labor? What does that mean? I guess it's better to be sentenced to hard labor than to walk through the street with a policeman on either side for the preliminary hearings every day. Oh, yes, you're such a kind man, Sir," said I, "and really good-looking. Now, there's a man who wouldn't have acted like Corentin, letting me have that baby all by myself." "I'll tell them the little fellow died of illness," said the lawyer. He gave a good speech.

"Her fault it is not," said he.

"No, my fault it is not," said I.

"Go back home again," says the judge.

I didn't know what was happening. What I could see was, there was someone in the courtroom signaling to me. My father it was! My mother was sick at home. My father tried to quit his job at the paper-mill, but the manager said he didn't want him to. Then afterward he got in a fight with Gloaguen because Gloaguen said I was a slut. Then after that there I was at home back again.

"Come to Sainte-Anne with us, Marie Lebolloch," said Sister Euphrasia. "It'll be nice for you there!"

"Marie Lebolloch is coming with me," said Corentin Leborgne.

"Oh, Corentin!" said my mother, "if you would have spoke up, misfortune wouldn't have come upon her."

"Ashamed I was, Mrs. Lebolloch," said Corentin.

"Misfortune is upon you, Marie Lebolloch," said Sister.

"My goodness, Sister, if the misfortune wouldn't have happened, Corentin wouldn't be married to me. Who do you think would have paid to support that little baby? Could *I* have supported him? How was *I* supposed to support him? Begging along the highway for his bread! The Good Lord is unjust, that's for sure!"

"Marie Lebolloch, you're in a state of sin forever," said Sister Euphrasia.

"In a state of sin I may be, Sister Euphrasia, I don't know about that; but I do know I'm married, that's for sure!"

◆

The Lawyer Who Meant to Have Two Wives
Instead of One

They would be flattered if I came.—J. PASSER, attorney at law

In a provincial town

It's enough to turn you completely cynical! How can any woman be so depraved? Really, men are much too restrained in front of women when it comes to discussions about fooling around. What good does it do for us men to be so shy? It doesn't get us anywhere. My God, but these women are brazen! Who could ever for a moment have imagined that Miss Virginia Hélary would play footsie with me the way she has? I will grant the existence of mitigating circumstances.[1] Admittedly I'm the handsomest man in the city; I have a ready wit; I even have a mocking, teasing little way with me, but not going beyond the bounds of propriety, I need scarcely add. Anyhow, I'm worth falling for! But does it make any sense that a girl from a decent family should be as eager for love-making as a nightclub entertainer? She was the one, the shameless creature, she it was who led me by the hand to her little bedroom after lunch, I swear she was the one . . . to show me a box of seashells; she even quite bluntly told the little nephew who was dogging our heels to go away. Consequently, in case we had been caught in the act, as when her brother young Master Paul came to look at himself in the wardrobe mirror, in such a way that there was simply no doubt we'd been seen, in such case the person liable to a reprimand wasn't me; all I had to do was leave the opposing parties, as we say at the courthouse, to get themselves out of the mess . . . obviously. But he didn't act as though he'd seen; he played innocent. All the same, though, the nerve of her!

"See here, my girl," I said to Virginia in the evening at the fair, near the bicycle merry-go-round, while the family kept an eye on the little nephew as he got his two pennies' worth of exercise, "jokes aside, I'll have you know that I'm a responsible man. Nature is

1. Max Jacob studied law and throughout this passage his lawyer narrator uses the jargon of his trade.

48

nature and all that, but why should I risk my reputation? The Prefect has plans for me; I'm a political figure."[2]

"Eleven o'clock, in front of your place, on the embankment," she answered, mouthing the words.

To sum up, then, there I was, standing like a ninny at the rail of my balcony with my mouth hanging open. I was not easy in my mind, for there were a good many folk passing by. This time it's her, I've got her . . . ? No, it was a country fellow clumping along on his wood-soled shoes! This time? No again, it was the vicar, coming back from his dinner at the Dufourmantels'. You get good cooking at the Dufourmantels'; why is it they don't invite me to dinner occasionally? . . . They would be flattered if I came. So is it just tact or shyness that prevents them from inviting me over? To the Devil with tact and shyness! Oh, goodness, that's cut me down to size! The next person to go by was a legal colleague of ours. As for him, it must have given him quite a turn to see with his own eyes the best courtroom lawyer in town standing there on his balcony at around eleven at night. Probably on reflection he decided I was working on a case, but let's suppose that the girl had been caught in the act of waiting in front of my house: in the long run I would have been compromised where public morality is concerned, all on account of a brief moment of amorous satisfaction.

"Oh, the family just goes on and on and it's so hard to get away," Virginia said to me. "Well, now, where shall we go?"

"I can't possibly take you to my place because of my maid; it wouldn't be prudent."

The result was that we walked up into the streets behind the embankment. "Love thy neighbor every time she's available!" That's the motto of all true males in the matter of womanizing, and it's my motto as well, with all due modesty. I would have been very willing, but it would have meant the total loss of my reputation. "Maître Passer walking through the streets with an underage girl![3] If you can't trust a chap like that, whom can you trust?" they'd all say. Oh the sidewalks and stairways and stretches of pavement we covered, pressed close to one another, but each time she started to

2. The prefect is official governor of a *Département*, one of the (at that time) ninety-five administrative units of French territory. Prefects are appointed from Paris.

3. French attorneys (barristers) are referred to and addressed as *Maître*.

kiss me, I would say to her: "Not here, not here!" It was apparent to
me that *she* knew where she was going, as she turned this way and
that: the wall between Saint Mark's Cemetery and the Convent of
the Daughters of Repentance is where she was heading. There her
eyes rolled up till only the whites . . . indeed, that happened several
times, since I . . . well, you know . . . but oh, Lord, was I frightened!
Lord! And the next day at the courthouse! It so happened that the
case I was currently pleading involved statutory rape, and there
was the presiding judge never taking his eyes off me! Oh, I paid a
heavy cost in fear and anxiety for that speech, I can tell you! I kept
saying to myself: "He knows . . . he knows. . . . For pity's sake, Your
Honor, come right out and call me to account, instead of gazing
at me without saying anything!" Afterward he accosted me: "How
very fresh your complexion is, Maître Passer!" he said to me. "You
must go in for very close shaves! I observed yesterday that you wore
light-colored ties; now, why? I should prefer to see you in black,
like everyone else. Black is suited to your character!"

"I can see that you're a very observant man, Your Honor. Since
yesterday, I've been using Astringent Lotion, but I shall give it up,
for the stuff is sticky and it stains false shirt-collars. And laundering
is expensive!"

I had laid out the money for a half-bottle of Astringent Lotion,
for it's an established fact that you can correctly deduce from a
person's complexion the imprudent amorous activities he has been
indulging in.

Virginia, when she suggested to me that I go and play on her
mother's piano, knew that she would surely find a way to get me
alone for a brief moment (I don't set much store by music; all that
stuff is just a lot of foolishness for simpletons, but I learned piano
as a youngster, for the simple reason that I was gifted at everything); what Virginia did not know, however, was that her older
sister, being a much more responsible person, would strike me as
preferable to Virginia and even give me a real distaste for her.
Indeed, Miss Eugenia, with her level-headed judgment, showed a
better understanding of the kind of man she was dealing with. Oh,
Virginia, I still loved you, but how sorry I was that you couldn't be a
reserved, properly behaved person, the way your older sister is! In
short, summoning Eugenia to appear in the case, or rather in the
garden, considerably altered the proceedings or, at the very least,

and joking aside, introduced some unexpected elements. While the older sister and I were walking in the garden, Virginia was playing the Sparrow Polka. "Have you never gone out on a spree?" Eugenia asked me. As I am considered a man of consequence and a political figure, I took it that Eugenia was poking fun at me. Finally, upon reflection, I realized that her inquiry was a way of showing me that she held me in esteem; this being so, since I was hoping that Eugenia would want to have me the way her sister did, I was bound to plead accordingly, don't you agree? So I told her a stupid story about a corporal, seeking to let her understand by oblique references that the corporal was in fact me. This corporal was a rather silly individual, but he made a specialty of saving drunkards from being punished and helping them stay safely hidden from the eyes of the officers till they could get spruced up. Thus I further impressed the young lady as a man who rescued others and yet was indulgent toward merrymaking: "Oh, but surely you've gone on one teeny weeny little spree yourself! Tell me about it; tell me; I want to know!" "Come on, now, I can see that you're all set to bring in your verdict," I answered. To have committed a few indiscretions as a student, provided you don't repeat the offense after you've reached the age of reason, doesn't detract from the basic seriousness of a man's character: thus there was no reason to deprive the young lady of her pleasure, so I told her how, in X one night, between my eighth and ninth term when I was doing my law degree, I smashed up all the furniture in an apartment, having, as a result of inebriation, come to the wrong floor. "What a sweet reward!" I said as she kissed me, but I must admit that these little introductory caresses don't interest me. At the table I prefer the roast to the appetizers. For real buck-rabbits like me it's the full exercise of male rights that counts; and the best of luck to all you gents who merely flirt. . . . In the evening near the home for the elderly, after Virginia's eyes had finished rolling up, she was erasing the evidence of the misdemeanor, to put it in lawyer's terms.

"It was definitely a mistake for you to go and stand across the street from the lamppost when the new postmaster walked by."

"It's safer for us not to hide; I prefer . . . oh, obviously I wasn't acting with your best interests in mind, Virginia, but rather my reputation."

"It's quite clear to me that men are all like pigs."

"What good is billing and cooing? That sort of foolishness is all right at the beginning, but nature says get on with it, and when a case has to be decided, nature's your best guide every time; that's my carefully considered, official opinion. Of necessity women never take it into their heads to consider nature, for the simple reason that only sensible, responsible men appreciate the value of nature."

"I keep getting a crazy urge to tell you that I took you quite at random, out of curiosity."

"You were determined to have me because I'm good-looking: I have a lovely ruddy-gold complexion; I have a Grecian nose; I have a full, handsome face; I have a nice big bushy black moustache. It's impossible not to love such a fine-looking man."

"You're so suspicious! You have an unpleasant voice!"

"I can't possibly have an unpleasant voice for the simple reason that I'm a famous courtroom lawyer. Pull yourself together, Virginia; you aren't making sense. It's laughable."

"Yes, but not the way you mean! Ha, ha, ha! Oh, you make me laugh all right! . . . You aren't always considerate of others, you know."

"Was it a desire to be considerate that led you to conceal the fact of your going away tomorrow so I wouldn't go with you to X tomorrow? You can't hide anything from the Law, Virginia!"

"Obviously you would have insisted on being told why I had decided to go alone to my aunt's place in X. Well, well! So you're jealous!"

"Virginia, when a person holds office, what difference does it make whether there are several individuals allowed to share in the benefits of that office, as long as the individual shares are not reduced as a direct consequence? There's no incompatibility involved."

To clean a silk top-hat which has fallen on the ground of a rainy evening, the best way to remove the dirt is to dry the hat out and give the muddied part a vigorous brushing; then you rub the stain with a rag soaked in spirits of turpentine.[4] A hat with an estimated value of twenty-eight francs! That's a fair amount of money, but

4. This sudden unannounced shift of focus, like a cut in cinematography, is typical of Jacob. The connection to what has gone before is made clear when we have read on. There is a resemblance to the poetic technique of Jacob's "cubist" period.

it's always better not to consider expense once you have definitely decided to make the outlay because then everyone thinks you are wealthy and also it's more economical to have a well-made item that will last you several years than to have a piece of rubbish, a valueless object, junk. Of course there's no need for my maid to know about this one little mishap: it sounds scatterbrained but actually it was perfectly natural to be eager for love-making. It was essential that I attend old Mr. Crumble's funeral since all of society was there! I mean, look at me! The handsomest, most intelligent lawyer in the county! It's no small thing to call yourself that! People would hold me in even greater esteem if I were to tell what I have here in the pocket of my frock coat: it's quite remarkable that I should have here two letters, from two girls who move about in society, the two sisters. Wouldn't you be edified about your daughters, papa Hélary, if you knew the unlikely fact that I have a letter from each of them in my pockets? As regards the letters, I hadn't had an opportunity to read them, but I thought I would read them at the café after the funeral, when a bunch of us got together to play *manille*. At the café I would have been very stupid to forgo a glass of chartreuse, seeing that the father of the two young ladies was paying for the drinks: chartreuse is a very good liqueur; it costs a franc twenty-five a glass, but old man Hélary's financial situation is first-rate.

I here transcribe the two documents:

Dear Sir;

Did you study the Fables of La Fontaine in high school? I'm told they are real masterpieces and I have no idea if that's so, being merely an ignorant girl. But it's a definite fact that there's one of them that fits you: the one about the dog who drops his dinner to try and gobble up the reflection of it in the water. You've been courting my sister, but of course we have no secrets from each other, so I know. Well, it's all over between you and me! o-v-e-r, over! Dreadfully sorry, my dear Sir.

from one who holds you in contempt,

Virginia.

You would have to be as stupid as a jury not to make a presumption of spite on the part of the young lady in the letter. It's plain

53

that I'm tired of her and as a result she's in a rage. Here is the other document in the case:

Dear Mr. Passer;
    You are my younger sister's lover and I was aware of the fact. Your bachelor stories interested me considerably, but, and you had better heed this warning for it will not be repeated, courting two people is no way to keep one of them.
    I am your most obedient servant, noble Sir.

                                                    Eugenia Hélary.

Having collated these two documents, I realized that the little ninnies had had the effrontery to make me the butt of a joke, but when I reviewed the case a major development made me realize that the whole thing was merely an intrigue on Eugenia's part to catch me. In fact Eugenia had figured out that I didn't need her sister any more, now that I had had her, and she was sending me her daddy, authorized to offer her in marriage. While I was folding the letters back up to put them in my pocket, the father of the two girls was saying to me:

"Are you aware, Maître Passer, that those young missies of mine will each have a dowry of forty thousand francs in cash?"

"Without prejudice to their rights as your heirs, Mr. Hélary."

"Ah-ha, Maître Passer!"

"They will come into their inheritance along with their brother, Master Paul!"

"There'll be enough for everyone, Maître Passer."

"There's no call for me to go into financial calculations with you, Mr. Hélary."

"Which of the two would you prefer if I were to propose a marriage to you?"

"The question of marriage is a serious question and one which requires a serious hearing. It cannot be denied that forty thousand francs is a handsome sum, but when you consider that I am a young man with a future and that I'll be in a position to become a Deputy and a Senator whenever I like, that amount seems trivial because of election expenses.[5] Now, then! If I were to say 'yes,'

5. France has a National Assembly (Chamber of Deputies) and a Senate.

there is no doubt whatsoever: Miss Eugenia is much more mature and responsible than her sister; I would prefer Miss Eugenia."

And, being nobody's fool, I sat there thinking: surely my sister-in-law will want a lusty buck-rabbit like me to start making love to her again, and that way I shall have two wives instead of one.

◆

The Man Who Had Never Traveled First Class on the Train Before

"Sixty million . . ."—PAUL

Paris

My friend Berger who is a clerk at Saint-Lazare Station (railroad pass department)—really, he's a chap with a brilliant future ahead of him!—happened upon a First-Class rail pass bearing the name of the resort town patronized by my mother, from which he and I had been corresponding for three months, and in an inspired act of thoughtfulness forwarded it immediately to me. I'm one that really does like special privileges as long as they aren't too questionable. I am still young, hence I am still poor, hence keenly aware of the profound pleasures afforded by true luxury, so how could I fail to say an enthusiastic yes when offered the opulent bounty of Western Rail, Inc? So at last I was going to make my way through the elegant society for which I was born, . . . a society in which I would form connections at once useful and delightful. Light-hearted as a lad, I carefully tended my person, using my poor mother's ylang-ylang, and settled into a bath.[1] Was this not the very opportunity upon which my thoughts dwell each morning as I dress: the rich woman who suddenly becomes infatuated with me? . . . not that I . . . Heavens, I'm laughing to myself, how odd.

Through some mysterious whim of the AUTHORITIES, there is no fire burning in the solemn First-Class waiting room; there's a splendid one for the vulgar herd who travel Third Class. November pierces me with her northern winds, but I, savoring the green

1. Ylang-ylang—the fashionable scent of the fin de siècle.

velvet of these armchairs, shall not suffer: I am not a man easily chilled, accustomed though we are to the warmth of the shop.

Imagine if I were to have an idyllic adventure in a sleeping-car with a touring actress or with one of those mysterious, chastely veiled creatures who have just this moment joined their lover in a tryst fraught with complications! Well! Shall not my eloquence suffice to make my very real abilities apparent to one of those ageless aristocratic fashion-plates? I'm not bad-looking, am I now? Short in stature but brisk in my movements; smooth-complexioned; a thin triangular face. See how my fingernails gleam: my grooming is always just so. I mean it seriously! What point would there be in all my careful contemplative study of these matters other than preparing me to enjoy life to the full, enabling me to come forth and triumph brilliantly? To me, good hunter and marksman that I am, the ideal game is—an elegant woman! Come now! A bit of daring is what's wanted here: then more daring, and still more daring![2] I'm not short of daring and yet I am extremely shy. The same holds true where love is concerned: I'm prudish but passionate.

It does not occur to me to enjoy the delights of the national landscape through the big window out in the corridor. Discreetly I allow my gaze to probe in minute detail the profiles in the various compartments, and all my nerves are attuned to assessing individual personalities: there's one clutch of women who have noisy friends at every station; I can spot the provincial nobility—and the upper crust they most certainly are not! This train is stopping every time there's a brick wall: once my own abilities, the inheritance from my widowed mother and a rich marriage have combined to provide me with the wealth befitting a man who is hungry for the good things in life, all my traveling will be done in the South on account of the fast trains. Stout gentlemen, jaundiced or rubicund, sit there reading the so-called comic illustrated papers without cracking a smile; if I speak to them it will only be to pick a quarrel. Other brute beasts in my compartment, whom it would afford me neither interest nor pleasure to tame, look as though they were bound for some solemn political gathering. At last, a pelisse! You know, that was a

---

2. Danton, speaking to the Assembly in 1792, when the Prussians were besieging Verdun: "To defeat them, Gentlemen, what we need is daring, then more daring, still more daring, and France will be saved."

real pelisse, a magnificent fur-lined cloak; I'm very knowledgeable in that area! Not some shoddy garment, none of your felted cloth! Oh, I swear an unbreakable oath to myself that some day I too will wear a ring with a fat ruby, and a fur-lined cape. Into an ashtray, which I am proud to have discovered, I cast with the lordly gesture of one who regularly uses First-Class coaches a cigarette just barely burned away at the tip, after which I bring my closed fists together on the seat-cushions in a pose at once simple, imposing, and dynamic. "My carriage will be waiting for us!" fur cloak says casually to his traveling companion. Oh, yes, now there, there's a man who's someone! I shall set about finding an excuse to speak to him. . . . Hang on, what's he saying now? "Cablegram . . . Switzerland. . . . Hunting to hounds!" I'm immediately convinced that he is the owner of some mighty château and has any number of guests awaiting him. By Jove! Oh, how happy I would be, oh how happy, to have him invite me to his fabulous hunts. Never till this moment have I been aware that I am, when you come right down to it, rather short. . . . What's that? "Childbirth . . . masseuse . . . operation. . . . A blood-letting was the only thing that saved her!" Why he's nothing but a country doctor! Of course I do appreciate the conversation of learned men, but what a disappointment! A mere pedanticist! He took me in and I was well and truly caught! Have you ever heard of anything so idiotic?

My inner dynamism very readily brings on attacks of chills and fever; I don't like excessive heat. After hesitating a number of times, I thought I might attenuate the heat around me by having recourse to a crank-handle which mechanically controls the coach's calorific count. With that ignoble shyness of mine which fills me with disgust when I set it for comparison beside what I refer to as "my worldly adventurer manner," I wriggle my way in beside the handle. These people find me contemptible and are looking at me with covert hostility (the feelings are perfectly mutual) and I am ill at ease. Cool and deliberately dextrous in my capacity as a business employee, I am nervous in this situation, for I should not wish to break the precious handle: No, it's too stiff! "Pull as hard as you want," says the doctor with the pelisse.

I am very embarrassed. I need calmly and coldly to choose a line of action, but what is it to be? What dignified mask shall I put on? How am I to sit back down without looking an utter fool?

In what direction shall I feign to turn my interested gaze? Like a drowning man, I clutch at the lifesaving straw of an idea: the washroom! Damn and blast! OCCUPIED! Now what? Do I go back into the compartment to be riddled with those treacherous, contemptuous glances? Well, but how do I do it? Wearing a forced smile, or with cold, exquisite courtesy? No, oh no! And so I, the man to whom only the little things seem impossible whereas the major ones dismay him not, linger in front of that OCCUPIED sign and am deeply saddened by this nonavailability. A quarter of an hour spent in quarantine staring at OCCUPIED! Every day I read in the newspapers accounts of people found dead in water-closets. What is the particular mode of behavior for a wealthy man who discovers such a thing? In what terms does he break the news? And if the murdered woman is merely ill, what does he do? Would we be able to get a locksmith at the next station to force this lock whose mechanism is complicated by words: VACANT!—OCCUPIED? At last! With calm, exquisite respect and not with a timid smile, I stand aside for one of those stout, ruddy-faced gentlemen. Very good! So . . . it's an actual fact . . . no little cake of soap in the First-Class washrooms! Now see here, a good many people would really make a row over something like this! Of course! Some boorish egotist has stolen it, you poor elegant passengers! You must admit that stealing soap isn't in the best of taste. Oh, I beg your pardon! My mistake! . . . I do apologize, I'm just betraying my total ignorance about life in First-Class carriages. Oh, how very, very ingenious! Look, see that? A tube fitted with two funnels at each of its extremities and with a handle; the soap comes tumbling down into your hand "like grated cheese." What an amusing little plaything, don't you agree? A perfect New Year's gift item for the toy department. It's a soap-mill. Hold on, now! Thank goodness I am not one of those people who, in their vulgar perverseness, make excessive use of the resources placed at their disposal: no indeed, no one would ever catch me showing a lack of self-control: that's enough soap. Respect for others is an integral part of chastity, modesty, and distinguished behavior; let us be respectful to the social group into whose midst chance has brought us.

Redon! Then Rennes in a little while! This isn't Rennes yet! What's all this, could they be coming to arrest someone? That would be good fun. These two railroad employees who have appeared out of the blue are asking to see my ticket. I can scarcely claim harassment since they're doing it to everyone. Oh, I'm quite sure of myself, everything is perfectly in order, Gentlemen; only the main thing is—can I find the pass my friend Berger sent me? Woe betide me if I've lost the Key to the Kingdom; imagine being asked to leave the coach! Rather death than such dishonor! The hostile eyes are waiting, hoping to see me put to shame. O joy o rapture, you aren't doomed yet, Paul. But now here's another unspeakably idiotic accident.

You'll soon see that I'm to be spared no humiliation: some silver coins, falling from my vest, have rolled under the seat. I'm going to look like a fool stooping to hunt for them. No need to tell you that I would gladly resign myself to sacrificing the money in favor of my self-respect. I am strongly attached to what is mine, but I dread appearing foolish. How can a bit of small change have any possible significance for my future? So you're rich, are you, Paul my little friend? Well, I will be, but a person isn't rich with the 200 francs doled out to me by the Galeries Lafayette. But the faces of my traveling companions show every sign of taking an interest in the carpet under the seats and my lost fortune. "Pooh," say I, vexed and casual, "It's no great matter!" "Oh, but still," says an earnest-mannered lady, "it's unpleasant to lose money!" That small change has suddenly become more important to me than any bunch of coins in my whole life and it's spoiling my trip. I can't stand it! Alright then, hurry up, while everyone has gotten off at this lunch-stop; take advantage of the situation to grub around, with your face brushing the folds in the carpet under the extra-wide seat. Success! the stiff panels of material were hiding my treasure.

Something strange is happening: since that new gentleman got on a little while ago with all his pale leather baggage, the train has been going at full speed, as though it were happy at the honor of the task entrusted to it: carrying a real First-Class passenger at last. Upon reflection I am sorry to have to report that he looked at me with deep uneasiness. Why? Because the object of his rather disagreeable scrutiny exudes a "Third-Class" aura at variance with the aristocratic seat he is occupying. That man finds me ill-clad or repulsive. I am prepared to admit in all sincerity that my jacket shows signs of wear but it's well cut and made from English cloth; of course there are my shoes, which are scuffed, but in their time they cost me thirty-five francs and they have a good shine. I realize I do have ugly hands. Oh, I know! I see what's wrong! It's my detachable shirt-collar. He considers my detachable collar ridiculous. I bought this shirt-collar in a provincial town, which normally I never do, and it's much too wide. Or else my hair! Everyone says I have lovely hair, and I comb it in an upsweep. So I was quite put out for a moment. Pooh! That man may very well juggle with millions, it makes no difference, he's nothing but an old fool. You see, the previous generation is unable to appreciate the next generation. You probably know that for physiognomists, eyes set too close together are a sign of stupidity.[3] I won't deny that he impresses me as being a man of fashion. When you look at him you can detect the well-to-do, slightly naïve customer we get at the Galeries. Pass judgment on me, criticize me if you will, find every fault in me, make fun of me; all my energies, all my thoughts, converge on this hero. No matter if he is stupid, I would like to master my excitement and show him in a distinguished conversation what I really am, what I know, and put an end to that I'm-above-all-this-sordid-reality silence of his. Oh, Hell and the Devil confound it! I've just gone and made myself ridiculous again. Oh, well, who cares? Since my great man, who luckily was out in the corridor, didn't see me: phooey to everyone else! I don't care a hoot! But that's what comes of not having your sealed copy of the Chaix timetable prominently in view in a smart satchel: I had donned my overcoat and picked up my packages too soon, thinking that we were coming to the big refreshment stop. I was mistaken, and I had to put everything neatly back in the luggage rack. Let's forget it; why dwell on it? That's not the problem now; the problem now is a mahogany folding table attached to the door. I would like to sit nobly writing my letters on that table. . . . No; let's say, jotting down my modest impressions. Oh, you wretch, will you be as awkward and timid here as you are swashbuckling and skillful in your department at the Galeries? "Excuse me, I'll just monopolize this writing table if I may . . . do please accept my apologies, Sir . . . I hope you won't be bothered in any way by this table!" These words I dared to utter to my neighbor, my hero, in a modulated, low-pitched, serious voice. Huh! A lot he cares! He gave a noncommittal growl. That fixes it once and for all: it means

3. Mrs. Alberti, a character in the next sketch, has just such eyes.

I don't fit the pattern; I've been given the boot; opportunity, fare-well! It's a basic house rule; all these people who travel First Class are cautious; they don't go spouting to you all about their mother-in-law the way Third-Class passengers do. Well, let me tell you that even if I'm the one who has to suffer for it, I like it better that way: it's a cooler, more dignified, wealthier way of behaving.

Well, Paul, my dear fellow, now comes a change of rail-lines with a meal-stop. After lunch we're going to be an "Express Train." We're going to turn into a luxury train with no nonsense about us. Don't I make a trim figure standing here on the platform? A bit short in the legs, certainly, but a neat figure, wouldn't you agree? And the shoulders, what do you think of the shoulders? After all, who's watching me just because I happen to take a seat at an un-assuming table where they have a set menu? No one! No one in sight! Where do you suppose *they* eat? Let's keep our eye on the door while we're eating. Oho! Isn't that my phlegmatic neighbor over there? By Heaven, I'm very well pleased that he isn't having lunch: he's the kind who eats little and eats well. What state is your wallet in, Paul? As you see, it's in a state that runs to blue menu-cards with meals at one and a half francs and not the ones with meals for two, three, four, and five francs. I have long been aware that registered membership in any social group goes according to your fortune, but never till this day have I felt so confined.

Since we can never forget that we aren't a millionaire, by Heaven I mean to become a great scoundrel in this modern civilization of ours! No halfway measures. The moment I get home I hand in my resignation to the people in charge at the Galeries Lafayette and go straight into Banking Circles! I shall go running after wealth and fortune with giant strides, crushing everything in my path. Out with youthful hesitation, and in its place here's to the opening of Paul Hubert and Company, with a change of staff and items manu-factured specially for the grand opening of our chain of stores. Damn the torpedoes, full steam ahead! I'm sending back my winter line of merchandise, and I want no moaning and groaning from the manufacturers! In this life, do it with class! Especially First Class . . . (Do you suppose I could possibly be a wit?)

The train is moving along smoothly through meadows enlarged by the flooding of the Loire. What a lot of elegant dresses and per-fumes there are, in this corridor which only a short time ago was so dowdy! Now there we have my natural element! Let's see, what can I do to fit into this hum of conversation and all its elegant overtones without looking like a fool? They are talking only among themselves and that just raises them even higher in my esteem. I can't tell you how much I like to hope that all this fashionable crowd are off to enjoy themselves in Paris till it's time to seek out the gentle December sun in Monte Carlo. "Among those present, your reporter spotted Mr. Paul Hubert, wearing a suit of Scottish homespun and carrying accessories of Mexican leather." Tell me, isn't that stout, fair-haired lady, the one showing off her splendid teeth to the well-dressed gentleman, a well-known actress? (Now there's a man's suit that would cost 400 francs at Carette's.) I remember a dress rehearsal at the Gymnase which I was fortunate enough to attend. Let's go over here and listen to what's being said: they all look as though they were being quietly brilliant in some fashionable drawing room while you, poor Paul, are nothing but the most wriggling, squirming species of sales-counter glow-worm. Anyhow, isn't this a drawing-room car that we're in? You see, you do have a ready wit, so what's stopping *you* from being quietly brilliant in someone's drawing room? A secure million in the bank, chum, a million, that's what's stopping you! If I skillfully contrived to strike up a conversation with one of these ladies, I would claim to be a millionaire, a financial reporter, and an amateur detective. . . . No, no, no false moves!

Most men would blush furiously to admit this, but an intelligent man has to be modest: this is the first time I've actually heard someone utter the words "Tea is served!"—and they were spoken by a *male* servant! Well, let's take good care not to call the ticket collector a servant; he's a unionized brother railroad worker and he might have something to say about that! But anyway, how big a tip should I give? Is five francs enough? Now then, boy, have some lamps brought, would you please? The voltaic arc-lights pierce the gloom and beneath their crystal tubes people settle in to read the news which has come from Paris expressly to meet us part way on our journey thither. As for you, Paul Hubert, back to Paris with you, very shortly now; your day of days and your wondrous First-Class ticket are ruined. You, the man who can do anything, have not been able to wangle a single conversation with a real First-Class passenger as defined by you. I had contrived to talk "polite small-talk, hunting, literature," with a gentleman who looked as though he was a big modern entrepreneur. Wasted effort. He replied with a smile, when I expressed my admiration for his knowledge of geography, that this is in no way due to an attentive perusal of Elisée Reclus: his itineraries depend not on him but on the heads of the firms he is employed by.[4]

N.B.—The assistant manager of my department at the Galeries Lafayette is quite intelligent; he's an unfrocked priest. Why, when I naïvely read him my notebook with the impressions of my trip, did he heave a sigh? "Blessed are the poor in ambition," he said, "for theirs is the Kingdom of Heaven! Poor old France!" He's funny! *I* certainly have no ambition to be poor and I'll take the silky undergarments of a cozy little woman over the Kingdom of Heaven any time. France needn't count on me or any of my fellow clerks, it seems to me—that doesn't stop the bosses from doing 60 million francs worth of business, the lucky stiffs!

"So! You think I'm just a conceited little fellow, is that it?" I said.

"No. What you are is greedy, and if you don't get very rich you'll turn vicious. Well, anyhow, Paul young fellow, I hope you remain a decent human being, or nearly."

◆

[*If you are sure Miss Tripier's portentous style must portend at least an interesting personal anecdote, you are going to be disappointed: a mind so cluttered with hand-me-down thoughts as hers has no room for anything fresh or interesting. If, on the other hand, you conclude that Jacob intended only the portrayal of such a mind through an imitation of the style such a mind might use, you are going to be bored, for Miss Tripier as a literary stylist is an utter bore. Max Jacob, on the other hand, is not. It is characteristic of his method that he not only imitates a style but then uses his own imitation as a device for penetrating to the personality lying beneath such a style, as one might build a mirror and then step through it into another world. Notice, for instance, how much is revealed within a few lines of the beginning by Miss Tripier's casual reference to love as "mental illness" and her naïve belief that references to love in literature go back as much as 200 years*

4. Elisée Reclus (1830–1905), French geographer and author of early guidebooks.

*or more— "even further than the author of Bérénice." Beneath the pedant
is a tragicomic personality. It is what lies below appearances that Max Jacob
is interested in bringing out and he is able to do this unsentimentally or, in
other words, comically.*]

◆

The Unmarried Teacher at the High School in Cherbourg

Doing much better in English.—E. TRIPIER.

Cherbourg

In this report I make no claim to be tracing step by step the evolving emotions which led to Lucretia's becoming the happy bride
of Thrasybulus.[1] The unusual interest of such an inquiry might
well tempt a future Doctor of Letters to take up her pen, but I do
not feel that I have aptitude enough in experimental psychology
on the one hand, or a keen enough mind on the other hand, to
undertake such a study, interesting though it might very well be.
There is nothing more enthralling or more instructive than the
progress and perils of an amorous intrigue or rather, to phrase it
better, the development in the human heart of the "love" feeling.[2]
In fact, nothing very definite is known about this mental illness and
I think it pointless to tackle a subject which so many great masters, going back even further than the author of Bérénice, have
already treated far more authoritatively than I can hope to do.[3]

---

1. At the risk of being more pedantic than Miss Tripier, we will use these
notes to explain some of the things she is referring to, so the reader can get a
real insight into her character and see how limited is her grasp of literature.
Thrasybulus was an Athenian general (445–388 B.C.) who restored democracy
in Athens. Lucretia was a Roman matron who committed suicide in 509 B.C.
after having been violated.

2. Miss Tripier's passion for dragging in literary analogies, no matter how
trivial the occasion, leads her to represent her utterly uneventful meeting with
her future husband in terms of high romance.

3. In his tragedy *Bérénice*, Jean Racine (1639–99) gives an intricate psychological analysis of two tormented hearts. The newly anointed emperor Titus
learns that the Romans would not accept the foreigner Bérénice, Queen of
Palestine, as their empress. Despite deep mutual love, they obey the will of the
people.

Still, never let it be said that Lucretia (the nickname I was given in Cherbourg; Thrasybulus was the nickname given to my husband Mr. Lechat) . . . but to continue, never let it be said that Lucretia denied herself exquisite moments of remembrance on the grounds that she is no Larochefoucauld nor yet a Barrès nor even a Bourget.[4] The memory of Cherbourg is so precious to me now! For is it not true that in most instances the attachment we feel for certain places derives merely from the fact of their being the visible manifestation of a cherished state of mind experienced concomitantly with our gazing upon them? Let it suffice, then, for me to set down in these pages a sheaf of randomly harvested impressions which I do not consider worthy of a more systematic presentation. Even the dating of them shall, whether deliberately or otherwise, remain uncertain; you may, if you wish, assign them to the winter preceding our becoming engaged.

(A heavy, pretentious introduction. Oh dear, how difficult it is to be, in Boileau's words,

"Simple, without connivance; pleasing, without contrivance!")[5]

I would consider it superfluous to describe the "first day back at school" even if these modest jottings were not, and were not meant to be, strictly and exclusively for my own perusal. Everyone has read back-to-school descriptions and the Platonic idea of "back to school" is so far endowed with real existence as to render further delineation of it unnecessary. Moreover the emotion which it is customary to display when dealing with the topic "back to school" (cf. Sully Prudhomme) would in my case and this context be purely

4. Giving classical nicknames to teachers is an old practice in French schools. In the 1950s, a high school in Toulouse had on staff a grim-faced battle-axe commonly known as "Venus."

La Rochefoucauld (1613–80) expressed his biting moral and psychological observations in the incisive and elegant form of the maxim. Maurice Barrès (1862–1923) was a journalist, novelist, philosopher, and politician. In his *Cult of the Ego* he meticulously portrays the inner life of an egotist. In order to expound his philosophical ideas, he filled his novels with digressions. Paul Bourget (1852–1935) uses an analytical method in his novels to capture the meanderings of his protagonists' naked souls. In his famous work *The Disciple* he discusses in both analytical and moralistic terms the responsibility of the writer and teacher in molding the young generation.

5. Nicolas Boileau (1636–1711) was a poet and critic. Miss Tripier quotes from his didactic poem *L'Art poétique*, in which he formulated the guiding principles of good style for expressing truth and beauty in the classical manner.

verbal.[6] I do not, I admit, set great store by Mummy's morning mug of coffee and little Andrew's antics and all the other things we are torn away from both by our professional duties and by our attempts to study for our own exams using the textbooks we have on hand. If I exclude purely physical emotions and those afforded by great classical music, I think I can truly say that other emotions are unknown to me; and it will have required no less an event than the Thrasybulus Episode to bring me around to a contemplation of the emotive element in my personal makeup. I classify moments of "emotionally dictated remembrance" (see above) under animal physiology.

Within my general conception of what constitutes comfort, the Navy Hotel, the little hotel where I was staying, can be considered as the embodiment of an ideal. Not but what the plainness of my room has on at least one occasion been a source of embarrassment to me. This is how it came about: a girl from the Ursuline convent had got in touch with me last year about preparing to take the advanced school certificate examinations (the curriculum is very heavy), and I would have had to give up any notion of exposing that Church-trained youngster to the influence of the modern scientific outlook if I had not obtained permission to do the tutoring in the hotel parlor, especially because of her family.[7] It cannot be denied that my friend Alice's room presents a more luxurious appearance than mine: she has a table laden with papers, and a bookcase of her own with bound volumes gracing its shelves, but one could not indulge the practice of walking around in her room as is my wont when cogitating or reciting from memory. So far from harboring the slightest desire for private ownership of furniture however handsome, I can only view such possessions as a source of problems in the, alas, all-too-frequent event of one's being "reassigned."

I do not pretend to be drawing character portraits in these pages, but I must at the very least name the individuals who impinge directly upon my daily life. The first of these is Joseph, a

6. Armand Sully Prudhomme (1839–1907) was an Academic poet who often dealt with domestic topics in his stilted, didactic poems.

7. Since the separation of Church and State in 1904–5 religion has not been taught in state schools and a rivalry has existed between the two systems, each claiming to be superior to the other. The scientific-minded Miss Tripier, of course, looks down on the "Church-trained youngster."

curious example of a hotel handyman, who spoke very favorably of me last year, declaring me to be a "good-looking girl." When a man's taste does him such credit, you really cannot dismiss him as a person of no importance. One thing is certain: unlikely though it may seem, Joseph is not unattractive; he has "style," it would be unfair to argue otherwise. The charge of anti-intellectualism is simply irrelevant; when I compare him with that distinguished humanist Mr. Lechat, commonly called Thrasybulus, Joseph is, all things considered, far and away the better-looking man. "Is that you, Joseph? Nice to know you're still here!" I called out on the first morning of term when, Nemesis-like, he knocked at my door to awaken me. He didn't answer. Speaking of Joseph, I do not blush to disclose a meritorious act of mine: one of those monsters called creditors, against whom hotel handymen are no better protected than other mortals, had been coming every day to dun him for ten francs, and Joseph was on the point of being dismissed. Like Timon of Athens, I prodigally disbursed the ten francs.[8] This action earned me the approval of Viscountess T——, of whom more in a moment, plus this remark from Mr. Lechat "after we were married": "That ten francs contributed a great deal to the psychological picture of you which I was trying to construct at the time!"

In Viscountess T—— you have one of those clerical temperaments that beget a dignified, patronizing way of speaking. In our relations with the young naval surgeons I hope shortly to reveal another side to her character, a stranger character than one might at the outset be inclined to suppose. She is nevertheless a woman of great distinction. One day we entered into a splendid polemic on the subject of a concert to which she proposed to take me. I rejected the offer, using arguments drawn from my theory of the will: any emotion, insofar as emotions are most often physiological in origin, is bad by definition, and it so happens that from the very opening bars of any orchestral music, I begin weeping copiously and am left in a state of mind quite unsuited to studying for the Doctor of Letters examination. Viscountess T—— defended the thesis that emotion is necessary to the perfection of the intel-

8. In Shakespeare's tragedy *Timon of Athens*, a generous host and patron of the arts exiles himself from his city to a cave where he discovers that, once he is in financial straits, he cannot rely on his "friends." In the cave he finds a buried treasure of gold and lavishly rewards his faithful servant.

lect, since it is impossible to understand anything without love, and further arguments in that vein. . . .[9]

Despite the disdain with which I have always regarded all questions pertaining to clothing, I did feel the need for a short cape, and a model priced at nine francs eighty-five drew my attention and thence my custom to Aux Dames de France in Cherbourg. Viscountess T——, pointing to a chiffon of pink netting, remarked that it would give the cape a new touch as well as greater fullness. I rejected the suggested ornament on the advice of Lechat commonly called Thrasybulus. The Viscountess then expounded her thesis: ought one to neglect the embellishment of the human body? Ought one to be lacking in charity toward one's neighbor's eye in its desire for beauty, and further arguments in that vein . . . ? Though our opinions might diverge, I continued to hold the Viscountess in esteem despite the attitude of Thrasybulus who always considered her insincere and not to be trusted. She came here for three months while the battleships were being refitted, along with her husband who is a naval engineer and her children who are taken by the maid to the Ursuline school every day; in the event, they've been at the Navy Hotel for three years.

One of the distinguishing characteristics of young naval surgeons is that they have nothing to do: morning sick-call and, for whichever of them is on duty, follow-up call. It would be idle to deny that those of them living at the Navy Hotel are charming lads and, all things considered, exquisitely tactful. What I can state for a fact is that these young men are reserved to a fault in their behavior toward Alice and me, without however going so far as to be shy. If the things my brother Hippolytus said during the holidays are to be believed, nothing could adequately describe the coarseness of the male sex; thus it is quite conceivable that when Alice and I are not present they do not blush to display the true feelings that they harbor toward us. I much prefer not to think about it. They try unsuccessfully to have us share their merriment and their taste for dancing, things that even a modicum of decorum would preclude our being involved with. It would be if not unseemly then at the very least frankly ludicrous for us to join in those waltzes and

9. See the first of the *Letters from Max Jacob to Marcel Béalu*, paragraph 5, for Jacob's ideas on the emotions in poetry.

quadrilles at all hours of the day and night. At the very most we need feel no scruples about playing the piano for them, and until one certain day the Viscountess commended our behavior. That, it so happened, was also the day when I received a clear intimation of Thrasybulus's feelings; shortly thereafter I was to lose his good opinion. But before I begin my account of such stirring events, it is essential to present, with a few deft strokes, the principal of the high-school.

Would that I might possess the barbed pen of a Juvenal, the comic verve of a Plautus, the stinging whip of an Aristophanes, the virulence of a Swift, the humorous philosophic depth of a Laurence Sterne as well as his knowledge of mankind, or even the direct, candid manner of a Mirbeau, the better to describe Mrs. Alberti, the new principal of the girls' high school in Cherbourg, but alas! I am merely Estelle Tripier commonly called Lucretia, student in Letters and upper-year high-school teacher.[10] Now, then, O Muse of La Bruyère, inspire me, as they say in epic poems.[11] Mrs. Alberti comes rushing into classrooms and, tornado-like, whirls herself out again. This puffing, panting red ball, squeezed into her tight-fitting garments, complains about the way her digestion interferes with her breathing, the way the Minister of Education tramples her abilities underfoot, the way her hoarseness of voice destroys her authority, the way the teachers undermine her efforts at administration, the way the students make light of everything, the way their families show total lack of understanding, and the way the curriculum stifles any display of initiative; despite which she remains as satisfied with herself as she is dissatisfied with the world at large. Let her but appear before a group of students and her abrupt, husky voice is cause for merriment; let her but change it for a higher-pitched one which suddenly becomes a yap, and the

10. Octave Mirbeau (1848–1917) was a writer and playwright. Jacob makes fun of his staunchly realist novels such as *Diary of a Maid* and his comedy *Business is Business*, written in the same style.

11. Jean de La Bruyère (1645–96) was a moralist and satirist. A keen observer of both bourgeois and aristocratic circles, he wrote *Characters of Theophrastus Translated from the Greek, with Characters or the Manners of this Century*, which depicted his contemporaries in lively, always unflattering, often even cruel character portraits. The portrait of Mrs. Alberti is an excellent pastiche of La Bruyère's picturesque, ironic, concrete style.

hilarity redoubles; she squints, she is myopic, and her eyes suggest two buttons set close together and protected by an enormous pince-nez.[12] Her husband Maurice, a benighted bureaucrat, teacher's aid at the high school for boys, believes that nature intended him to be a university professor; Mrs. Alberti considers him, and herself too, not unworthy of such a position, and has bought him a microscope. "How to end up in the same city, that's the whole problem!" she says in her Teutonic-sounding voice. "What it is to have strong emotional ties! . . . Look at those children playing! *They* aren't aware of their clothes, whereas mine are always tight! I've been advised to wear flannel for the pains in my feet but I can't do up my ankle-boots in the morning as it is!"

It is impossible to conjure up an adequate picture of the principal's physical appearance on days when the school inspector is to come: on those occasions Mrs. Alberti wears a black dress with mauve trim, covered in black lace at the yoke and wrists, and also at the scallops in the hem which form a festoon. It's her evening dress, and I am strongly inclined to believe that she is even more uncomfortable in it than in her ordinary clothing: it is quite within the bounds of probability that she has put on weight and that the dress, static matter trapped in its skilled crafting, has been unable to adapt to the fatty tissue, living matter in a state of motion. During the most recent inspection, when I was teaching a lesson on Corneille's *Nicomède*, some happy impulse inspired me to talk about the Cartesian influence in the seventeenth century, a pet topic of Mr. Claus, the inspector. After that, he could hardly fail to be delighted with my performance, nor, in turn, could the principal. These smiles of officialdom, rather than my personal qualities, earned me an invitation to the principal's inner office, an introduction to the husband Maurice whom I'd heard so much about and who is the center of her emotional life, the promise of that New Year's Eve party which will remain a milestone in my life, and a private viewing of the principal's entire collection of personal photographs. "I always look as though I squint in photographs! There's not one that's a good likeness," she said. Naturally it was required that I should pick out which one was her in group pictures, girlhood pictures, pictures taken in bathing suits, family groups, and

12. See "The Man Who Had Never Traveled First Class on the Train Before," note 3.

school pictures: I brought all the vigor of my intellect to bear on this delicate operation and was sufficiently successful, I can state this with certainty, to win her good graces. She praised me to the inspector. What luck!

I shall leave the principal to work on her Christmas tree, organize little presents, make madeleine-cookies, wrap them in silver paper, tie ribbons around party-whistles, send out invitations to the parents of girls who have had four first-place standings during the term, parents of girls in their senior year and of girls who are on the honor roll; I grant her the virtue of having a great deal of energy, and turn my attention to my future husband Mr. Lechat commonly called Thrasybulus, Ph.D. in English. Ethics would dictate that I owe a debt of gratitude to the Viscountess, for her husband is a childhood friend of Thrasybulus and thus it was through her that I met him, but it may truly be said that it was through her that I almost lost him, and however helpful to me she may unwittingly have been, it was only because the two of them had a falling-out that I got him back. If one may judge from iconographic documents, my husband has the physical stature of great men, which is to say average height; he has a black beard laced with white hairs, and glasses. Among the many debts I owe him, I rank most highly my acquaintance with the Lake poets and with Burns, the British Pushkin; with Swift who is unknown in France and with the author of *Robinson Crusoe*, that slender volume which, if one may so express it, is merely the hypotenuse in the triangle of Defoe's work. Let me add that my husband is not only a humanist, he is a man of wisdom, and his theories are of practical use to me. Now as I have said, it was on the evening of the New Year's party that I simply had to abandon any remaining doubts about his feelings toward me. He took me aside to converse about an essay on Romeo and Juliette that I had submitted to him, took a volume of Shakespeare out of his pocket, and began to read in a low voice. Then, as though impelled by a current of poetic thought, he stopped (in the middle of the balcony scene), reached under his glasses to wipe his eyes, made as though to take my hand and turned away from me. In the domain of will power, I thought to myself, we are much superior to men. "Thrasybulus is in love with me," I straightway said to Alice. "Take care," replied my friend, "He's had several mistresses." "My brother Hippolytus says that two mistresses are better than one and a number of authors express the same view." Meanwhile Mrs. Alberti was achieving depths of stupidity worthy of the emperor Claudius: "Mister Gras," she was saying to the venerable vice-principal of the high school, "I want to show you the special esteem I have for you as a person. Here are two gilded nuts; one of them has a blue thread and that's your wife; and your daughter is the nut with the pink thread; don't you agree, Mr. Lechat?" "In Syriac the word for nut is *agon*," said Mr. Lechat sadly. There can be no doubt that these were the only words he'd uttered since the balcony scene: I was very moved, I mean physiologically moved (cf. above).

Alice and I had correctly conjectured that the naval surgeons would be celebrating at the hotel. And indeed we were obliged to decline their offers of champagne. Without becoming too profound in my analyses, let me simply note that the Viscountess could have had no reason other than the intrinsic baseness of her character for acting as she did; it was in fact quite pointless for us to drink champagne as she seemed to be insisting we do. When one of the doctors asked permission to kiss me, "This is New Year's Eve, my dear," she said. "Don't hang back!" "Kiss Alice as well," I said to the young man. He kissed me, blushing as he did so, but there was nothing in his action to shock my modesty. The Viscountess, meanwhile, under the appearances of hypocritical morality, was broaching a theory which was in fact licentious, to wit, that as long as the behavior of men is not dictated by the highest ethical considerations, that of women need not be more so. People say foolish things of that sort in conversation; I did, however, note with pleasure that the young men were protesting. After having a piece of the festive nougat, a confection to which I am partial, Alice and I withdrew, pursued by the bestower of kisses who was all for having another round, and by a very vivacious Viscountess who was insisting, in a disgusting and contemptible fashion, that we take part in these dissolute goings-on. So much for clerical mentalities when the restraints are removed.

To the best of my knowledge I had not failed that evening in any of my responsibilities and the only reason I could find for the coldness of Mr. Lechat's behavior was shyness, or a certain inflexibility of character. The fact is that upon meeting me after school at the corner of Lycée and Port streets, he stated, as he handed back my uncorrected compositions, that he would no longer be at home at our regular times. There could be no doubt that he was fleeing from me as from a Siren. Alas, poor Siren! I also learned, through Miss Guerlo commonly called Hercules Amphibian and Miss Bréhat commonly called Bradamanta, that he had made a trip to Paris, where he had applied to the Ministry of Education for a transfer.[13]

These two unmarried ladies who, as Protestants, enjoy considerable influence in high places, use identical dress and constant twinliness, if I may so express it, to display publicly a friendship comparable to that of Castor and Pollux, or Orestes and Pylades, or Saint Peter and Saint Mark, or Saint Gregory Nazianzen and Saint Basil the Great. If Bradamanta, who is a chemistry teacher, lingers in the empty reaches of the laboratory after four o'clock, it is common-room knowledge that Hercules Amphibian comes and waits open-mouthed for her friend to finish work before tasting the fruit of her own after-school freedom. But now here is something that should move us all deeply, though personally I feel no such inclination: they went together to the Ministry of Education in Paris, where they wept and pleaded in the office of the director of secondary education not to be separated in the event they were promoted. This fact was disclosed by the principal who was there soliciting a single posting for herself and her husband in the vicinity of Paris and also demanding that girls' high schools be granted the one-day holiday extension unfairly reserved for boys' schools. These details, it seems to me, are a faithful reflection of the academic world at the beginning of the twentieth century.

For six weeks, Lechat's total silence, and his behavior, carefully interpreted, seemed to signify that he no longer attached the slightest objective value to my person. And for that very reason (if we are to believe what writers tell us) he occupied a greater place in my thoughts. Considering my theory of the will, this situation should not have been such as to distract me from my duties. It is odd that so far these notes contain no reference to the children who pass through my hands. That is probably because I make a point of not taking an interest in them, so as not to expose myself to feelings that would interfere with my own academic studies. People are always comparing our style of education unfavorably with the kind

13. Bradamanta was a female warrior in Ariosto's *Orlando furioso*.

afforded by the clergy, which is paternal and loving: I've no doubt it is! But what sort of results does this give you in exams? The very worst; just look at the statistics! And in real life? Viscountess T——! I do, however, consider it my duty to point out to the girls which works of painting and music it is vital for them to admire. For our ecclesiastical colleagues, Paris may be worth a Mass, but for me, knowing what to see when you get there is worth a Pass! And without going to the point of criticizing how the girls behave in town, as Alice does—her teaching methods have a general taint of clericalism and are widely disapproved of (you perform your assigned duties and that's it!)—I do try to guide their taste in dress: "Young ladies, you do not wear a yellow hat with a red dress!" I heard one of the girls saying during recess, mimicking me. She's the one who handed in a narrative composition in which she was coming down the stairs wearing her *scandals*.

Anyone familiar with the monotony of life in the Public Service will not be surprised to find me recording as an event of some magnitude the appearance of a "new arrival" on the teaching staff. Miss Duménil, nicknamed Philoctetes because she is so solitary, wandered around in Cherbourg on her first night without coming upon either a hotel or the high school. Although I felt not the least bit drawn toward this fair-haired little person with her precious air and her mathematician's manner, I felt I should sponsor her; and all too often habit becomes a substitute for friendship, operating in the same sphere as friendship but faster. We would take our walks together and, with no fear of jesting too freely, we would make fun of colleagues whose sole concerns were their promotion and their husbands, all of them teachers at the boys' high school. One evening we were voicing sundry opinions on the subject of a Beethoven andante, and there was a sunset which I suppose was quite a decent one for that time of year, when she suddenly revealed the treachery of Viscountess T——. That lady was consigning me to the Gods of the Underworld for all to hear: apparently my conduct on the evening of the New Year's party had been entirely directed toward correcting or condemning hers, and she would never forgive me. I guessed intuitively that these feelings of hers were not unconnected with Thrasybulus's sudden coldness and I was not mistaken. Thus it was that the "new arrival," from being a mere distraction while I waited for larger events to enter my life, thus it was that her advent became the *deus ex machina* of my marriage.

The principal, who rightly prizes her hard-earned reputation for diplomatic social activity, organized a tea to mark Shrove Tuesday. I am pleased to report that the day was a failure for everyone except me. A gang of Mardi gras masqueraders invaded the caretaker's lodge; forty schoolboys, whose boldness has all my admiration, got into the dear old place, into the dancing room where the students' mothers had assembled from all over town to watch a group lesson. I do not feel compelled to follow them around describing their escapades. Excellent witnesses, reliable ones, have stated that they kissed Mrs. Morisson, one of the most respectable matrons in the city, while a certain gallant young gentleman was putting his arm round her daughter's waist (the daughter is one of my students); and that they danced in a circle round the principal while she, abandoning the final preparations for her school tea, tried to negotiate. While waiting for the guests to come, I was busy defending German philology to my usual little group. According to those same witnesses, the principal is supposed to have beseeched her dear Maurice to go and fetch the superintendent of police. A real scandal. Meanwhile, when the dancing lesson was over, the appointed time for the tea arrived, as did the ladies and gentlemen who had been asked to it; in they came, to find no sign of the principal, or tea, or a table suitably laid. Nothing definite is known about how the principal was occupied at that time. My friend Alice sat down to the piano to entertain the arriving guests. A teacher belonging to the young carnival-goers who were still in our midst, mistaking our stout school manageress for the head of the establishment (he's new), went up and made her a formal bow, to everyone's delight. "Mr. Lechat! Mr. Lechat! Is Mr. Lechat here?" This from the principal who came swooping in and whirled away out of sight again: "Mr. Lechat, go and find my husband!" Mr. Lechat started after her, but stopped in front of me.

"Miss Tripier," he said, "I have wronged you. Broadly speaking, I think that I . . . I paid heed to slanderous utterances whose very source ought to have made me suspicious. Philoctetes, I mean . . . the new. . . . As regards this whole matter, I hope that you will allow me to be your friend again."

The next day I went to give him back Marlowe's *Faust*, which I studied: the copy in my possession belonged to Mr. Lechat commonly called Thrasybulus.

"It seems you are fond of my library?" he said.

"Yes indeed! I don't suppose I could hope to find a better, not where English literature is concerned."

"In that case, allow me to say that this library can be yours for the rest of your life."

"Yes . . . yes . . . I know . . . I understand . . . Marlowe's *Faust* is far from being on a par with Goethe's, yet there is no question but that Marlowe can sustain comparison with Shakespeare."

While I was talking, he took my hand and slipped a ring onto my finger.

The police superintendent came after all the masqueraders had left. Maurice did not return until far into the night, in, I'm told, a state of intoxication.

Thrasybulus and Lucretia were married during the Easter holidays. I am making great strides in my study of English.

Don't Hang Up, Miss!
or, The Telephone Company Does It Again

A Tale with a Message

[*Jacob's* Ne Coupez pas Mademoiselle, ou Les Erreurs des P.T.T. *is likely to strike the critic the way the flower in a crannied wall struck Tennyson: understand and you understand everything. Indeed the theme is clearly communication and hence presumably understanding, yet not much else is clear, except the fact that we have here an example of Jacob's prose poetry: the piece is not metrical or so filled with images that we feel compelled to think of it as poetry, but it does invite the kind of attention that no mere prose composition of equal obscurity would. A central image or "pensée," perhaps, gives rise to others, seemingly at random, yet the whole composition has some kind of structure, for the last lines take us back to the first. Like all genuine poetry* Don't Hang up, Miss! *convinces the reader that unraveling the meaning is a worthwhile endeavor, even if the endeavor is unsuccessful.*

Whatever it should be called technically—it is rather too long to fit Jacob's definition of prose poetry—this cheerful flight of fantasy has not been republished since 1921. The luxury edition, published in one hundred copies, illustrated by four Juan Gris lithographs, is a coveted collector's item today.]

◆

The Muse

Alcofibras the Giant spied or thought he spied a spider's Milky Web, and said to himself: "What have we here! a headdress, light and airy, which I shall bring into fashion for next spring!"

And so saying, he pulled up the network of telephone lines serving a city of some size. Telephone and telegraph lines. And set them upon his head.

and oh the wonder
of messages sublunar rent asunder!
A cry of protest rose above the rest; 'twas this:
"Wait, Operator, wait! Don't hang up, Miss!"

Great Heavens! Don't hang up Miss Who? Who is this young lady that mustn't get hung up? Upon what horrible, earth-shaking event has he indiscreetly stumbled? Can she be some princess on whose fate the destinies of empires hang? Is she the female repository of some fearful state secret? That must be it! A girl has fallen into the hands of desperate criminals! She's in some sort of prison. An executioner is ready to Operate some dread machine: he's going to hang her up!

And all the world was watching, fearful for her fate. Alcofibras will take a hand in the affair. A giant he may be, but he is also a gallant gentleman, and he will not allow the young lady to be hung up. Too late! Too late! The young lady has been hung up. A conversation, between two examining magistrates, magically is heard: "Ha! That's right! On Holy-Martyrs Avenue! Holy-Martyrs Avenue? That's a good one!" How cruelly ironic are these words! Like the story of Miss Troubesco's trunk!

"Besides," he thought, "how am I to set my giant foot upon that puny pill they call a planet, even if I plan it? One foot on Paris, and ffft! no Paris!"

Behold the despair of Greatness, tied firmly to the shore, as the saying is, by his greatness.

◆

The Poet

How many times might not we men of rank have usefully inter-
vened in the quarrels of our inferiors, if our very rank had not
bound us within the status quo. I appeal to all you men of goodwill,
so numerous on earth: what despair is yours on such occasions, for
instead of peacefully digesting your Sunday chicken there in your
armchair, you experience a pang of pain brought on by *their* dis-
agreements. Yesterday evening a woman who, I could sense, was
still young and beautiful, was trying to steer her husband away
from the doors of a bar, he being in an obvious state of intoxication.

"Lay one hand on me and I'll slug you!" he was saying.

"Supper's going to get cold, I tell you!" she kept saying. It was the
time of day when men go for their predinner drinks.

He abandoned reality, as represented in this instance by a
woman, in favor of the gilded dreams to be had from alcohol. The
husband slugged the wife. Do you not think I might have inter-
vened to good effect? I would have laid stress on women's rights! I
would have pointed out to the man that his duty is to support and
protect, regardless of social class. But did I do so? I did not; my
dignity kept me away from the place to which my conscience was
summoning me, my dignity and perhaps a certain native cowardice
as well . . . but let's not go into that.

At the time of the telephone mix-ups which we referred to
earlier and which, as the reader will no doubt have surmised, were
caused by the bold hand of Alcofibras the giant, courteous relations
were being maintained between two heads of state: the Emperor
of China and the Mikado of Japan.

One of them, whom I call X, had inquired by wire (he's entitled
to send telegrams free of charge) after the health of the other:

"Is Your Majesty enjoying the excellent sleep which you so well
deserve, and what of Your Majesty's revered Wife?"

Ah, then a fearful mix-up did ensue, and led to fearful crimes!
What answer do you suppose the head of state received? Alas for
that fateful, fateful mix-up!

"Get lost, you jerk! Come off it, fathead!"

This second wire was intended for a respectable wholesale

dealer and came from the pen of another wholesale dealer with whom he had been unable to reach an agreement on the pricing of the new toilet tissues to be used for Japanese handkerchiefs. Apologies were tendered and the staffs at the embassies were changed. The Minister of Communications was put to death. The clerk who was supposed to have transmitted the telegram was guillotined after first being gift-wrapped and publicly displayed in a barrel. All to no avail: it was considered that a war was required.

Hidden behind a pile of clouds, the giant watched in silent horror as Asia and a number of Pacific islands went up in flame.

Don't hang up Miss . . . !

That universal cry! That cry, like a refrain! Entreaty, ceaselessly repeated! The changeless chant of universal woe!

"Oh!" cried he, "let me hear you echo in my ears once more; I want to hear that cry again, and on that cry, to die!"

The giant did not doubt but that the young lady with the hang-up was at once the cause, the martyr, and the legendary heroine of the war.

The Muses, and Homer whose greatness never ceases to be sung in the Azure Land, told Alcofibras the Giant the story of Helen of Troy.

"Did your Miss Helen get hung up too?" Alcofibras wanted to know.

And the voice of this hulking, sentimental giant was to be heard as he howled in the night:

"Don't hang up Miss . . . !"

From *The Dullard Prince*

[*The French title of this book is* Le Roi de Béotie, *"The King of Boeotia."
The ancient Boeotians were reputed to be dull, uncouth, blockheaded; and
the French word* Béotien *still refers to such a person.*

*Jacob wrote to Jean Cocteau: "If they ask the meaning of the title,
sing them:*

> *'Please find enclosed and pray accept
> A most unworthy offering:
> The heart of a Boeotian king.'"*

Jacob is referring to a song in Offenbach's opéra bouffe Orpheus in the
Underworld, *a song that begins "When I was king of Boeotia. . . ." So the
reference is specific, but the general sense of Boeotian is unchanged; hence*
The Dullard Prince.

*With a great variety of structures and style, the author re-creates here the
texture of real life, but using nonrealist techniques. This applies particularly
to the second part of the volume. The first contains seventeen narratives,
some long, some short, most of them written long before the book's publication in 1921, whereas the second part recalls Max Jacob's car accident, the
ensuing pneumonia, and his agonizing experience in hospital. The images,
style, and structure of these pages simulate a feverish mind, moving swiftly
back and forth between the conscious and the subconscious, transcending
reality in apocalyptic visions.*

*More than twenty years later, Jacob reread his book and found that it was
"filled with emotions, follies, and accurate details about mankind." Why?
Because, as he said, he took the trouble to write straight from the gut.*]

◆

Surprised and Delighted

To Mrs. Emma Henry Hertz

[*Although this story is written in the first person under the name of Max, it cannot be read as a "true story." Jacob believed only in creative invention, so much so that even when he was dictating his life story to his biographer or told certain incidents of his life to his innumerable correspondents, he always colored the bare truth. A particular blend of autobiography and fiction appears systematically throughout his works, probably because he was never able to get used to himself. He played being someone else in* Film-Flam *and* The Dark Room, *or he invented another biography to suit the occasion. Nevertheless the end of this story rings true, for at the age of twenty-three Max Jacob had burned his bridges, turned his back on his family, abandoned forever all hope for a peaceful bourgeois existence, and entered instead upon a "life of privation and suffering."*]

Let me confess that my attempts to take part in barrack drills were so ineffectual that those whose task it was to conduct such drills eventually found their patience exhausted. And when after six weeks the kindly vigilance of the military authorities put an end to my labors in order to spare me further fatigue, I was more successful in concealing my shame at being relieved of my responsibilities than were my superiors in concealing their joy at having discharged theirs. The school in Paris which was to prepare me for my probable future as a civil servant had not expected me that year: so military discharge meant holidays, and on holiday I still am.

I became an artist or I learned that I was one or I thought I was or I learned to be. My sensibility, artificially heightened by leisure time and free of the restraints imposed by school routines, filled me with new excitement; at the same time I learned the joys of freedom in a country setting, and found these joys so much to my liking that I was unwilling to give them up again. My native city, where my family still resides, is in a valley surrounded by innumerable other valleys full of rocks, trees, and brooks: occasionally I wept as I cycled along the roads. Suddenly it seemed to me that other people didn't understand great works of art; their opinions struck me as ridiculous. Out of a sense of modesty I hid my sacred dreams and the outward signs of these new feelings from those who would have scoffed at them, and I was consoled for my silence by a dawning sense of pride which lay beneath. Unfortunately, pursuing the lure of a none-too-solid friendship, I broke my silence, wounding in the process both myself and those who loved me.

Doctor Marius Alexandre and I were of the same age, came from the same town, had attended the same high school. He had recently renounced the companionship of his teachers at the medical school in X to run a country property which the death of his parents had left unmanaged. But neither his fortune nor his inclinations would permit of his medical studies going to waste. The populace of his native town was apportioned among a small number of doctors whom he had no hope of dispossessing. In our public asylums, the Insane busy themselves with Agronomy and Cattle-raising; Marius Alexandre bought them a little cow and was chosen as their doctor. East of the city, the property occupied by the Insane Asylum forms a round green hill by day, and at night a necropolis by virtue of its crown of low white buildings. One of these is the living-quarters for the doctor, the student who assists him in providing medical services, and an inmate who acts as their domestic servant. The two learned gentlemen have a dining room in common and their bedrooms are separated by a door. I ran across Marius one day and went with him to the Asylum. The white wood panels in the medical building betrayed its decrepitude, and their state of filth similarly betrayed the habits of its three occupants: plates still wet from being washed, and glasses gray from dust and red from wine were on a bedroom writing-table rather than where they belonged. I recognized the collection of walking-sticks belonging to Marius' late father, but you, O walking-sticks of noble Mr. Alexandre Senior, would you have recognized, beneath last winter's military conscript, the smartly dressed youngster of former days sadly contemplating a passage to be translated from the Latin?

Through the open window Marius showed me the miles of green country that lay between him and Anael Valley, his inherited acres; and the valley itself, a line of rocks on the horizon.

"I love Anael's little brook," he said, "its white rocks covered with holly, and its moors where you can simply vanish from sight."

He began to laugh for no reason.

"You loved that place from the time you were a child. You wanted to be a farmer, not realizing that your love of the land was a poet's love."

"Me, a poet? With my belly and my medical studies? Come now, you must be joking! It was always you that got the top marks in French; you were the poet."

"I've become one."

I went on to reveal my new inner feelings, and asked him to keep them a secret. I had now found someone to confide in, and I did so repeatedly.

I liked coming to the Asylum and letting my eyes roam over the stretches of countryside that my feet had roamed when I was a child. Marius regularly complained about the Asylum, the director, the intern, the servant, the town, and life in general; he drank cider and laughed. He became red in the face, he danced, he played the mandolin. On the horizon the rocks of Anael Valley hid the river from view. Gangs of us had gone there as schoolboys and swum stark naked. Around the hazels and the reeds, we had played hide-and-seek beneath the water.

One summer's morning when I had my back to the window in Marius Alexandre's living-quarters, my eye lit on a piece of paper lying on the floor near the doorway connecting the two bedrooms. It had a line of handwriting across it and was placed as though door and floor had moved it, revolving wicket-fashion, from one room to the other.

"Ah, Marius, Marius, your neighbor has a woman in his room at night! And you try to lure her to your side of the wall, I dare say when your subordinate lies sleeping. This note contains her answer: 'I can't! You know darn well I can't!' "

Marius stammered like a young kid caught in the act.

"You can stop playing Sherlock Holmes, old buddy; I'm not going to tell you a thing!"

He snapped his fingers; he was very proud of his ability to snap his fingers.

"The woman is from a middle-class background at the least; I infer that from your silence as much as from the elegance of her handwriting. The note was written last night; otherwise it would have been swept up by now. Husbands are not much in the habit of granting overnight leave to their wives, so your neighbor's visitor is unmarried. Heavens, Marius, you're looking so embarrassed! How foolish of you! Surely you know me well enough to rely on my discretion."

This incident distracted me from contemplation of the drastic changes taking place within me, and freed me from the delightful anguish caused by my suppressed emotional states. The game of amateur detective seemed worthy of a future writer; when I left, I took along the piece of paper, intending that its handwriting and style should provide the basis for an investigation.

More old books are read in small towns than in big cities; local libraries are better patronized than national ones. For one hour each day, all the best and all the rest of society in X, plus the kindly offices of Mr. Majet, director of the town library, created something like a semisilent literary salon in that graveyard of 3,000 volumes comprising the finest novels of the nineteenth century, a few of the worst, and some enormous relics that had survived the burning of an abbey in 1789. The caretaker at the library, old Mr. Lanson, an ex-policeman who wore mittens to cover up the fact that there were fingers missing from his hands, and whose eyelids no longer covered his china-blue eyes, would hold a ruler in his mouth and point to a thick register showing the titles of books that people took out after signing for them. I suddenly realized that old Lanson's register was a dictionary of handwriting that included all my fellow X——ians: a single glance produced a second specimen of the handwriting in the note, and also the name I was seeking.

At Home and Abroad 1863, *volumes II and III*

old Lanson had written. A friend of my sister's and my mother's had signed for the books: Amelia Geay.

"What's so funny, Mr. Max?" said old Lanson. "Not me, I hope? No, eh? I must say I would have been surprised . . . you're a decent young fellow, with respect for others, not like all those kids who just come here so they can poke fun at me!"

With the discovery of Amelia Geay's name in the register, I ceased to be an innocent and began to picture society in new ways. Whatever his previous experience may have been, a young man who prefers good to evil is deeply shaken when he discovers the real world. Moreover, this little victory made me aware of my mental abilities and encouraged me to use them further. On reflection, I decided that the informal tone of Amelia Geay's message implied the shared pleasures of an orgy, that is, the presence of a second woman in the medical annex of the Insane Asylum at night.

In provincial towns, fallen women come in mutually sustaining pairs. Without ever having verified this law of behavior, I felt its truth so keenly that I was moved to seek Amelia Geay's nighttime associate among her regular daytime ones.

Amelia was part of an intellectual aristocracy whose female representatives liked to assemble around Miss Malvina, the young teacher of English at the girls' high school. A desire to scoff and a vengeful scorn for the madding crowd, along with a liking for tea, Beethoven, and limp fabrics, strengthened the mutual sympathy of these clever young ladies. My family was well known, and this gave me the right to venture into their midst. I went to borrow a book from Miss Malvina. I contrived to ask for an author the teacher was studying, to turn up on a day when the lady intellectuals were holding a general meeting, to foresee that a student accepted for admission to a school in Paris would also be acceptable to them, and to steer the conversation toward such remarks as must further my investigation.

"I'm sure a man-about-town like you gets bored in a little place like this," said a big, jolly, dark-haired girl named Mary Quenel.

"But the countryside is so lovely here!"

"Don't you get fed up with all that green stuff?"

"There are certain spots I could gaze at indefinitely and never be weary of. Take Anael Valley, for instance; sublime!"

"Oh, yes, magnificent!" was the chorus. "And you should see it by moonlight," said Miss Quenel: "just like a stage-set."

This moonlight effect was received with admiration by the gathering and with satisfaction by me. Oh, Mary Quenel, what an unguarded tongue is yours! So you'd been walking at night among those rocks, far distant though they are from town, . . . with your good mother, I suppose! Or wasn't it rather the owner of the rocks, one Marius Alexandre, who had chosen the poetic hours of darkness to show you round his estate?

The following night found me boarding a train for Paris after the most painful scene in which I have ever played a part. I had been so overjoyed at my discoveries that although I was honorable enough not to confide them to anyone else, I was not cautious enough to keep them from Marius.

"Marius," I said, "in the evening you, your intern, Mary Quenel, and Amelia Geay go driving over to Anael Valley. These outings are followed by little private parties."

Marius went red in the face and raised his eyebrows.

"You mean to say you know all that! You? Who told you? Who knows enough to have told you all that?"

"No one else knows about it, and no one will, not from me at any rate."

"You're mighty clever! I've got to hand it to you, you're mighty clever! But it was very wrong of you to do what you did; I never expected an old friend to spy on me like that."

"Exactly what wrong have I done?"

"Do you know the legal term for what you did? It's called breach of trust."

"But you hadn't entrusted me with anything."

Whereupon Marius began to laugh. His belly shook.

"This is funny! This is really funny!"

He snapped his fingers, held out his hand for me to shake and resumed his usual litany of complaints.

Doctor Alexandre and my father were both members of a certain club. That evening, feigning the very tenderest of feelings, my friend had told my father all about my aspirations and betrayed the fact that I intended to throw away my career. My father was upset by this stunning piece of news to the point of being laid low by a stroke. Marius Alexandre was the first doctor to treat him; it was Marius who ordered that he be taken to hospital. Painfully surprised at the tragic outcome of his revenge, he explained to my mother with tears in his eyes how such a terrible misfortune had come about, and when I appeared at the sick man's bedside my mother ordered me to leave for Paris that night.

Then began the life of privation and suffering which is mine to this very day.

◆

Cousin Joseph

Cousin Joseph's physical beauty was the pride of the entire family. When Gualbert was young he was a good-looking lad, but his own mother could be heard to declare that Gualbert's good looks were as nothing compared to Cousin Joseph's. Nature, who has made some men too long and others short, setting here a pallid face upon a heron's neck, there a beet-red visage on a bullish stump, had, it seems, decreed pleasing proportions among Cousin Joseph's limbs and between these and his countenance. To Gualbert, this Cousin Joseph whom he had never seen was a kind of mysterious god. When he did see him, Cousin Joseph was sixty, a widower and the father of several children, and he looked the way a wine merchant would look if the wine merchant looked like Rochegrosse the painter.[1] I should add that in order to look like Rochegrosse the painter you have to trim your hair to form a bang and your beard to form a point. Cousin Joseph made the most of the pleasures afforded him by this resemblance. Cousin Joseph, feeling that his physical beauty was leaving Gualbert unimpressed, tried showing him some hundreds of photographs to see if that would help. There was one of Cousin Joseph as a soldier, one of Cousin Joseph as a hunter, Cousin Joseph wearing a straw boater, Cousin Joseph wearing a dark suit, Cousin Joseph in the country, on a balcony with his children around him, with his friends around him, a back view of Cousin Joseph, Cousin Joseph photographed full face, in profile, in three-quarters, with direct illumination, with no illumination. Cousin Joseph at dawn, at dusk, at noon, by lamplight, by gaslight, by electric light. Gualbert, who had a perverse disposition, considered that right from childhood onward, his old cousin had looked the way he still looked today: the way a wine merchant would look if the wine merchant looked like Rochegrosse the painter. Cousin Joseph was a wine merchant.

1. Georges Rochegrosse the painter did exist, in ironic contrast to the nonexistence of Cousin Joseph's reputed beauty, his talent as a sculptor, or his much-praised generosity toward his family and friends. The deflated Joseph is soon revealed by his verbal tics and the author's irony as another example of the eternal bourgeois.

In his boyhood, Cousin Joseph was a sculptor. At an age when others are winning prizes at high school, he was winning his at schools of sculpture, and such talent as he showed at that time augured well for the talent he would one day possess. He satisfied the prevailing taste in art well enough to inspire predictions that he would continue to satisfy such tastes as might prevail in future. At twenty he was still talented, but mostly he was kind-hearted. Cousin Joseph kept nothing for himself that he was not happy to share with others as occasion arose. His sculpture studio was a refuge for sculptors with no studio, his meals the meals of his fellow artists. At celebrations and festivities, noble, smiling, somewhat sad, he seemed to take delight only in the delight of others. So Cousin Gualbert had been told, and the behavior of Joseph the café owner seemed to bear out the stories one heard about Joseph the sculptor. He paid his employees for services that illness had kept them from providing, and paid them a higher wage than any other café owner for the services they did provide. His daughter Georgette complemented and completed his virtues with her own. A word from her could calm a noisy argument; she could mete out justice without provoking mutterings of discontent; and generosity vied with economy in her management of affairs. His sons were nimble with their wits and with their hands. So Joseph's heart brought him happiness, but not so his career: the heart in fact did the career no good. A love of sculpture is not always a happy bedfellow to the loves of a sculptor. Cousin Joseph's loves came along when he was twenty. Against the attentions of a handsome man who in addition looked like Rochegrosse, what woman could have possibly been proof? He wed the mother of his child, and as he wished them greater material happiness than the rewards of impoverished artists annually afford, he tried to go and find it in America. In those days America was still Eldorado, a land of golden checkbooks! For a time, poverty shook his faith in the transatlantic paradise. One day, however, a Fifth Avenue department store ordered some wax dummies to decorate a show window for the Christmas season, and Cousin Joseph caught people's attention with figures representing international celebrities: Sarah Bernhardt, General Boulanger, and so on.[2] More such orders followed year by year,

2. Georges Boulanger (1837–91), "the man on horseback" of French history,

89

bringing affluence; and just as well, for Cousin Joseph would have suffered greatly had he been unable to give his four children the education he felt they deserved. He really was a kind-hearted man. So kind-hearted that he could not bring himself to say no when his wife wanted them to go back to France, although it ruined them financially. Napoleon in wax, along with Rodin and Sadi-Carnot, made the trip across the waters without being damaged.[3]

The World's Fair of 1889 stimulated public interest in wax figures to such a point that the Grévin Waxworks Museum was no longer enough. Poets of the time recorded the fright they had experienced on seeing exhibits of wax figures in cellars; philosophers held forth on the subject of waxworks displays; a painting called *Man and Mannequin* attracted much favorable comment. The potential morality and immorality of reproduction by means of wax were weighed one against the other by a preacher. Clearly wax figures were "in": Cousin Joseph made the most of it, and to get rich quicker he exploited two human foibles at once: the passion for wax figures and the passion for alcohol.[4] All Gualbert knew about Joseph's career was what he'd heard from other people; only recently had he begun to see his handsome cousin socially. By this time Joseph was making 20,000 francs a year in a big café-bar on the main boulevard. The wax figures had been sold. Joseph was a widower and boasted that his sixty years did not prevent him from pleasuring a mistress who loved him for his physical beauty and not for his money. As for sculpture, he made sure to devote some time to it on Sundays, showed an interest in its high priests during the annual Paris Art Show, and was convinced that on the morrow of his death all his Art Institute friends would walk behind his flower-covered coffin. His was the middle-class home of a man who liked painted plaster figures; he kept an exquisite table; he delighted in pouring good wine; and his little gray eyes grew misty

---

was a minister of defense who in 1886 attempted a coup, failed, fled to Brussels to avoid arrest, and committed suicide at the tomb of his mistress.

3. Sadi-Carnot (1837), president of the French Republic, was assassinated by an anarchist in 1894.

4. For Jacob, who hated realism and naturalism in all its manifestations, this vogue for wax figures was the epitome of bad taste.

when he spoke of his children to whom he was lavishly generous. His behavior was patriarchal.

* * *

"What about Georgette?" said Gualbert, a young man of Protestant mien, as he carved the wing of a turkey stuffed with foie gras. "Aren't you going to find her a husband?"

"Well, you know, my boy, she's very useful to me at the café," replied the great-hearted man as he dipped his gray mustache into a glass of Burgundy (the big 1903 vintage).

"And when you're not there any more, who will she be useful to then, Cousin?"

"Don't you worry, my boy, her dowry's been provided for. But you've no idea how vital it is to have her at home. She's the only one who can keep harmony between Paul and Lucien, and I so much prefer to have harmony around me. You just don't know how I love harmony. The mere thought of being separated from my loved ones! . . . Naturally there'll come a day when I have to go, the same as for everyone else. What will become of my family line if Paul and Lucien don't get along with each other? She's the only one who can—"

"Will Georgette be less of a peacemaker when she's married?"

"Now, see here! It's easy for you to talk! A married couple added to my household. Fine! And why not have Paul get married while we're at it! And maybe Lucien will take a notion to get married! And! And! And!"

Gualbert spoke wisely but his behavior was frivolous. Except when specifically invited, he did not have much contact with solid citizens other than at funerals or festive seasons—New Year's and Easter, for instance. Gualbert did not like people who knew him too well and he suspected the family of broadcasting his shortcomings. He required admiration, and his cousins were slower to comply with this requirement than were his friends. Still, Cousin Joseph did do well by his dinner guests, and in the absence of admiration Gualbert was prepared to settle for a good meal. So it came about that he was seated one day at the café owner's table.

"Well, lad, you'll be pleased to know that Georgette is getting married."

"I'm glad to hear it! You're so good to your children, I couldn't imagine there was any limit to what you would do for them."

"No indeed! She's marrying a young Englishman, a very decent sort of fellow . . . very kind-hearted . . . great future ahead of him. . . . I must admit that from all I've been able to discover he sounds first-rate. He works in the cutting department of a big tailoring establishment. He comes from a very respectable family, very close-knit; he's steady-going, has a solid character."

"And how did he and his fiancée happen to meet?"

"Here! At the café! He saw her behind the till! They're in love! She's very happy."

"People who think ill of love matches are wrong. They claim that stormy passions don't thrive in the calms of married life, and it's true that violent love can lead to violent hate, but it's equally true that in the bond of friendship which comes from sharing life's experiences, the cement can be provided by memories of that violent love."

"You put it well, my boy! But that's not the problem. . . . No, that's really not the problem! . . . Quite honestly . . . I don't like the fellow."

"Oh . . ."

"That's right: I don't like him. He had dinner here and he didn't behave properly."

"You don't mean it! What happened to the famous British stuffiness?"

"British stuffiness? There wasn't any British stuffiness in sight on that occasion, let me tell you! During dessert he jumped over the table pivoting on one thumb. He never stopped making puns in French the entire evening, like some young fool of an artist. He took off his jacket. In short—he misbehaved!"[5]

"Oh, Cousin, how little you know the English! Didn't you have any English friends in America? All those eccentricities are accepted in England. An Englishman is paying you a compliment if he behaves like a spoiled child in your home: it's his way of show-

5. The young Englishman bears some resemblance to Jacob, who in his Montmartre days, measuring up to his reputation as a clown, used to dance in red socks on tabletops to entertain the dinner party. It is also a fact that making puns was so much his second nature that sometimes he besought God to withdraw this talent from him.

ing you that he considers himself one of the family. Take, for instance, some friends of mine who have very high-up connections in London. And I mean very high-up! Big businessmen, bankers, judges—"

"Always laying it on thick, aren't you, Gualbert! Exactly like the rest of your family: anything for appearances! Your mother was just an unsuccessful socialite; your grandmother positively dripped polite manners everywhere she went; your Great-Aunt Adele had no use for any man who didn't have medals or decorations. The heart took second place to the title, in your family."

"To come back to my friends . . . last year they invited two English noblemen, who were making a short stay in Paris, to come and stay with them over Christmas. Two venerable old-fashioned gentlemen, splendid to behold: black suits, white side-whiskers, portly figures, precious stones and rare. Well, you'll find it hard to believe this: at one o'clock in the morning, these two gentlemen, who must have had a combined age of a hundred and twenty at least, were playing leapfrog, and my friends were wondering whether the ornaments on the console-tables would get smashed!"

"I don't believe a word of it! You're bound and determined to see Georgette married. Your family are all alike: none of you would balk at telling a lie in order to achieve your ends. Do you know what Falguière said to me one day? 'The fact is, Joseph, an artist who lies is a rotten artist.' "

A few months later, Gualbert and Cousin Joseph met at Aunt Jean's funeral. Gualbert was really heavy-hearted as they walked along behind the casket: as a schoolboy he had spent his summer holidays at Aunt Jean's and she would teach him songs or at any rate whatever bits she could remember from the light-hearted ditties of an earlier day. Aunt Jean sang off-key, and the tunes to the songs came out sounding like nothing on earth, but Gualbert could never think of them without wanting to cry. It was Aunt Jean who had taught Gualbert to dance, and Gualbert now recognized that while as a singer echoing her refrains he had brought no special credit to his aunt, as a dancer he did distinguish himself and would have gone on doing so had he not considered that tangos required more work than they were worth.

Cousin Joseph, clad in solemn black, was saying through his tears:

"Aunt Jean was a fine woman. What a fine woman she was! You have to realize, my boy, with her death we're seeing the end of a generation. The younger generation is selfish; it's not the way it used to be; nobody cares about other people. Yes, a fine woman!"

"You knew her quite well?"

Cousin Joseph wiped his eyes. "I saw her once at Aunt Amelia's funeral and then again at my mother's funeral. I was six years old."

"Ah, yes, a fine woman! Morals have been attacked repeatedly over the last hundred years. Moreover, the introduction of universal, or supposedly universal, education. . . . When do we marry off Georgette to her Englishman?"

"Never, not to that fellow! A man who jumps over tables after dinner!"

"But that's English humor, Joseph!"

"You don't mean to teach me English, I trust!"

"Teach you English, no, but teach you about the English, yes; someone needs to, from what I can see."

"I may as well tell you, my boy. I've made inquiries about him, and the facts are really deplorable. To begin with he has no qualifications; he's just a general employee."

"Very well, then, his wife will be at his side through the upturns and downturns in his fortunes."

"What's more he drinks, steals, lies, and chases skirts; he's dirty, lazy, violent-tempered, and philandering. What's to become of my poor little Georgette? She'll be mighty unhappy with such a barbarian!"

"That's quite a list of faults! The average specimen of humanity would settle for just one of them. Where did you get this charming portrait?"

"From a reliable source, a woman who came specially to tell me all about him: his mistress, no less! A very respectable person and a good-looking girl, what's more."

"You're very naïve, Cousin Joseph . . . or rather . . . there is none so blind as he who will not see."

Later Gualbert met his cousin again. Georgette was married to the Englishman. "She has no heart, that girl," said Joseph; "I think she puts her husband and child before her father. I don't matter to her any more . . . I mean it seriously, I don't matter to her any more!"

◆

Another Night—"Understanding with
Your Eyes Shut"
[from Hospital Nights and Dawn]

[*On the twenty-seventh of January in 1920, as he was crossing a boulevard
on his way to the Opéra to see* The Three-Cornered Hat, *Jacob was
struck by a car and rushed to hospital. How he caught pneumonia from a
car accident is dramatically told in the series "Hospital Nights and Dawn,"
which forms a section of* The Dullard Prince.]

"No, really, you mustn't encourage them to think they can just ask
for things whenever they want!" (The patients, that's who; that's
who: the patients!) Implication: "I trained as a nurse so I could
GET you. Now I'm out for blood!" When she shut young Blondie
in with a dangerous elderly lunatic, was that deliberate? Blondie's
screams pierced the walls, but screams in the night are nothing
new here. Fortunately, they came round to check the dishes and
plates! Blondie, brandishing a dish, had fought for her life. They
punished her for breaking the dish. And what about the big cabinet with all the medicine, the one they take away every evening. . . .
Okay, everybody, let's at least get a little shut-eye at night, shall we?

That's why nights in hospital would put me in mind of Hell if
I were Dante. At night, not a glass of water, would you believe it!
The drinking water is in the big cabinet, the cabinet is under lock
and key and the key isn't here. And then there's the intern who
looks at the newspaper you're reading before he speaks to you. . . .
Hold on, now, what's got into me? Have I come here to check up
on how the place is run? Am I going to slam the door when I leave,
like a chambermaid? I was brought in here out of charity and I'm
using the opportunity to make a fuss; is that it? Yes, it is; telling the
truth is so helpful! On the other hand, it's almost always harmful.

I shut my eyes to understand the outside world. The picture
of X in the mirror at night. Ye gods! Is it true that—? Surely he
wasn't always so "lamplight-colored." I prefer him in something
less fancy-dress-ball or just Gay-Nineties, headed for Hell or Purga-

tory down a frozen highway. The road that Swedenborg describes. Don't worry; he's not dead! He's very much alive! He's gone to the loo, loo as in blood.

(Needless to say, the person in question is me.)

I've never been able to hunt for something I've lost except with my eyes shut. Using inner vision I located twelve dozen towels belonging or formerly belonging to the National Health, which no one could see even though the towels were right there in front of their eyes whereas I, eyeless, saw them plainly: red and green with pale binding. But today I have all the gurgles and gargoyles of Notre Dame between my stomach and my belly and on upward.

We must shut our eyes; we must shut our eyes in order to find the life that was lost. We must shut our eyes to imperfections in order to rediscover truth or the flesh incorruptible. The reason the flesh of Jesus is incorruptible and corruptible is that He combined the understanding you achieve with your eyes shut, and the other kind. And I say we must imitate Jesus and shut our eyes till we have won the right to open them. In order to acknowledge Him we must know Him, and in order to know Him we must imitate Him.

"Remarkable! Remarkable!"

"Fine; now go to sleep!"

At eleven o'clock, a great commotion! All the lights go on! Enter upstage left a self-powered palanquin (me again).

"What's the matter with you?" asks a nurse.

"*You're* supposed to tell *me*!" answers the patient.

"Well! Of all the nerve! If you've come here to talk in that insolent manner, you can just go away again!"

And somehow you find the self-control required to express what everyone is suffering . . .

Now is the time for terror!

. . . Now the lampshade, and the comings and goings of veiled figures under the lamplight, the papers and official forms lending importance to those very respectable ladies, under the lamplight. And then begins the night watch, under the lamplight: the male attendant and the nurse take up their positions, under the lamplight. And stretching into the distance, away from the lamplight, is the kingdom of groans and moans, cries as of dogs at play, monkeys' cries, and all those chest cavities are musical resonators conveying an accurate or nearly accurate sense of the martyrdom people are suffering out there with their eyes shut, far from the lamplight. The (electric) lamplight.[1]

"Stephen, you hold the strip of gauze while I wind."

"Yes, all right. But don't hide your face behind the lampshade so I can't see you."

"Please hold the strip straight or I can't wind it straight. None of your teasing, now, Stephen; be serious."

"You're the one that's laughing, Stephanie, so how am I supposed to stay serious?"

Stephen is asleep, Stephanie is dozing. Me, speaking from my bed, with my eyes shut:

"He's from your hometown, and he's engaged to you."

"I'm willing if he is."

"He's a mechanic but he's got to give it up because he's going blind."

"No matter! When he has to stop working I'll work enough for both of us."

Little red-headed Breton girl, secretly taking grammar lessons at night, you're not like that stuck-up, strutting nurse we have in the morning; God will bless your modesty and courage, and your love revealed by the lamplight.

"You have to understand that your situation and ours are not the same: you just turn up one day to lie there moaning aimlessly on that high-quality metal bedspring, whereas we, on the other hand, know that in three days' time you'll be feeling fine and that in two weeks you'll have forgotten all about the hospital." That holds true 2,000 times a year. At the foot of the crack in the wall and the split tile there is a patient who has the gift of self-expression; he howls only as much as it hurts; he's a nice man; this time it's not me.

"When I saw they were putting me in the section at the far end of the ward, the thought never crossed my mind that nobody came out of there alive, because I had my eyes shut and I wasn't thinking about anything. But through my eyelids I saw that the hospital is between two railway stations so that for every searing pain there can be an answering train whistle." Come, then, robin red-breast,

---

1. The insistence on the lamp is an allusion either to Florence Nightingale, "The Lady with the Lamp," or to Christ as the "Light of the World." That the lamp is "electric" implies lack of compassion.

pigeon transpierced, nature's intimations of pneumonia: manifest yourselves to those whose eyes are shut.[2]

Return to animalism, madness, howling. Pain striking at your chest with a pickaxe to hasten the coming of the Sacred Heart of Jesus. Animalism, madness, howling, pain is divine for death is divine, but pain is animal, so. . . . Editor's note: it's how the pain is received that's divine.[3]

Let me shut my eyes. . . . The portrait of X in the lamplight-colored mirror is me, me minus the fever which doesn't exist but I call fever what you call illness. I saw you again and I can see you still, you my second self, my double; your face doesn't look the way it used to in the old days. Still a touch of depravity in the eyes, a touch of weariness around the eyelids. Something that will never remind people of the Mona Lisa. That's not a man, it's a woman! In fact Mona Lisa isn't even a woman, it's a performer's name, like Mayol.[4] And anyhow, why the long, swarthy, Oriental face? Am I finally—finally!—going to play the Great Poet, or the husband-and-father who makes you think of Louis XVI in Le Temple?[5] Just look at this brand-new ward! The workmen smoked so much before the tenants moved in, they smoked so much that at first sight you think the place is already full of furniture. It's the beds. In my case what I've done is to furnish the whole ward in the style of ancient Rome so I'll have no trouble being Caius Julius. . . . "When we're alone together, pussy-cat, just call me Nero, your little Nero-kins, to take my mind off all that imperial pomp." Is there a dead man somewhere about? There's a dead man somewhere about. And everyone thinks this dead man is a living person. There's a living person here who everyone thinks is a dead man because he has his eyes shut. Very smartly dressed crowd; among those present your reporter noted a considerable number of chest ailments. The coffin is too small; there must be some mistake. No, the one you're

2. "Pigeon transpierced": See *In Defense of Tartufe*, "Meanings," note 4.

3. See *The Artist Introduces Himself*, note 2.

4. Jacob is probably referring to the very popular singer and song writer Félix Mayol.

5. Louis XVI, charged with treason, was stripped of his rank and imprisoned in the tower of Le Temple (Paris) in 1791. He was condemned to death and executed in 1793.

burying is not your sister or brother; it's me! But whatever mistake has been made, a dead man there must surely be, for a coffin there definitely is; it's hard to imagine one without the other. And if the man is in the coffin, then why these white-clad resurrected figures still recumbent but who will very shortly be standing around the lamplight-colored portrait of me in this mirror-pond of death? I'll never manage to get into that coffin; it wasn't made for me; it isn't for me.

Summary portrait of the modern lay nurse (to conclude this particular night): "Fénelon High School in white clogs, or how to look as though you have the knack or how to have the knack of looking as though you're studying for an exam when you've never learned to read." Dialogue in the night, among harmless ghosts howling with their eyes shut.

INTERN: Mrs. Richeaubé Teyssières, for too long now I've shut my eyes to what's going on around here. I cannot stand to see sixty patients left without anyone who can give them an injection once in a while, merely on the grounds that it's nighttime. I ask you not to let these men undergo needless suffering when tomorrow they may be dead.

NURSE: Oh, as far as medication or injections are concerned, it doesn't change matters whether there's anyone here or not. Everything's under lock and key, the key isn't here and the lady who has the key won't come in till her regular time.

INTERN: If that's the case, Mrs. Richeaubé Teyssières, and if those are the rules, the rules and the system, then I'm terribly sorry.

NURSE: It's no fault of yours, or mine either: those are the rules.

INTERN: They'll howl all night and the rules say no glass of sugar-water unless they've put in a request in the morning.

The little coffin is in front of the mirror and the mirror is reflecting my lamplight-colored face. In the wards there is in fact no mirror; there's just me, seeing with my eyes shut.

My eyes, already shut so as to make a start at understanding life, which is feasible if you understand death.

Among those present, your reporter noted the distressful cry of a dog, and that of a bird . . . and that of an actor: my own cry when all's said and done.

◆

Daytime—"The Tale of the Handsome Arab" [from Hospital Nights and Dawn]

[This passage has two distinct parts: a humorous anecdote about an expatriate Arab whose mistresses keep depositing him at a hospital, followed by a serious account of Jacob's own admittance to hospital after a car accident. The transition between the two, unmarked by any special spacing, is complex: after the tale about the Arab, the author invents himself a literary persona. This character first considers what was a real dilemma for Jacob after his discharge from hospital: whether to write a letter, tactful or blunt, denouncing the inhumane way that the hospital was run. Then the persona experiences Jacob's car ride from the scene of the accident to the hospital and his admittance thereto.

If the Surrealist (the word is used advisedly) juxtaposition of elements is bewildering to the reader, it is because the succession of events was bewildering to the accident victim.]

In this narrative we will not meet the regular guests of the Marquise de Lariboisière, the moans and groans and peaceable ghosts who haunt the upper windows of her splendid hospital.[1] Instead we have a handsome Arab, more specifically a Syrian knowing no French and, until the time our story opens, none the worse off on that account. I am informed that in his own country he was a "schoolmaster" and had in his charge 200 pupils, but in France his occupation is rather different: after the war he was given shelter by one of those fair damsels who wait for the butchers from La Villette to come past in the morning and for anyone else who may come past in the evening.[2] Through a chain of circumstances unknown to me, the fair damsel eventually developed a distaste for her lodger and as she could find no way to get rid of him, and as

---

1. The Marquise de Lariboisière, 1794–1851, founded the hospital that bears her name. Completed in 1854, it is still a teaching hospital. Jacob several times refers to the long-departed Marquise as though she were personally and graciously presiding at "her" hospital.

2. La Villette is the nineteenth district of Paris, where large slaughterhouses were located till very recently.

he is possessed of Herculean strength, and as there is none so deaf as a Syrian who refuses to understand French, she resorted to a stratagem: she took him, as though for a walk or a pleasure outing, to the hospital nearest their place of residence, recommended him to the care of a passing male attendant as being an extremely ill man and took her departure. An intern came over and asked him questions, but what medical details can you hope to obtain from a Syrian who is in good health and who would be hard put to describe his ailment even if he had one? They tried Spanish. No. English, then? How about Italian? Or even German? Sorry; he speaks only Syriac.[3] Surely you don't expect us to go out in the middle of Paris and hunt up an interpreter for your Syriac. I mean, if we did that, we might end up understanding one another, and we can't have that, can we? . . . They tried to listen to his various pulses and heartbeats: he wouldn't let anyone come near him. What could be going on in the mind of this Eastern schoolmaster? He began to weep! He moaned gently: they decided he must be in pain. The intern had an idea: he sedated the Arab so he could control him; they undressed him, and carried him sedan-chair fashion to a ward and onto a bed with a note reading "Under Observation."

He remained under observation for two months: they found several diseases for him to have and cured him of every last one. Eventually he disappeared: he slipped quietly out of the building one day in his hospital robe and no one went running after him. He remembered the place that had housed him before and found his way there: the Perigord Hotel! Room 33. By this time Room 33 had acquired a different hostess, but he was made welcome nonetheless. One day when the two tenants from Room 33 were taking the air on La Chapelle Boulevard, they happened to meet the previous occupant of their room and bed. The ladies knew one another, joined one another in laughter over their little adventure, heard one from the other about the adventure at the hospital. The Syriac followed not a word and stood calmly aloof. But the new occupant of Room 33 was left looking thoughtful.

One day she took the Syriac back to the hospital. This time, however, the Syriac had grasped what was happening: he allowed

3. At this point, perhaps to add to the absurdity, Jacob switches from the correct "Syrian" to "Syriac," a misnomer for both the Arab and his tongue.

himself to be abandoned, displayed more incomprehension of the French tongue than ever and caused more perplexity than ever amongst interns, externs, and trainees. He would be there to this day but for an incident that no one could have predicted: a French lady turned up, with a variety of documents including a valid marriage contract; she explained that the Syriac was her husband and that she herself was Syriac but a French citizen. She then earnestly entreated the medical gentlemen to explain to her why the Syriac had always declined to make that use of her which a husband may make of his wife, and she further entreated that the Syriac should be taught how. The medical gentlemen replied that this aspect of the patient's well-being was not their concern. The Syriac, for his part, refused to go with his wife, and since whereas the law requires that a wife shall go with her husband it makes no provision for the opposite contingency, there was initially no attempt made to compel him. The little lady had to prove to the representatives of the medical profession that her Syriac was not sick before they would agree to throw him out. I wonder what became of them.

The author of these pages has begun to realize that he has an aptitude for writing. This being so, he chooses a hero who will be as likable as possible, to wit, himself; he then wonders whether an account of the events that brought him to this vale of tears called a night hospital would make a splendid book, and he begins to write. The hero must be exotic; a name can be so poetically evocative! But first there is his character to be considered. Authors today do not give sufficient attention to character portrayal: when they try to make the portrait profound, it comes out vague, and when they think they've made it accurate, they've merely been superficial.

My hero will be called Schwevischenbund.

Schwevischenbund did not dare go in and write the exquisitely tactful letter; out of timidity, he wrote only the rude, vulgar letter; even that letter he didn't actually write, but was unable to decide on any course of action. As they sped through the city streets, he could see the single word "Hotel" standing out against the glass bowl of every hotel lamp that they passed, but the automobile that had run over Schwevischenbund was not taking him to a hotel; it was taking him to the Vale of Tragedies, the Vale of Tears.

"Your surnames, givenames'naddress. Y'r mother's maidename!"

He had lapsed into unconsciousness in his tight-fitting black suit. They had left him sitting on a garden chair for two hours, in a ward consisting of a rectangular patch of asphalt paving, to wait for a "bath-lady," and as the bath-lady, when she arrived, had been a bit more gracious than the many, many city policemen in plain clothes and the other city policemen in uniform who inquired so solicitously about his mother's maiden name, the bath-lady's services being the only thing available for the moment in the otherwise sleeping hospital, Schwevischenbund had burst into a torrent of maudlin expressions of gratitude and goodwill.

The human race, according to our hero, could be divided into people who look like one another and people who do not, and it suddenly seemed to him an undeniable fact that he looked like the bath-lady, who on that evening was late in arriving. So he thrust aside his moaning and his shattered ribs which he had no clear awareness of in any case and softy called out: "Mommy!" This endearing utterance resulted in his being given a bath two hours later, for there was in the hospital neither cold water nor hot. He remained in the bath long enough to contract the pneumonia that still has him in its grip and he was moved to emerge again upon hearing the words: "Listen, you, there are other people waiting for the bath too, y'know!" It was after midnight. Bath time, very likely! But any time is a good time to catch pneumonia. This is the right place for me to mention that Schwevischenbund was wearing a black suit, since he had been going to the Opéra that evening.

"He's the delegate representing Perm to the people's Soviet," said one of the patients. Was he referring to the city of Perm or was someone representing the interests of hairdressers?

"And at parochial school, let me tell you, the Sisters had a pretty low opinion of my brothers."

With the coming of daylight, the circle of hyenas surrounding the camp melted away; the howling died down and you might have thought that the animals had left the white marble cemetery. There now appeared on the scene a bunch of those children who have stopped going to school and studying books and begun going to hospital and studying people. They poked the painfully tender flesh of my breast, striving in a delightfully obsessive way to find their teacher's latest mistake, the same spot that he had touched and which was abundantly obvious to anyone with a pair of eyes. Surely the spot must have been obvious to anyone, gentlemen, if it was obvious to you as well. Patiently getting ready to take their medical examinations, but not yet ready to give medical examinations to patients. No one is developing their capacity for love; yet love is the foundation of science.

N.B. In the foregoing passage, the author, who numbers among his friends many interns and externs for whom he has the highest regard, is putting words into the mouth of an "entirely conventional" hero, for it is understood that one must always speak ill of any institution through which one has passed. The author owes a debt of thanks to all those who looked after him. He does not share the opinion of Schwevischenbund the Hun. That is what makes this ironic book so interesting.

If, for instance, it is impossible to find needle and thread, button and seamstress, in this citadel of death and resurrection, surely that is not the fault of the blue-eyed interns.

Schwevischenbund, despite his delirium unaccompanied by fever, kept thanking everyone effusively and repeating his name and his mother's unmarried name to everyone who asked for information on these two points. It seemed to him that the duty of a man who has just been hurled violently into a completely new environment is to repeat his name and his mother's family name [. . .]

◆

Night to Remember, Better Known as Medical Walpurgisnacht [from Hospital Nights and Dawn]

Seven and it's winter and not three . . . o'clock and that's the degree of time in the night. Splenetic melancholy now contracts upon itself, the patients drawing comfort from the nurse's round: it brings the expectation of morning, freeing the doorway and driving out the demons and all the powers of darkness there encamped. They've turned off the electricity so now there aren't any enchanted scenes to look at nor even the patients' heads lined up like something out of the Dupuytren Museum.[1] The nurse is im-

1. Baron Guillaume Dupuytren (1777–1835) was a pioneering surgeon. The Anatomical Museum of Paris was named after him.

patient to start composing her entry in that book of falsehoods up there, the logbook of hours, where for each hour the same lie is inscribed: "The patients are quiet." She writes: "Bed 31 was given syrup of ether and bed 32 his injection of camphor oil." The truth is that there is no syrup, or ether, or camphor in this room where people die. They've turned off the lamps, and the light will no longer stifle the moans, nor set its luminescent foot upon the chests of these human animals. Cuckoo! Cuckoo-clock of despair! Entrusted to the night. The cuckoo brings good luck; the vault overhead is lucky: it covers pain; it's made of stone, so it's not involved. Who is involved? The sympathy of the passersby as they look up at the blue lightbulbs: "Someone up there is suffering." It doesn't occur to anyone that what's killing me is the power of the dark.

But no evening roll-call, which makes it a change from the barracks. Around the lamp, with the young nurse and her notebook, these sounds: the doglike yelps of suffering, the chattering as of monkeys congregated in the branches, and the rending, childish laughter of a senile patient, and sounds as of people quarreling and making up and the repeated calls for "mother" who can't hear me from so far away and doesn't come.

The patient in bed 42 has sat up, shroud-clad:

"Paris, city of indifference, every spoke of your wheels is in my chest . . . Go ahead and whistle, streetcars, little pendulums cutting right below the breastbone."

"Back in your bed, 42! What's got into you?"

The patient in bed 39 has sat up, shroud-clad:

"A jackal's eye in among my ribs, to look inside, to look and see! An eye to look in among my ribs and see what's broken."

And all the jackals form a circle round the lamplight where it reigns supreme, around the young nurse and her notebook in which "the patients are quiet!"

"Yes, I think that Satan exists to wrack our bodies."

The patient in bed 28: "I . . . I . . . I . . . came here while I was eating, I came on account of having eaten . . . I shouldn't have . . . have . . . have eaten cake."

The patient in bed 37 has gone from among the reeds, 37 has gone from among the snakes in the reeds. So soon! So soon? and not the little white marble foot that I was expecting. This evening the patient in bed 37 has gone from among the jackals who are there in the shadows. The bedsheets have shattered the windows of the night with that cry of pain which is the cry of cars in the street.

In response to a signal, a whistle.

The nurse and the lamp are worried. She's a "newcomer" to the staff, and they've brought her into this darkened room in amongst the ghosts and she keeps turning her head this way and that.

The matron comes. The junior nurse confides her worries to the senior nurse.

"He coughs, does he? What of it? So do I cough! Everybody coughs!"

And they write in the book of hours: "The patients are quiet."

You can never tell.

Next day, Doctor Massenet said:

"Well, now, what's all this? 'We wanted to leave art-school.' "[2]

and with a single one of his piercing glances reduced his moaning tribe to fascinated thrall. Mind you, daylight had come and at those hours the occupants of the beds have ceased to be ghosts and the power of the dark has been conjured away.

But that, my good (if male) or charming (if female) reader, was afterward. We left the nurse struggling between her French composition (of which I have spoken) and her French compassion, and doing (can you guess?) rather more justice to the former than to the latter. And our hero said:

"Receive my embrace amidst my groans, Wagnerian ghost, o shade of Buridan; which side can I lie on so as not to moan with pain, tell me, Buridan, tell me, Margaret! Margaret! Sewn in a sack and flung in the Seine, is that the answer?[3] But already sings the bird, that the peoples may be saved. That bird is the red-breast, emblem of the bronchitic; no! it is the pigeon transpierced, delightful emblem of those with lung congestion. You who have not loved death and pain, you do not know." I'm in pain! Well, it's better that way . . . at least one has a reason for being here.

2. Perhaps Jacob had said this in his delirium and a nurse had scrupulously made a note of it.

3. Buridan was a medieval philosopher. Legend has it that the lecherous Queen Margot had him sewn into a sack and flung into the Seine. (François Villon refers to this legend in his poem about the snows of yesteryear.) For the semidelirious patient, the connection may be twofold: like Buridan in his sack, Jacob cannot find a comfortable position; and in his indecision he is like the ass postulated by Buridan, which cannot decide between two identical haystacks and so starves to death.

Moonrise! Like a belly heaving into view, exposed down to the navel! How ugly are the hues of human flesh! But moonrise hailed as by much water at the boil: the many bird-songs from a single tree (O rounded shadowed patch!)

> Worthwhile topic
> Erstwhile top hit
> First I'll stop at Dantan's
> Subway stop: Dantin
> (Down-town)

Dedicated to Jean Bastia, who imitates my style in *Comoedia*, thinking he's imitating someone else.[4] And boasts about it.

I can accept the idea of a locomotive being referred to as a bird of shadows and fire, but not the reverse; I mean I can't accept the idea of a bird of night being referred to as a locomotive. And yet . . .

This whole chapter is botched; I'll start again.

The world has gone, and now is the hour when the mirrors will come alive, moving to the sublime tune of human lamentations all around us; the spirits of the night are about to present their *tableaux vivants* for those who have eyes to see. Item one: portrait of a doctor, outlined by the spirits on the mirror at the far end of the ward—there is no mirror, no far end of the ward—one way to get the upper hand over that I'm-gruff-but-underneath-I'm-a-great-humanitarian look is to use philosophic reasoning, or your heart, in order to see people who are not of the same world as you. The world of spirits is the only world I care about, my dear Doctor. That's why I have invented myself a hero and that's why I have bestowed upon him the ironically allusive name of Schwevischenbund. Let us return to our nocturnal portrait: you'd never find our hero preferring to use the chief physician's wash-basin, not like those nice interns and externs, dear me, no! He is courtesy incarnate in the person of a gentleman. You'd never find *him* sticking his fingers in his nose, or going around holding his fingers as if they had just been freshly lifted out of the water, or *drumming*

---

4. *Comoedia* was a literary journal which Max Jacob mentions having read in the 1940s under the Occupation. There is no doubt that the Surrealists owed a great and unacknowledged debt to Jacob (a debt now recognized by some critics), so that writers who believed that they were writing "like the Surrealists" were in fact writing like Max Jacob.

them together on the nurses' buttocks (hear the ironic sound of the locomotives in the nearby railway stations, rising and falling like the voices of people known and loved).

I'm never hungry any more, I guess I'll never be hungry again, not hungry for tobacco, not hungry for bread. Oh God, this listlessness; with your head there on the white and unable to. . . . I've already spoken of the policy of keeping your eyes shut, or of the true understanding acquired from close proximity to mortal suffering. Faced with unbearable pain that no one seems able or willing or knowledgeable enough to relieve, I have but one recourse: to learn to love my pain, and transmute it into ecstasy. But what can never be transmuted is the impotence of being there in bed, the weakness of your arms, your movements clumsy as the movements of a one-armed man, and the majestic majestic majestic indifference of others toward you and of yourself toward others, others. . . . But as opposed to all this, . . . clumsiness isolates you, weakness makes you listless, and indifference lets you see, see, see, with your eyes shut. A very young nurse from the country turns down a perfectly legitimate gratuity and later says: "So it's true! You're a literary man, a writer! I've been looking after a writer!" Hear, O Literature, and you, Muses, hear this homage! Savor it in all its rarity exquisite. And you, Night, all shivering with skulls both unforeseeable and unforeseen, dark and atmospheric ocean making up this night, tremble at the homage this shepherdess has paid to literature.

The whole Lariboisière family, young Schwevischenbund, the stag, the murdered man, and not a single borrowing from novels or from films among the lot, nothing but fresh new material . . . but the pen in my hand is not able to render them on paper.[5] The moment young Schwevischenbund has authority he abuses it, but generally he is shy. He often suffers from having authority. This young man uses the term "sweetheart" in addressing a girl on whom he gazes quite chastely, and he takes a philanthropic interest in her, till one day . . .

I have a natural aptitude for writing; I'm quite convinced of that now, and I intend to take advantage of my stay in Dr. Massenet's

5. The sense of the stag and the murdered man, perhaps further productions of Jacob's fevered mind, has not come down to us.

establishment to write a novel. I shall start at daybreak, that is to say three-quarters of an hour hence.

And so, rising above the (admittedly attenuated by the arrival of dawn) cacophony of weeping and wailing, our hero took up his pen.

◆

Cockcrow
[from Hospital Nights and Dawn]

Farewell scene: gentleman in street clothes, going from bed to bed; my friends the (other) patients are ill at ease. We were equals and now suddenly I'm a gentleman. For the cabbie, I'm a future customer; for the waiter, the man who might leave a tip. The heels of my ankle-boots feel awkward on these cement slabs intended for slippers: to the male attendants I'm no longer the patient in bed 33, I'm Mister Jacob. As for the intern . . . but I promised myself not to speak ill of anyone. Goodbye, hospital corridors, I'm a stranger now. Goodbye to the fever-inspired visions, the living spirits in these walls, goodbye to the little chapel that they keep locked up, goodbye to the hospital chaplain reduced to courtesy and smiles by the impiety of everyone around him, goodbye to the good kind nurse, and the other one! Goodbye, you pleasant-mannered, unappreciated orderlies. Listen, everyone, friends, lying there pale in your beds, I'll be back, I'll come back on Thursday. And I did come back.

Two of them were dead; the North African had nearly died, death was written on his face; the little butcher's boy—such a remarkable lad!—had been operated on. All his verve and fun had gone: his grandmother was very worried, and the whole family, an attractive poor Parisian family, were gathered by the bed.

Goodbye again! This time I won't be coming back. I have some traveling ahead of me! The south of France has been recommended for my cough and my weakened condition: so off I shall go, and what a fuss and bother it takes to put my affairs in order and lay my hands on a bit of money! Going to see buyers, carting with me paintings weighed down by their frames, when my miserable broken shoulder can't even move a chair; . . . but there's a glimpse of pure blue sky ahead. Hang on. Visiting the special people in charge of the compensation my accident entitles me to, conferring with publishers, thanking friends, accepting and turning down invitations, buying trunks, cashing checks. Ahead there's a glimpse—hang on! There's a glimpse of sun and sea, the pines and railway coaches that I like, and undisturbed work, which I love. Painting and writing poetry and blue skies! Blue skies! There's a glimpse of blue sky ahead! But oh, my poor dear fellow patients. . . . For you, the pavement of the city streets! Oh to be able to take them with me, all the patients in Grisolle Ward, and while I'm at it the supervisors and all the staff as well.

◆

It's Still Only Daybreak
[from Hospital Nights and Dawn]

Written in the streets of Paris

You really haven't changed that much, Paris—despite electricity and all the life going on beneath your streets—from the days when somber-visaged Musset drank your mud, the color of gray absinthe, mud that stains.

Your skies are mild, Paris, but how poor the land! Everything black with dust, black hats, houses. The passersby are pleasant, kindly, but what a defensive posture to their bodies, bent by those scourges that weeping women haltingly confide in doctors' offices! Moderate, sensible, polite, the Parisian thinks himself king of the world when he might be merely its proud slave. Oh, hide your sewers, their smell is a foreboding! And yet, some time or other, intoxicated by the drinks at one of those bars which Paris calls by strange names in order to escape reality, you may be deluded by your own secret lusts into seeing beauty in the women around you, you may mistake the expensive trappings of a South American snob for real Parisian luxury, mistake the idiot inventions of fashion for creative imagination, or a repainted wreck for a new automobile, or the brow of a doddering specialist for that of a wise and learned man, or mistake the raconteurs of anodyne anecdotes for men of wit, or the laughter of streetwalkers for true gaiety; if you love truth, turn inward, and try having a look round our law-courts; that's the place to discover the real stuff of which Paris is made, and where the money comes from when money there is, and what may be hidden behind a woman's calm exterior and her husband's wholesome, loyal bearing. I tell you, Hospital, Paris does not think about death.

Hospital, mausoleum of the living, there you sit between two railroad stations; and you're another, with Departures people don't come back from. In my mind I kneel before your door, Hospital, and give thanks to God for leaving me among the living here on earth. I sit here on this bench and my weakness and my weariness are like the agony of death. Head still so weak, and the head controls everything else! You poor limbs, like limbs grown old, with your poor head which is still so weak, still so weak your poor head! Oh, agony! weariness! weakness! Hey there, all you people rushing by in your cars, you're going to die, y'know! You're all going to die! Hey there, all you sex-fiends, the young ones and the old, you're going to die! Women tied to your kitchens, you others who live in style, you bluestockings, you're all going to die, friends! Listen, you people in your automobiles, will you just listen to the knell I toll: I say you're all going to die! I got the information just now in the hospital and here I am on Magenta Boulevard shouting out the news for you to hear: you're going to die, all of you, all of us. An appalling statement but a true one nonetheless, the only true statement, a statement that you can't shift or budge but can only reach out and poke carefully with the fingertips of your mind, you're going to die. Will you just listen to me instead of rushing past: in a little while we're going to die. . . . Forget it, I didn't say a thing; on this bench sits a cowardly little man: me—me, the man that didn't die under the wheels of that car on place Pigalle; me, the man that didn't die in Grisolle Ward (bed 33, Grisolle Ward, Lariboisière Hospital). The cowardly little man is pale; he didn't say a thing. Thanks anyway, but the fear of looking foolish is just too much and besides in Paris they immediately mark you down as a loony. Loonies, all of us! If that's what you think, I don't suppose you've tried bringing your mind to bear for a moment on the flesh rotting in that cold bed there, a bed that was warm yesterday! To you, God, I owe what little struggling life I still have in me, to you I owe the hospital which opened the door to life by coming between me and death! As

111

you have enlightened me, Lord, enlighten also these people going by. One Sunday in November they'll go to the cemetery to remember the dead; that day let them shudder at the dead remains which they themselves will shortly be. Yes, shudder! Of the dead we know nothing, save that we shall be like them. Dead! We shall all be dead: that woman walking by, and me, and that stout man whose hat is blowing away, will be dead, and that Dufayel delivery-man will be dead, and that street vendor and his wife who has dust all over her, and me! I'll be dead too.[1] Everything turns the other way round, the sun, the potential for evolving, the city, family, neighbors, and you're left with nothing but the doorway into empty space. You leave behind . . . you leave behind whatever constitutes life; God tears up that particular page and throws it away. But the difference is that *I know*! I come trembling and repentant with the hope that Your Majestic Understanding will not dismiss with scorn my striving toward Good, but what of *them*? What of those others who go rushing by unchecked, as though the devils were whipping them already . . . rushing where? . . . You, who died for them all, all the Homeless Ones! And for me, the sinner; O Death you frighten me so!

The blood on the rock! The rock is a handsome limousine from the best manufacturer, so say the witnesses to the accident. Don't worry, all you oversensitive people who tremble at the sight of blood but not at the sight of suffering, there's no blood in my story, there's no blood in my story! But it's time I set the record straight. It's cars that are the trouble! My heart shakes its fist at cars. The same civilization that gave us cars gave us cannons; they're about equally dangerous, wouldn't you agree? Do you gentlemen, who represent the forces of law and order in this city, mean to tell me that you tolerate vehicles whizzing through its streets with speeds of that sort at eight o'clock in the evening? No, admittedly: the shells the Germans used to lob at us were no less dangerous than cars; we used to go down into basements and hide from them. Is that what we're going to have to do in order to live safely with cars? Live underground with the rats and the subway? But to resume: 'twas a fine winter's evening; the Opéra was offering its second public performance of *The Three-Cornered Hat;* one of my friends

1. Dufayel refers to a department store specializing in furniture.

was involved, and I was to go and applaud his talent.[2] With no particular enthusiasm, I had arrayed myself in the style such occasions require, and, enjoying in my soul the peace that comes from doing one's duty, I worked out in my mind the series of underground rail-lines that would take me to where my duty might duly be done. I had walked the length of the rue des Saints-Martyrs which leads the sinner from the Sacré-Coeur Basilica down to the Profane World but also back up again toward Him, and I was just coming to place Pigalle, the roundabout where all the vices of this Earth converge, when suddenly I was surrounded by cars all going faster than trains. May God forgive those bandits as I forgive them in writing this, but may God save us from their assaults as well.

According to a witness, a corpse wearing a black suit was picked up on the wooden pavement of place Pigalle. The head was sticking out past the wheel. Horror! At least now I know what the underside of a car looks like. Shut your eyes now, gentle convalescent, and you can see again the black dark roundabout where all the vices of this earth converge: place Pigalle! No policemen about; two kindly men propping you up. Here we are outside the pharmacist's; closed.

"My left suspender is pressing into me."

"You aren't wearing suspenders."

"Does that mean my collarbone is broken?"

That's all you can remember, except the car I'm in, the one that ran me down! My, what a splendid car, like being in a first-class railway coach. Someone's asking me things. Can I possibly find the strength to answer? Words come at random; my wits are wandering. Why am I being asked the maiden name of my worthy mother? Now you can't remember anything. So this is death! Death in the street, with no priest, no family, among nameless strangers. So this is where you've come to claim me, unforeseeable Death! So this is how you come and claim us. . . . And how would I have appeared before God, all laden with my sins? What would have become of me, summoned to the presence of the only Judge before I'd had a chance to reflect upon my soul? What a fearful lesson! Remember the parable of the Foolish Virgins: you too will suddenly know the coming of Final Justice and woe to the Foolish Virgin who has laid

2. Jacob's friend was Picasso, who designed set and costumes for the ballet *The Three-Cornered Hat.*

up no provision of grace for her soul, for her lamp no provision of oil. I would like to remember and I cannot . . . I am being carried or I am walking, I know not . . . there is a very big clean open court-yard, a dim light, an iron chair painted bright green, and I am sitting on the chair. A man came and asked me my worthy mother's maiden name, and then a very proper young man:

"Your left collarbone is broken."

"Yes! my . . ."

Should I call you Doctor, young intern, out of respect? Doctor, then; you seemed so kind, so thoughtful and humane; why leave me here, half-naked and alone, sitting upon an iron chair? It's not that I'm in pain, but in my present weakened state what further ills must surely come my way, left here like this! Doctor; it's not my own cause I'm defending when I write these words, but the cause of the poor, in the name of Our Lord Jesus Christ! I'm not the one—I, a middle-class bachelor poet—I'm not the one who's going to catch pneumonia on account of your negligence: all of society is going to catch pneumonia thanks to you. Hate and possible reprisals don't worry you, Doctor; apparently you fear man no more than you fear God. I'm a very indulgent fellow, you know! I know what it's like to work all night, the demands made by work and the pur-suit of knowledge; I know a person hates to be disturbed and that when the routine task is done it's back to your microscope, back to your discoveries, or more simply back to studying for the next exam or for your thesis; I even know what it's like to have bureau-cracy encroaching on your life . . . let's not be unfair here . . . no one can be a hero around the clock. I'll tell you what: I'll go even further! You've given me pneumonia through your negligence and I say thank you very much! You've taught me death and suffering, and I would like these things to be taught to everybody: it's very salutary. How long I stayed sitting on an iron chair, half-naked, in an open courtyard, on that cold January twenty-seventh night, I do not know. I'd lost all sense of being. I believe they enumerated my personal effects and what was in them, and drew up a formal list which had to be signed; they asked me once again, I believe, to state the maiden name of my worthy mother, and then I was left alone, still all alone on my chair. Do you hear me, Doctor? All of Human Society was left alone on an iron chair in an open courtyard cold and naked while you studied the topics for your next exam. Is there a course in applied ethics at the Medical School in Paris? If there is no course in applied ethics at the Medical School in Paris, I suggest they create one. But I fear that would just mean one more exam! One more subject to study! One more excuse for the interns, whom I respectfully address as Doctor, to abandon the whole of Human Society on an iron chair in an open courtyard.

Someone, at last! A very nice, decent woman; poor thing, she's all hot and flustered! She takes off her hat and her good coat. Behind her comes a male attendant:

"We've got to give him a bath; I'm sure there won't be any water, just like the other times! I guess I'm late, eh? My mother-in-law took sick. What a nuisance!"

"Look at his pants and shoes: he's a gentleman; gentlemen aren't dirty."

"No matter; we've got to give him a bath."

They strip me of my remaining garments and now the water won't run. Yes it will! The water's running: it's running cold. The nice, decent woman, with great devotion to duty, washes me with a sponge; she also washes my clothes, which are then put into a bag.

"Well," says the male attendant, "is this guy gonna stay in the bath till tomorrow or something? There're other people waiting to take his place."

I'm shivering; I can hear cries in my chest, cries welling up without my being able to hold them back. Every time I breathe, the torn flesh is pushed up. Truly, for the first time since the accident I am suffering pain. Are there more formalities? I don't care, I tell you! I'm in pain, I'm groaning, I'm in pain, I'm in pain, the world doesn't exist, my pain has taken over the world. In the past hour I've become a bundle of pain, and the bundle of pain is on a stretcher. Corridors and more corridors. That ice-cold courtyard! Every motion lulls my clamoring pain. Now here's a ward full of tobacco smoke, and full of beds. I discover firsthand that tobacco smoke makes the patients cough; I discover firsthand that coughing is indescribably painful for people suffering from pneumonia. Since at that hour (as I found out later) no medication is available, I endured an entire hellish night of coughing, tobacco, chest pain, and an immense faintness that kept me from invoking the one succor available to me in my abandoned state. I was forgetting about God and I didn't have the strength *not* to forget about him. You mean, die without thinking about God?! The chaplain wasn't there and certainly it would never have occurred to anyone to go and fetch him.

The next day, men in whom distinction vied with learning stood around my bed and tried to figure out how the wheels of a car could have brought on pneumonia. "Trauma!" A word I learned that morning.

"It's a latent pulmonary congestion that was just waiting for a chance to break out," said one of them.

"He was in an exceptionally weakened condition," said another.

Out of compassion for those who took me in, or out of compassion for myself, I did not state my own version of how the condition might have arisen. But today, sitting on a bench in Magenta Boulevard contemplating the mausoleum of the living, and knowing that after me there are bound to be others in that place, I feel I would be adding to their woes if I failed to point out one small imperfection in the otherwise admirable hospital system: dangerous acts of negligence when the patients first arrive. Before allowing myself to become involved in recriminations against a group of administrators to whom I owe a debt of gratitude, I sought advice from a man of wisdom: Not to point out an abuse is to make yourself a party to it, he said to me, and I'm sure he's right.

From *The Central Laboratory*

*[Arlette Albert-Birot explains the title of this collection of poems published in 1921: "In it is centralized all the research representing Max's poetical activity between 1903 and 1920" (*Qui (ne) connaît (pas) Max Jacob? Rennes, 1987, *our transl.).*

As poetry, Le Laboratoire Central *is outside the scope of this anthology. We have chosen an exception, a passage of prose contained in one of the poems. The poem, "All Honor to the Sardana and the Tenora," was inspired by a short trip to Spain, taken by Max Jacob and Picasso in 1913. When they visited the town of Figueras in Catalonia, the poet participated in an exuberant sardana, danced by the whole village to the music of local composers. Later he captured the experience in a poem, whose style and tone shift constantly. Jacob first creates his impressions of Catalonia in an avalanche of humorous, juxtaposed images; then, suddenly switching to a passage of classically balanced prose, he describes the village band and particularly the instrument called the* tenora; *finally, returning to poetry, he transposes with perfect pitch both music and dance in dynamic, circular images to express the sheer joy and fun of his joining the whirling dance.*

The middle passage, in prose, is the one given here, with a few lines of the poetry that follows. In the 1990s, the sardana has acquired political status, having become very much the official dance of a Catalonia aspiring to independence.]

♦

All Honor to the Sardana and the Tenora

All my life I shall remember the musical instrument known as the *tenora*; it is about the length of a clarinet and could, a musician assures me, hold its own against forty trombones. It emits a dry, strident sound like that of the bagpipe. I heard the *tenora* at Figueras, a town in Catalonia, in a little band playing on the public square. The band was composed of a cello, a valve horn, brasses, and a flute that did short, charming solos. The sardana was being danced, and before each dance the orchestra would perform a long, stately introduction. The *tenora* declaimed loudly, supported by the other instruments in close-packed concert. The members of this splendid band are musicians from the town; their names are unknown in France except to Pathé Brothers, Ltd. No sacrifice is too great for this gramophone manufacturing company when it comes to . . . etc. After the introduction, the rhythm of the dance begins, a rhythm so strong that I can't imagine wishing for anything more: a polka rhythm broken by sudden silences and long flourishes. There are moments in the sardanas when the music catches fire and you think you have had a blazing glimpse of splendor. The sardana is danced in a circle, the arms of the dancers held out girandola-wise and almost motionless, except in the passages where the music catches fire. You watch the dancers' feet, which are kept taut and execute graceful little grimaces. In the middle of the circle there is another circle, and in the middle of that circle another; and the movements of the three circles are the same but don't coincide, because the leader of each circle is feeling the music in a different way. There were several rosettes of dancers on the cobbled street in the evening, on the public square in Figueras.

> Sardana, you are like a rose!
> And all these girls are dressed in rose.
> The dancers circle, the dancers spin.
> Why do the houses not join in?

From *The Dark Room*

[The Dark Room *was first published in 1922. The French title not only refers to the photographer's darkroom, but hints at the censorship office (*le cabinet noir*) which evokes the censoring of the subconscious by the individual himself.*

In this series of thirty-two letters, with or without commentaries, Jacob takes up the style and persona *of various imaginary correspondents. With a mixture of colloquial vivacity, specialized jargon, and a vocabulary in accordance with their astrological characters, the authors of these imaginary letters reveal a long series of human foibles. Max Jacob does not make fun of the shortcomings of his fellow humans from a lofty position; rather he denounces them after detecting these very failings in himself. As a born comedian and mime, Jacob can easily assume the personality of his correspondents one after another. This untiring observer of society and behavior captures the singularity, the basic attitude of each protagonist in turn, with remarkable accuracy. He achieves this with a dazzling variety of voices and by a constant shifting of style, vocabulary, and structure.*

In The Dark Room, *Jacob does not follow the tradition of the eighteenth-century epistolary novel, but, as in* Film-Flam, *pursues something closer to the seventeenth-century "character portrait." Save for a few light moments, this summary of the author's experience of humankind up to that point in his life is almost as dark as the title suggests. Is this dark picture of cynicism, prejudices, and stupidity in all its privileged forms, as pessimistic as the typical novels or short stories of the time? No. The light, ironic handling of human behavior gives not only comic relief, but hope. If, in these imaginary epistles, we can recognize our own weaknesses and laugh at ourselves, we will be saved.*]

◆

Another Letter Written While in Hospital

Bed 77, Brouillard Ward
Holy Charity Hospital

Dear Sir,

Here I am back in one of these gloomy wards which there is no need for me to describe to you, and it isn't very pleasant to have, in the beds next to yours, people you would not have wanted as servants.[1] By a stroke of good fortune, and thanks to Mr. Turlin's recommendation, the head doctor shows me special consideration; for me he's a familiar face, as he was a medical student when I was a waiter at the d'Harcourt Café. But as you will readily understand, under the circumstances it's not for a down-and-outer to shake hands with a Medical Practitioner. I don't have to tell you how much I dwell on the past and the way I stupidly went through money like water. If I could just have the money I used to spend in a single night when I was at the Stock Exchange, or if I had just one of the pieces of jewelry that I gave Martha Leverrier, or if I even had a situation the way domestic servants do—those servants whom I used to dismiss from service so casually.

My dear Sir, I am stricken with cerebral anemia and weakness resulting from lack of nutrition. My general physical condition is poor. I couldn't cope any longer with living in the street. It takes a bit of money to subsist out on the pavement these days. It's not like when I was young: you could get along with a few pennies earned opening carriage doors or shining shoes or running errands for the ladies. A croissant cost a penny or two! But now things are hard for the poor! And the rich man never thinks about the poor man any more, in fact less than ever, for it makes people feel very comfortable to say that everyone's been getting good wages since the War. When I was rich I scarcely gave it a thought either; I realize . . .

I wasn't able to come to an arrangement with Puiset. I under-

1. Max Jacob chose poverty as a way of life and felt deep sympathy for the "downtrodden and the humiliated," but never expressed it with the sentimentalism of a "bleeding heart." Thus his sick and destitute protagonist stirs our sympathy for his misfortunes without being at all admirable himself.

went the humiliating experience of going to that man, who had known me when I was wealthy, and asking him for a job playing bit parts or sweeping up in his theater. It was hard to do, but I thought he would make the grand, noble gesture, for I've often invited him to dinner or lunch at the Café Anglais or the Café de Paris. He declined to be of service to me and offered me ten francs which I turned down as you can well imagine. He's a millionaire, they say: well, every dog has his day! I don't believe a small helping hand, held out in my direction, would have hurt him very much. It could be argued that seeing me around in his theater might have been unpleasant for him: no man likes to come to work every day and see among his subordinates a fellow whom he once saw driving a smart carriage in the Bois de Boulogne, with a monocle and buttercup-yellow gloves, and who has now come down in the world. Which goes to show, dear Sir, that friendship the quality of yours is rare indeed. If it hadn't been for you, I would have starved to death. It's of some consolation to me that I've seen it all, for a man who has been orphaned at the age of eight, has worked at every sort of job in London and Paris, who has by a lucky stroke been a stockbroker's servant and then himself a stockbroker, who has been through every conceivable form of lawsuit and had his private townhouse sold from under him, that man can truly say that he has seen it all, give or take the geography one gets from traveling. If it weren't for this cerebral anemia, now, I wouldn't be in hospital, because then I could still be a "translator" in the office of a certified translator at the Stock Exchange, or handling dispatches for Radio News Agency or Havas or Reuter's or any such. But with cerebral anemia, what's a person to do?

And besides, dear Sir, I'm behind the times; I can't keep up the struggle in this city of Paris which kills off its destitute, its weak, its sick, its old people and children. I just haven't got what it takes any more to cope with things as they come along. The fact is, I've had enough. After a certain number of punches, you just can't take it the way you used to. And anyway, this life of flophouses and soup kitchens wears a man out. They say to you: "Pay for your night in advance or out you go!" and the next night it's the same story, and the next, and it's just plain murder! Of course, there are the little public gardens if you know how to get in, or the Wine Market. And then you can sleep at the police station once in a while, and once in a while at the nuns' place on Méchain Street. When I wasn't in such bad shape as I am now, there was also the dodge of taking foreign tourists to find a woman, because the rule is that if someone brings a girl a customer she finds him a place to sleep. But who can you walk up to on the street when you haven't even got a clean shirt-collar? No sir, no pals any more—men or women; nothing left to do but go from hospital to hospital like an old jailbird that's never out for long. Sir, I have, you might say, simply run out of steam. I am aware that my mental outlook dates from 1882; I'm a woolly mammoth, a dinosaur, a creature from prehistoric times that no one today understands. Drop me a note, send five francs for my tobacco and I'll be happy.

Please believe me when I say how grateful I am and that I remain your devoted friend,

Alexis Guillet

Comments

This letter provides an answer, as though it had been written for the purpose, to our hard-working, hard-hearted friends who crush the poor with the words: "All they have to do is work! After all, *I* work!" Let's just see you go several kilometers on foot in order to find the heap of sand that your buddy has told you about, way out in the suburbs, and *then* let's see you manage to get to the other end of Paris in order to be at some municipal soup kitchen by sunup: "Too late! Can't you get here on time? As if you had so much to do!!!" (actual words). A person's strength is sapped by this cross-country begging![2] But go ahead and tell us about it, you people, all sleek and shiny like well-fed plough horses! Go ahead, fellows, tell us about work and how every man since Adam has had to earn his bread by the sweat of his brow. Adam, indeed! But Adam didn't have to get a half-pound of bread at the Sacré-Coeur in Montmartre at seven o'clock on Sunday morning when he'd slept the night on a bench in Vaugirard. And in Paris at least there are a few things you can fall back on; Parisians are humane people, and city policemen are not as brutal as the cartoonists would have us

2. Presumably the "heap of sand" is a pile of sand that someone wants moved, implying the prospect of a bit of paid labor. Only in 1984 did the French government recognize the absurdity of expecting the poor to travel across the city; that year the government began to distribute free subway passes to the unemployed.

believe! But oh, the plight of the poor out in the country! No hospitals there! There the indigent is considered a tramp, that is to say, something you go after with dogs and pitchforks. For every farmer who is a good and worthy man there are a thousand who are hostile and suspicious.

People of my generation knew the poet Cornuty who was a friend of Verlaine's and was present when Verlaine died.[3] Cornuty had considered it poetic to "take to the road" and was always glad to tell people his impressions and adventures.

"The tramps you see on the highways," Cornuty told me, "show each other the way to the farms where you can be sure of a handout. On January first, everyone gives, and you have the right to beg; on other days you don't have the right to beg. On January first tramps will often change clothes in order to turn up at the same charitably disposed house several times." One night, Cornuty froze his legs sleeping in a haystack; his companions carried him to a farmhouse and woke the people up, and the farm people took him to a blacksmith's forge "at the risk of killing me," added Cornuty. "It was a policeman who taught me the rules of begging; I wish there were more like him!" On one occasion, Cornuty said to a farmer: "All I have is seven cents!" They gave him soup and a plate of meat and a room with a carpet. He heard the man say to his wife: "It was God who sent him here!" They didn't take his seven cents.

◆

Letter to Mrs.Goldencalf

[*In Max Jacob's picture gallery of the French bourgeoisie, there is no marital bliss. Married women are stout, shrewish, and hard as nails. They consider their husbands only as "providers" and turn their libido elsewhere. They either shower their unspent love on their unworthy offspring, usually their sons, or they invest their energies in building up a glamorous social life. They rigidly keep up appearances, take elegance and fashion with deadly seriousness, and religiously respect social etiquette.*]

3. In his prayer book, Max Jacob kept a list of the living and dead for whom he prayed daily. Cornuty's name was on this list. The dying Verlaine's last words to Cornuty were, "Be pure of heart, open to the world of miracles."

Le Blanc Sainte-Même (near Guéret)

My Dear Sister-in-Law,

I can't keep this boarder you've wished on me. He's turning my place into a shambles. When he goes to the toilet—excuse me for discussing such matters—he puts his feet on the bench instead of sitting down like a decent person, so that he gets the bench dirty, and if the lattice fence round the garden was not firmly supported with iron stakes he would smash it down. He smokes too much, which smells up my living room, and we find cigarette butts and pipe dottle on the paths in the garden. He helps himself to fruit that is lying on the ground and you know I like to save it for Jenny Caugant's pigs. He went to the village dance and came home after midnight. The maid was obliged to get up and unbolt the door for him; she had almost nothing on, and it's all quite improper, for he made a remark that was rather disrespectful to a person her age. At the dance the only person he led out onto the floor was the school-teacher's wife because she was better dressed than the others; this did not go unnoticed. Lastly, I consider that those white striped suits, called beach-suits, are much too unconventional for a small community such as this. He's very nice for getting up a flirtation, but as for marrying him to Miss Landsdowry, I assure you the thing is impossible: he's too loud and flashy. He hangs around in taverns, and, to make matters worse, cracks jokes that other people don't always understand! In short, your son has manners which don't suit us. I'm not accusing you of bringing him up badly, since I understand he's going to be a doctor and have a university degree and all that, but he hasn't been brought up to suit the taste of people in these parts who tend to be sticklers for etiquette. Find him a wife in Paris or at the watering resorts, since you're in a position to marry him off young and that's the best thing you can do.

Love to your husband, little Germaine, and yourself,

Amélie

P.S. You can consider yourself lucky to have picked a husband who is a nice man and turned out to be a good provider. In my case . . . well, you know Alfred, don't you? Well, he hasn't changed.

Comments

Mrs. Goldencalf was enraged! She crumpled the letter and threw it across the room, but then as a precaution asked a servant to pick it up and hand it back to her, carefully smoothed it out, reread it, and filed it away. Nicéphore was intelligent enough and rich enough to marry whom he wished and when he wished.

Mrs. Goldencalf gets up at nine. She has been awake for an hour, going over in her mind all the grounds she can find for being angry at everyone. She faithfully promises herself that she will catch the maids doing something they shouldn't and that she will get her dressmaker's cutter dismissed. She will write to *Illustration* that she's canceling her subscription if they go on publishing photos about X; she will write to the author of that novel to tell him his book is hateful; she will write a recriminatory letter to that sister-in-law of hers in Le Blanc Sainte-Même. Behold her risen from her bed! Her meager bun of hair rises snakelike above a face which, bereft of makeup, has no trace of womanliness:

"What's this? No hot water waiting for me? A lot of good it is to have three housemaids! Oh, but I shall make a clean sweep of all my domestic staff!" She rings to summon her servants, but as none comes running to do her bidding, into the hall like biting North Wind she swoops: "Is that how you do your job, you bunch of nincompoops? The shoes haven't been shined! My breakfast isn't cooking! And what about my toast? What a disgrace! Oh, I shall make a clean sweep, let me tell you!"

She lingers a moment in her husband's bedroom, hoping to think of something disagreeable to say to him: "Naturally, the lord and master is still in bed at ten o'clock!" No answer from the lord and master. "I, on the other hand, have been up since seven. The fact is that if you want your house well kept. . . . Although I must admit that for all the work *you* have to do, you might just as well. . . . Ye gods, what it is to be afflicted with a sluggard the likes of you! Look at him: no interest in anything! Never reads anything! Never goes anywhere!" No answer from the lord and master. He lies there smoking; he's thinking: "Since I was stupid enough to buy those shares from that fool of a man Bearmarket, I'm going to give him a piece of advice: let him simply shut down his shoe factories; then nobody will have shoes any more, and then he can sell them at whatever price he likes!" His good lady, having lost all hope of provoking her mild-mannered spouse, moves on to the dining room: "This coffee is unspeakable! What's this cup doing here? I've said a thousand times that I want my cup and no other, my cup with the initials on it! My rounds of toast are too dark! How is it the dining-room floor still hasn't been done? Oh, just you wait, I shall make a clean sweep of the whole lot! And the same for my dressmaker: she'll have to make a clean sweep of her employees, too, if she wants to keep my custom. Have you ever *seen* such a housecoat, it doesn't fit me anywhere. Just look at this, Marie! . . . No, don't touch me! Clumsy girl! Stupid thing! I don't know why I don't smack you! You pricked me! Get out! . . . What about Nicéphore? Is master Nicéphore up yet?" "No, Ma'am. But the hairdresser's been waiting for you for an hour, Ma'am. He says he's pressed for time." "Pressed for time? Pressed for time! So our gentleman is pressed for time! Well, I'm going to keep him waiting till noon and if he doesn't like it he can stay away for good! That'll show him who I am!"

Nicéphore is a medical student. He ought to be at the hospital listening to his teacher, but of the two positions, vertical and horizontal, he prefers the horizontal. Nicéphore is musing:

"Once my parents are dead, medicine can go hang! There'll always be enough income from the Crédit Lyonnais for my sister and me. If need be, I'll take over the management of Voltaire Warehouse and Storage. It's not a bad establishment and running it doesn't take too much work."

The time is noon. Although the gentleman of the house has not come back from the tobacconist's where he went to buy cigars (the five-cent cigars for people he invites to his home; his own favorite brand is reserved for a few distinguished guests), his good lady is already at the table with Nicéphore and Sweetie-Pie. "A fine time to be coming in!" says the lady to her husband who is ten minutes late. "Marie! What sort of hors d'oeuvres are these; they taste like boiled leather! This is slop! Take it back for the kitchen staff!" Mr. Goldencalf, having ventured to make a remark about Nicéphore's excessive expenditures, is sharply taken to task. Mrs. Goldencalf bursts into tears and leaves the table, followed by her daughter. Do you suppose she is going to have an attack of hysteria? By no means! The lady gets dressed and finds something to blame the housemaid for: it's her fault that her mistress is getting stout; it's the dress-maker's fault that not one dress fits her properly. She will spend the day handing down her judgments in other people's drawing rooms, to which she brings a supercilious, imperial manner of the kind that makes tradespeople tremble in their boots. There is only one person she is really afraid of and that is her dressmaker, because that lady was clever enough and daring enough to say to her cutter one day: "Just don't pay any attention, Mrs. Lucie! If she isn't pleased with us, let her take her custom to someone else! This is simply the behavior you get from people with more money than breeding!" From that day on, the good lady became very mild-mannered when visiting her dressmaker. She gets her own back whenever she mentions the dressmaker in conversation.

And indeed, try and find anyone whom she mentions favorably! She tears the reputations of her friends to shreds, accuses her servants of the blackest crimes, and the latest books, newspapers, plays, and paintings of being "enough to make you shudder." She shows emotion only when speaking of gowns or when praising her son Nicéphore, whom she smothers with frantic kisses in public. There is no stratagem she will reject if it's for him: to supplement the allowance paid out to him by his father, she submits forged tradesmen's bills to her husband and the sums paid out in settlement of these supposed accounts go to pay for Nicéphore's extravagances. She is absurdly unjust toward her husband; she persists in thinking him stupid although he has made her a fortune; she becomes angry at everything he says to her and considers it perfectly natural that he should have worked all his life only for her. She is incapable of giving up a single minute of her life to say or do something that would please him, or a single one of her opinions to make him appear to be in the right, and does not scruple to laugh in his face when she thinks he's being ridiculous. She, who understands everything, has understood not one thing pertaining to the character of this man. She imagines herself to have a superior mind because she is extremely proud, and indeed she is quite clear-sighted! But the only human trait she has is her love for Nicéphore, and even that love is more suggestive of mental disorder than of tender motherly affection.

Let us do her justice! Mrs. Goldencalf is an excellent hostess; that is probably why she is much sought-after socially. Another reason is that her biting opinions impress her unsophisticated friends. But oddly enough, when she is in her own drawing room she becomes very mellow and even that biting turn of mind is quite absent. When she was a girl, a humble clerk with whom she used to flirt before, during, and after High Mass in her native town of X, but whom she had spurned as a husband because she was ambitious, had in revenge nicknamed her *the Disdainful Dish*. His joy at having thought up this quip consoled the poor lad; he is not the only person to have found consolation for his sorrows by indulging the spirit of vengefulness. We record this witticism because it describes not just Mrs. Goldencalf but an entire social caste: self-satisfied, well fed, more contemptuous than were the aristocrats of days gone by. The triumphal operations of the Goldencalf family are formulated and pursued with nothing to fear save falling foul of the law, and normally the law protects such a family. Now the fact is that at five o'clock, in her drawing room, the lady is no longer "disdainful" at all; indeed it could scarcely be said that she is still a "dish." She saves her pronouncements, condemning deeds and men, for her friends' drawing rooms; when she treats her hosts as people of no importance and tries to come down to their level, she reveals what she herself is like. Have no fear: she will take her revenge this evening by making slighting remarks about each of the ladies who were so incautious as to be drawn to her poisoned honey!

An "absolutely reliable person," one of those Parisian ladies who know everything that has happened in Paris over the past thirty years, none other than Mrs. Krauss-Cognon, has just now informed me that I "don't know the first thing about the Goldencalf family." According to her, Mrs. Goldencalf is supposed to "have a very shrewd head on her shoulders." She's the one who is said to have made the entire Goldencalf fortune. Mrs. Goldencalf, according to this account, is an "angel of charity," spending her entire life giving gold and advice to the humble.

Quite possibly.

◆

Letter from a Working Girl to Her Employer's Son

Dear Mr. Fernand,

My Aunt Jean says that trouble makes a person think and I'm sure doing a lot of thinking right now, Mr. Fernand, because I've got a lot of trouble in my heart. Aunt Jean is the lady that was always there and by the way, she thinks you're very polite! Oh, Mr. Fernand, I was too happy that evening on Philippe-Auguste Avenue and Aunt Jean says it only happens once in a person's life and a person has to understand how things are.[1] But okay, I've thought it over carefully and your mother understands better than we do. It's no fun, let me tell you, Mr. Fernand! I've set the photograph from Saint-Cloud on the mantel in my room and I put it in a wooden frame that cost me two francs thirty-five at the Galeries Gambetta. Saint-Cloud was real nice; Saint-Cloud is a place I'll always love. Every evening I talk to the photograph we took in Saint-Cloud! And then I think how you'll never get to see what it's like where we live, 'cause my mind is made up. Yes, indeed, my mind is made up and it hurts me to have to say it. Whatever you do, Mr. Fernand, don't go thinking it's on account of I don't love you enough. If that's what love is like then I guess I do love you but my mind is made up. Oh my goodness, I'm so afraid you'll think it's on account of I don't love you enough! But it's better only one of us should suffer and that's why I'm writing to you. The funny thing is I always used to say I'd never fall in love with a man who wore glasses or a fat, dark-haired man.

Now I can guess that the reason you won't tell me the truth is that you're so kind and considerate you don't want to hurt my feelings. Oh, I could tell that your feelings had changed . . . compared with Philippe-Auguste Avenue; and I know the whole truth and it's such a heartbreak for the one who loves you, honest it is! I had a little ray of sunshine in my life and it was so precious! When

1. Did the writer of this letter have a once-only Cinderella's ball experience on Philippe-Auguste Avenue with her prince? And was Saint-Cloud, the Paris suburb referred to later, the site of their love-nest? Octavia and Fernand remain sole possessors of their shared memories: the reader is allowed only a glimpse.

Mr. Quellien, the foreman, shouted "Octavia" out in the hall, it was just like I felt a chill come over me. "This is it," I says to myself, "this means the end!" I was working happily away with the big tailor's shears. Justine Marrois said to me: "Well, go on, Octavia, they're calling you! What's the matter with you?" I had to go, didn't I? "Well, Octavia," Quellien says to me, "so we've been spinning out Love's Sweet Dream with the boss's son, have we? Well, I've got orders to pay you your wages up to date; you're through!" As far as finding work goes there's no problem about that but I figured it was really an order from your mother about you and that was that! It meant goodbye to those kind, gentle eyes of yours, Mr. Fernand, goodbye forever unless fate takes a hand. The trouble is that out of pride I was stupid enough to come out and say you'd promised to marry me and all the girls called me Mrs. Fernand and that hurt me worse than anything. But I forgive them, Mr. Fernand, I forgive them! And I forgive your mother, too, even if she did say I was "old and wrinkled before my time, a little snip covered with freckles and always in a rage!" After all, we all know what a mother is, I mean we're bound to, aren't we? But Justine Marrois is the one who's all wrinkled and has freckles. And your mother knows Justine, because Justine went to Joinville to take a package of scissors out to your place last July. Oh, why won't people just leave me to cry in peace! Aunt Jean has found out that your mother was always rummaging in your pockets and that she'd found my letters tucked into that pretty red notebook of yours and read them. But it's better this way! I'd rather know!

When I go past your little house on Charenne Street, of an evening, I can see the light in the dining room, and I imagine you all there together, the four of you, all very happy. I can truly say that I had a great affection for you and for your father, because he's good to the workers, and the same goes for your sister and your mother. And to be the cause of a breach between you and your mother, Mr. Fernand, is something I'll never do. I never knew my own mother, 'cause I have no one but Aunt Jean, but I would never have set out to disobey her because that's the kind of thing you should never, never do! Of course I know that if a person's whole life could be like on Philippe-Auguste Avenue that would be nice. It would be so nice! When you stop to think about it, I don't belong in that house; I should have realized that sooner. And even supposing—what would be the use? A penniless girl there, among all those rich people, upsetting everybody? Mr. Fernand, you're the man I love and I have to say goodbye. Goodbye, Mr. Fernand, goodbye. I'll never forget. Spare a thought once in a while for a humble working girl who loves you true, Mr. Fernand, and marry someone from your own class. Some day I'll see you going by on the street with a little child, another woman's child, and I'll come over and kiss the child, Mr. Fernand, on account of Philippe-Auguste Avenue and on account of Saint-Cloud too. I've thought it over very carefully, I really have, and my mind is made up.

I'll always think of myself as your fiancée,

Octavia Loiseau

P.S. Aunt Jean says as how I'm a fool because a person has to stand up for her rights, is what she says, but God is my judge in Heaven, Mr. Fernand, and my mother will be my judge in Heaven too.

◆

They Sat in the Bar and Laughed Over It [1]

[*Jacob confided to Jean Cocteau that Anna Bourdin's letter was one of his "inspired" texts. He wrote "They Sat in the Bar and Laughed Over It" in one sitting, as if suddenly possessed by his own invention. He generally wrote his prose very quickly and afterward started the painstaking work of testing for quality, examining every paragraph, every sentence, every word, and ruthlessly discarding whatever did not ring true. "I measure out my prose with an eyedropper," he said.*]

Dear Charles,

After what has just happened, I feel a need to write to you!

I greatly fear that the days of turning cartwheels on the beach are over, and the sundial of our hearts now marks a much less happy time. I think you realized that, Charles! An author whose name I forget said it all: You don't trifle with love! You trifled with

1. We have seen Mrs. Goldencalf, the staunch, stout middle-class married woman, bluntly ordering around an aloof, subdued husband. Now we see Anna Bourdin, her slimmer, younger counterpart, obliquely manipulating an ambitious but lazy partner. Anna parades her little love affairs and sexual appetites as "grand passions" and herself as a "martyr to love."

mine, Charles! I sold my piano: what for? or rather, who for? There are three kinds of interior decoration: stylish, functional, and artistic. My apartment was stylish. You don't like white lacquer and you bear the responsibility for changes that were made. We started with the sort of banter people exchange under sunshades on the beach; now you tell me that I have wrecked your career and that you ought to be with United Shipping, Ltd. Do you think changing my furniture because you don't like white lacquer was a mere trifle? Or selling my piano because I can't resist the urge to sit down and plink a tune? You say: "Anna, you've caused a permanent rift between me and my mother." You forget, Charles, that I went seven months without letting an egg into the dining room on the grounds that the sight of an egg makes you throw up. I have a self-sacrificing nature, Charles. I'm a blonde; as you know, my blondeness owes nothing to the hairdresser's art: all blondes have self-sacrificing natures. A friend of mine said so—one of the friends you drove away with your sarcastic remarks. A charming man: he recited monologues and people enjoyed listening. He also used to say that naturally wavy hair is a sign of patience. So you see how clever he is. You fired my housemaid, or it amounts to that: you didn't like the girl, and she left. I had a tablecloth of Genoese velvet: it's in the attic at my house in Le Tréport because you burned a hole in it with your cigar. Do you think a woman who prides herself on a smart-looking apartment can keep a tablecloth with a hole burned in it? She cannot. To do you justice, Charles, you looked all over Paris for material of the same kind as my tablecloth! But did you find any? No, Charles, you did not.[2] So what's the use? Now you come and tell me: "For your sake I missed my chance to marry a girl with 413,000 francs." Instead of thanking me for the nobility of my feelings, Charles, you find fault. As a woman, I simply refused to let a man whom I have loved, whom I still love, demean himself in my sight. Where did her money come from? From ill-gotten gains, Charles,

2. Anna's concern about her tablecloth curiously echoes real-life complaints about Max Jacob made by Princess Ghika, the former demimondaine Liane de Pougy, a notorious beauty. She and her husband often entertained Max at their villa in Brittany. Later she described how he "leans with all his weight on frail white lacquered chairs. . . . I have seen him lying in his filthy clothes and muddy shoes on a precious bedspread of white silk damask" (Liane de Pougy, *My Blue Notebooks*, New York, 1971, p. 116).

beneath the dignity of a man who is nearly . . . anyway, the purity of
my love saved you from committing an act of infamy. Do you really
think I'm not aware of your contempt for women? Do you think my
pride wasn't hurt? Do you think I wasn't hurt each time you arrived
a few minutes late? There I was, a woman who had given herself
freely and lovingly, proud to be deceiving the man she had ceased
to love and to be immolating him to the man she loved now, and
that's all the respect you showed for my feelings. Oh, you can be
tactful occasionally, Charles, thank Heavens; you broke off an ad-
vantageous friendship on my account and you never threw that up
at me. But don't you understand, Charles, it's not tact I need. I'm
a woman, and woman is a creature of unthinking passion. I gave
up Aristide for you, and he was an up-and-coming man, whereas
you never managed to get a position with United Shipping, Ltd.
despite your Doctor of Law degree. I'm not blaming you, but don't
talk about sacrifices to a woman who is a martyr in the cause of love.
Don't you dare to complain when here I am without even my poor
little piano to help me sing with a broken heart. Buy another piano,
I can hear you say, but pianos cost the earth and besides, who will
give me back those nimble fingers that skimmed the keyboard in
my days at the convent? So then what's the use? The same with my
houseplants. I would have given anything to keep my auracaria.
You didn't like my auracaria. Things reached a stage where I was
ready to hand you an ultimatum, as the saying goes: take me as I
am, auracaria and all, or leave me. But I loved you and I am a tactful woman. I don't like it when things become ridiculous. I confess
I loved you to the point of giving up my artistic tastes and pleasures.
But you know, Charles, it's artistic pleasures that lend nobility to a
woman's life, and make us different from the animals. Yes, the days
of turning cartwheels are gone; and gone, oh, gone, the games beneath the sunshade on the beach! You were a tyrant, Charles, and
I your slave; I see that now, but I couldn't then, so blind is Love.

You write: "First you ruined *my* life and now you've thrown me
out of yours!" I do like your writing style, Charles, and I shall preserve all your letters however imprudent that may be, for it is no
concern of anyone's, after all. But when did I throw you out of
my life? Weren't you the one who left because Aristide came back?
You say Aristide and I are lovers again. What proof have you? And
even if you had proof, what would that prove? Aristide came back

133

because he doesn't live in Montfort-sur-Meu anymore, because he quarreled with his wife's family. Aristide is a particular friend of mine and if—which I do not admit—if Aristide and I were what is called "lovers," I would ask, Is that reason enough to accuse me of ruining your life? Am I the sort of woman who would ruin a man's life? Where did you get this notion that I am a heartless woman? When have you ever seen me hurt anyone? Haven't you seen me giving to the poor? Just ask my servants how they are treated in my home, for Heaven's sake! Didn't I shut my eyes when I realized that Maria Vaillant was stealing from me? Didn't I marry off Yvonne to Mrs. Protaize's coachman? Do I or do I not provide my mother with a living allowance? Didn't I set my brother Edward up in business? Didn't I give 200 francs to the survivors of the S/S *Elan* disaster? Well then? What can you mean when you say I have no heart? Knowing all this, can you still think I'm the kind of woman who would ruin a man's life? Yes, the time for cartwheels and games beneath the sunshade is over! Here we are, forced to face reality, two poor wretches thrown into one another's arms by love. I rest my case! No, Charles, my door is not closed to you, don't ever think that. If you come to my home you may be sure that I will always be glad to see you. Believe me when I say there is still enough love in my heart to help me forget your cruel behavior and your last cruel letter.

Ever your friend,

Anna Bourdin

Comments

It has to be acknowledged that Anna Bourdin has a stylish apartment, but how far must we go along with Charles's mistress when she states that he was partly responsible for the drastic domestic upheavals referred to here? Be honest, now, Anna Bourdin! Weren't you the one to be much struck by something Mrs. Protaize said: "White lacquer is quite out of fashion"? The same for the piano: if you got bored with the piano, why blame it on Charles? Charles likes music, but why not admit that your playing was simply awful? It's not exactly enjoyable to listen to someone stumbling her way through one of Mayol's songs using one or two fingers. Yet never once did Charles utter a complaint about your musical pastime;

you were the one, let me tell you, you were the one who got discouraged one evening when you saw how well Mrs. Protaize plays: she can really work her way quite handily through waltzes, tangos, and even bits from *Manon*.

You sold your piano in a fit of rage or sulks, lacking the strength of character either to work at the Craft of music or to contemplate with detachment the obvious superiority of your friend Mrs. Protaize at the keyboard. As for the friends that poor Charles is supposed to have driven away, don't make me laugh! At the time you were deeply in love with Charles, I know; your friends were trying to wean you away from him for reasons I need not go into here: you chose love over friendship, which is very natural, and, in order to establish love in all its authority, what you established was a couple cut off from everyone else. I won't look too closely at the business of the housemaid except to say that she knew too much about a past you wanted to forget. Or at the Genoese velvet tablecloth. Here the fault lies with Charles; he burned a hole in the Genoese velvet tablecloth and what's more he lied when he led you to believe that various steps had been taken with a view to replacing it: he took not one such step. As for the auracaria, you cared for it mainly because it was a present from Aristide and that was also the reason why Charles did *not* care for it. So let's hear no more about your artistic tastes: as regards the auracaria I assure you that the artistic tastes, which no one ever denies that you possess, are quite unrelated to the plant that Aristide gave you. Nor do I deny your kindheartedness, but do I really need to point out that ruining a man's life for love, and giving or not giving to the poor, do not come from the same compartments of the brain or the heart? You know all this as well as I do, you aren't that naïve: what we really have here is . . . how shall I put it . . . is a bit of bad faith on your part, wouldn't you say? Charles accuses you of ruining his life . . . we'll examine that contention in a moment . . . what have you got to say in reply? It's a bit awkward. Are you going to deny having ruined his life? If you were a worse person than you are, it would flatter your vanity to have had the power to ruin someone's life (there are plenty of women capable of that) but you are not a bad person. If you were as good a person as you claim to be, you would find in your heart gentle words of consolation. But what you mainly are is indifferent and God alone can fathom the indifference of a woman who has fallen out of love. And all you are capable of feeling in your indifference is the need to prove how virtuous you are.

Let me move on to Charles! Charles won't admit, Charles has always refused to admit, that he is subject to seasickness! When United Shipping, Ltd. offered him a position that involved trips to the four corners of the world, Charles, who likes emotional scenes, came weeping into Anna Bourdin's arms, swearing never to be parted from her. Much moved, Anna Bourdin stroked his bald head. The next thing we know, Charles is accusing Anna of having wrecked his career: he's not being fair. Charles says to Anna: "You've caused a permanent rift between me and my mother." There is an element of truth in that statement, but only very indirectly. Charles's mother admonished her son one evening because he was going out after supper every day. Charles replied that he wasn't a child any more. Charles's mother tried to take him with her on a visit to the Talabardons, who have friends in Parliament. Charles, who was expected at Anna's, refused to go with his mother. His mother said tearfully: "You're seeing a woman, Charles; I know you are!" "Well, and supposing I am? You know very well I can't get married because you and I have just barely enough to support the two of us. Do you expect me to live like a monk?" Whereupon Charles' mother fainted or nearly, Charles walked out and went to live at Anna Bourdin's until such time as "I find a situation." It may be seen from the foregoing that Anna Bourdin is for all purposes not responsible for the rift between the most worthy of sons and the most loving of mothers.

Now, a word about marrying the girl with the 413,000 francs! No such marriage was planned or even contemplated. Miss Talabardon had 413,000 francs coming to her from her grandmother who was also her godmother; the day that Charles's mother discovered this interesting fact, she conceived the notion that her son, by virtue of his intelligence and his distinguished qualities both innate and acquired, was eminently deserving of such a fortune. She gave utterance to this thought several times in Charles's presence, whereupon Charles's demeanor changed to that of a sulky schoolboy. One day, speaking to his mother, he declared that he would never marry because he didn't want everyone to say he'd married for money. Charles went to Anna Bourdin with the tale that they were trying to marry him off for 413,000 francs and that he was saying no because he loved only her. Let me add for the sake of truthfulness that Anna Bourdin replied: "Go ahead and say yes, darling; you wouldn't be the first husband who went to City Hall and swore to be faithful while silently making plans for a love-nest." And now we have Charles writing to Anna: "For your sake I missed my chance to marry a girl with 413,000 francs!" And Anna writing back: "Where did her money come from? From ill-gotten gains," etc., thus casting opprobrium and discredit upon the good, decent Talabardon family.

Enough of this! What manner of man was Aristide? Who was he? What is the relationship between Aristide and Charles? Aristide is a property owner at Montfort-sur-Meu and a member of the Talabardon family. It was through him that Charles met Anna Bourdin: "I've got a cozy little woman; you should see her, Charles! . . . a woman who moves around in society, I mean real society, not just somebody who puts on airs, nothing like that! And she has a good mind; she plays the piano." For a time, Charles provided a pleasantly distracting third party for a couple who were bored. The day came when conversation faltered; Aristide realized that he was now in the way, and since he had in any case to leave for Montfort-sur-Meu he gallantly bowed out. Upon his return from Montfort-sur-Meu he came walking into Anna's apartment and into her arms. Charles, who is not a fool, guessed or understood. Since he happened, at that particular moment, to have what he referred to as "a little something going for me on the side," he was indulgent toward Anna's having one as well, until the day when his "little something on the side" got jealous; he then assumed a cloak of dignity and made embittered comments about Aristide. You will be relieved to learn that the two gentlemen are still very good friends. Charles even read Aristide the letter we have reproduced here. They sat in the bar and laughed over it. Women who misbehave are soon objects of contempt to the very men who have catered to their vanity the most. Mind you, the women couldn't care less about those men; in fact, the Devil is the only one who comes out ahead in this sort of transaction.[3]

3. The Devil, who always takes malicious pleasure in lending his support to those who make fun of others, is not simply a figure of speech to be lightly dismissed. Jacob believed as strongly in the Devil as in God. He sees and represents

♦

Advice to a Young Doctor from an
Established Practitioner

Dear Albert,

All you have to do is convince the caretaker's wife that you saved her life when she had a head cold and all the tenants in the building will want you as their doctor. There will be a whirlwind-cum-snowball effect: that apartment block will bring the entire street and then the entire neighborhood into your office. When Cousin Charles set up practice in Rodez, he made his reputation the day he arrived by treating a cerebral stroke with a blood-letting; it turned out he had saved the life of the head waiter at his hotel. You've often heard me repeat the old saying: these three things a doctor needs: knowledge, which has its uses and is the same for all; know-how, which is much more important; and how-to-get-known, which is indispensable. The caretaker's wife trumpets your name to the world and gets you known; the know-how lay in convincing her that you had cured her. A little knowledge saved the head waiter in Rodez, who also proved to be a first-rate trumpeter, if memory serves.

To begin with, get it into your head that for you the least important member of a household is the patient. It's not him you've got to satisfy, it's the rest of the family. If you want to establish a reputation, first of all you have to consider other doctors as enemies. You must develop a knack for implying that in such-and-such circumstances Mr. So-and-So's condition was not treated as it ought to have been, that Mr. Z's life could have been saved, and that, whatever the case, the wise and learned specialist who should have been brought in was you. Strive to convey all this in a voice combining authority with great flexibility, and display a firm, scientific attitude. Inquire about the health of the whole family, but no familiarity, please: inspire a certain amount of fear so you won't be asked too many questions, and maintain presence of mind and steady poise. On one occasion I was treating the son of a head nurse; as you might suppose, my dear Albert, such persons, generally disagree-

---

him under a hundred disguises, but finds him most assuredly present in his own bosom as the eternal tempter.

able at the best of times, are quite knowledgeable and not easily impressed. I had prescribed quinine hydrochlorate, though quinine is usually given as a sulfate. "Why hydrochlorate, Doctor?" asked the head nurse. I answered as though my mind were elsewhere and without taking my eyes off the patient. "In cases such as this, Matron, there's no question; only hydrochlorate can give satisfactory results!" Now as you and I both know, my dear Albert, the two salts are chemically analagous. So self-assurance is the thing, Albert; self-assurance, authority, composure!

The most obnoxious kind of patient is the hypochondriac. If you can cure him and get him off their hands, the rest of the family will appreciate that more than anything. You may say: "The hypochondriac is not the proper concern of the doctor!" Wrong! What is Medicine? Does it consist of using drugs to relieve symptomatic distress? Obviously that's part of it. But only part, Albert; the whole purpose of medicine is to achieve that euphoric state we call health. And here allow me to quote what Farabeuf said: "Health is a precarious state which bodes no good!" The hypochondriac, on the other hand, is a person who thinks he is sick and needs to be convinced that he is not. I would not have brought up the question of the hypochondriac, except that he takes us right to the heart of medical practice, the problem of the usefulness of the doctor and his value to society; what I intend, in fact, is to move on by way of the hypochondriac and talk to you about confidence.

I had a Chronic Rheumatism who was very attached to me. I've always remembered this patient because whenever I prescribed for him he would utter the strange ritual words: "Okay, Doctor, but do you figure that stuff will do me any good?" Obviously he had confidence in me, but he wanted to have even more confidence, as though he were obscurely aware that where there is no confidence there can be no cure. The odd thing is that in his desire to have his faith in me confirmed and approved, the person he turned to was me. He was really asking for me to be as positive in my manner as I could possibly be. A doctor is a man who sells hope, and next to hope comes faith. So it is up to you to inspire in your patient a frame of mind such that the drug will have greater effect prescribed by you than prescribed by someone else. The drug must be the means by which you convey confidence. I had a Neuralgia who had tried all the known drugs. One day I had an idea: I handed her a compound as though it was something brand new, when in fact it was just a mixture of two drugs she'd often used before to no effect. I had ground a particular kind of pink pill in with a particular kind of white powder. Presto! I cured her. A hypochondriac, you protest? Rubbish! A hypochondriac is a person who imagines she is ill; but where is the dividing line between the real and the imaginary in illness? Notice, by the way, the role played by the idea of "brand new"; if my powder had not been "new," would I have succeeded in curing my patient?

When I was young, I would occasionally replace a colleague; I did *locums*. You can't imagine what a success I was, simply by virtue of coming from somewhere else: they looked at me and saw Paris, modern science, the latest inventions . . . who knows what they saw? Thus the community must always regard you as the man bringing them whatever is new in the world of medicine. Refer as often as you can to recent discoveries, take a medical journal out of your pocket, keep science reviews in your waiting room. And this feeling that "he knows what's new in the field" will help you inspire confidence. But whatever you do, don't imagine that when the members of a family are seeing you regularly, they will be more apt to do what you say if you become their close personal friend. A doctor, my dear Albert, has to preserve his sphinxlike character. If you show a tendency to explain the illness and the procedures you mean to use for curing it, you lose your air of mystery, your authority, the effect of surprise; in other words people stop thinking of you as the man who knows what's new and they lose confidence. In conclusion, Medicine is an art, not a science. Science is a set of formulas that anyone can apply. Medicine is a set of psychological techniques that are only as good as the person using them. These psychological techniques are what give medical science its therapeutic value.

You say in your letter that you haven't yet decided what sort of patients you will try to acquire or where you will set up practice: "You have practiced in a number of different social settings, Uncle, and in a number of different countries, so please advise me!" Well, take my word for it, the social stratum comprising the well-paid worker and lower middle class is still the best bet. The memories your question stirs up! . . . The hours, Albert! The hours you can spend on one patient, in the homes of the rich! Imagine an entrance hall! You wait for the man-servant! Then you wait for the lady of the house! The lady of the house appears and the lady of the house embarks on a series of endless anecdotes. The lady of the house has time to talk and it never occurs to her that you don't have time to listen. After half an hour you venture to ask if you may see the patient. Then you have to act utterly fascinated; you have to treat the child—let's say it's the child that's the patient—as a unique youngster whose case is exceptional. And bear in mind that the remedies to be prescribed are not the remedies that will do for just any class of society: for an exceptional case you have to have special drugs to start with, and then you have to talk about "watering resorts, nursing homes, sanatoria, fresh air treatments, moving the patient, a stay in the country." There are fashionable remedies which you have to know about and discuss the merits of. Now don't imagine you're all done and the house call is over; onto the scene comes the grandmother and back you go to the beginning: not only will you be repeating for the benefit of this lady everything you've already said, but the grandmother will be repeating everything the mother has already said, with occasional contradictions. On your way downstairs you'll meet the father just coming in; he has opinions of his very own and apparently feels that the utterances of the women are none too reliable. These are the sort of people who read the expensive magazines and this gentleman is very well informed. "I wonder, Doctor, whether you've thought of prescribing X or Y." And if you have not thought of X or Y, your only way out is to answer: "You're quite right, that would be very desirable, but the child's condition hasn't yet improved to the point where he can stand treatment with that drug." At last you're able to get away, and you reflect on your way out that while you were taking all those measures and precautions you could have been making four or five ordinary calls and earning a fee with each one. As it is, you will wait till the end of the year to be paid. In that connection I remember telling your family one day how an extremely fashionable lady, Baroness A——, handed me a sealed envelope after I'd made my call; at that time I was charging twenty francs for calls, and the envelope contained only ten. Mind you, in the days when housecalls were three francs, a Russian noblewoman once handed me a fee of twenty. In so doing, she was honoring herself rather than me. As a general rule the doctor should be more fashionable than his patient and represent a higher social class. Think for a moment how vexed you are if you come walking onto someone's good carpet when you're all spattered with mud like something the cat dragged in. How can you hope to inspire confidence? But now think for a moment of the respect you inspire in a simple workman if you're wearing a top hat. The doctor who is no better dressed than his patient has to make up for it by trying harder: he has to compensate by showing a more positive attitude and greater knowledge; it's simpler to let your clothes speak for you. Incidentally, once you have decided what sort of patients to have, abide by your choice; otherwise you'll be forever racking your brains to try and remember the differences in rates from one household to another and your memory might play tricks on you.

The nicest patient to deal with is one from the lower middle class. The rich make you bring in specialists, professors who will check up on you and put you in the wrong, and the rich will take their word over yours because the specialist is charging them 600 francs. There's none of that with the lower middle class or the working-class people. For the worker you're on a higher plane than an employer, you're a mysterious being; with him you can be relaxed, plain-spoken if need be, or even colloquial; no eloquent proofs or explanations will be required. You might, however, quite possibly fail to be understood and find yourself hampered by a serious difference in social caste. The person from the lower middle class, on the other hand, even if he allows himself to be dazzled as easily as the worker, will understand you more readily; he'll try to show an interest, which is flattering and creates a bond. Moreover in certain working-class homes you can't prescribe drugs that are too costly; with the lower middle-class family you can tell how far you should go.

Closely connected to the problem of how much to charge is the problem of how often to make calls. In this respect the small Paris shopkeeper is the ideal patient: you can go and see him whenever you like. With the rich and the poor you don't go unless you're called. In rural areas the patient either complains that you're exploiting him or complains that you're neglecting him.

I also want to talk to you about the patient's feelings toward his doctor in general and about gifts in particular. Thank Heaven, the custom of giving gifts is starting to disappear: the bronze ornament, the massive inkstand, the porcelain vase. When your Grandfather Adolphus died, we gave Doctor Ballu—you knew him—two Sèvres vases, very ugly things I must admit, but apparently quite valuable. Doctor Ballu, who, as you may remember, had always been extremely devoted, suddenly turned sullen and distant. Your mother discovered through Mrs. Aimée's housemaid that he'd been expecting to get the Empire clock which spent so many, many years in the window at Mr. Lecomte the clockmaker's. Poor Doctor Ballu! I met a colleague in Paris who used to put all the gifts he got from his patients into his parlor in the hope that some day someone would at least steal a piece of bronze. Nobody ever did, poor devil! Quite the reverse, in fact: seeing the parlor filled with what they took to be expressions of the doctor's taste, his patients would give him more of the same. I could write you fifty pages about the gratitude of patients: it is never in proportion to the service you have rendered. You can sweat blood to save a patient and nobody takes the least notice; after all, you were just doing your job! The man who showed me the greatest degree of gratitude was a farmer whose wife died at the market of a stroke without my having a chance to do anything to save her. Early in my medical career a very frightened mother called me to the bedside of a young man. Not as much was known about flu as is known today; I thought we had a very serious fever on our hands. A week later my patient was on his feet. The gratitude of that good lady has followed me about ever since. Gratitude is an awkward emotion and the gifts it brings you will all be quite absurd. Don't confuse "gratitude" with the vainglory of the caretaker's wife I was talking about earlier, the one in the apartment building. The caretaker's wife is very proud to have discovered a doctor capable of curing people; hers is the pride of the keeper showing off a trained elephant.

Don't flatter yourself that if a patient remains faithful to you he's doing it out of gratitude; he's doing it out of habit. On the subject of faithful patients, allow me to tell a rather amusing story: a friend of our family's, Doctor Duval, who has his practice on Voltaire Boulevard, was very surprised one day to be called out to Montrouge. At the end of the house call he asked his patient why he had sent for a doctor who lived so far away: "Oh," was the reply, "I looked in the phone book! I saw the name Duval, and that reminded me of a doctor I'd had who was very nice, so I thought maybe that name would bring me luck!" Certainly faithful patients are what make a practice. In Paris it's feast or famine, either you're starving or you have patients beating at the door. When you buy a practice in Paris, you're not buying anything, and your roster of patients is constantly changing. In the country your location in a district with no doctor forces people to come to you. Don't imagine you're going to get rich! You see private houses belonging to retired lawyers; you don't see any belonging to retired doctors. Nor will you be richer in Paris than anywhere else. Paris has its advantages: you don't have transportation costs; you can put aside your medical manner and walk around the streets anonymously. In provincial towns you'll always run across someone who will take you to task for going out with your fishing rod while the lawyer's wife lies dying or the postmistress is so sick, or someone who asks you for news of a patient whose existence has for the moment slipped your mind: "Do you think you can pull her through, Doctor? Will it be a long illness? Will she lose her hair?" It's the hair that finally brings to mind who this patient is that you'd been unable to place.

Anyhow, why go into it at such length? No one has ever benefited from someone else's experience. Follow your star, Albert, seize opportunities; if, as I believe, you are able, lucky and honest, you'll be successful; I hope you will be.

Regards to your father and my sister,

Gilbert

P.S. Watch out for dinner invitations. You'll find yourself being taken to very nice houses to dine. Generally when people invite the doctor over to dinner that's the only form of payment they intend him to get. Or don't accept the invitation unless it's a home where the family has been paying you regularly. Besides, these dinners out will be made hideous for you by each of the other guests wanting just a wee bit of medical advice.

"The Maid"

[*Using the time-honored techniques of dialectic, the author divides himself in two, to discuss the rights and wrongs of a contemporary murder case. Memories of his real-life mother, as well as fictional middle-class ladies and their servants encountered in his readings, blend with newspaper reports of the trial to produce a disturbing piece of social commentary.*

"The Maid" (La Bonne) is an unpublished manuscript, owned by M. Didier Gompel, to whom the editors of this anthology are most grateful.]

◆

"You aren't going to argue about the verdict, I don't suppose. But if I know you, you'd rather they'd been put in the Insane Asylum. There's a certain breed of criminal who deserves only cold showers and bromides."

"Obviously judges ought to make a bit more use of the Insane Asylum than they do. They're aware of this, but probably there are questions of economy that come into it. That's not what I wanted to talk to you about. The Papin sisters have ceased to interest me.[1] I'm thinking now of domestic servants and the women who are their employers."

"My dear fellow! The investigation showed that the Papin sisters did not kill for revenge. Their victims were the kindest of people,

---

1. This is a reference to a famous court case involving two maids who killed their mistress for no "apparent reason." The Papin sisters entered literature again when Jean Genet based his play *The Maids* on their crime. The most readily available account of the trial is in Janet Flanner's *Paris Was Yesterday* (Popular Library, 1972, pp. 98–104). Jacob incorrectly refers to two victims.

145

and no one, not even a female orangutan, could have taken it into her head to hate them."

"Granted! . . . Now let us suppose, if you will, that the opposite is true. We have here two domestic servants who have killed their masters. Let's suppose that they did it for revenge. Why not? It's quite plausible."

"Are you suggesting that today, well into the twentieth century, there are still employers so inhumane as to inspire that kind of hatred?"

"Twentieth-century ideas may have affected big industrial employers who, consciously or otherwise, have hitherto displayed a peremptory manner in dealing with their employees. But you don't suppose the same progress holds true for a kitchen in some provincial town, do you? Imagine two women of limited mental horizons, with nothing to amuse them: the maid and her mistress. They have no other thought than thinking about themselves. You know very well, my dear friend, that man is naturally inclined to abuse his authority. . . ."

"Yes; the sergeant-major, the foreman, the police constable."

"That's right. The maid becomes morbidly sensitive; her mistress's every utterance becomes a source of irritation, and the mistress, if she has the least touch of Mrs. Lepic in her, gives herself free rein.[2] Besides, doesn't it seem quite natural to her to count the silverware every evening without for a moment suspecting that to do so is an act of distrust?"

"Not at all! A simple matter of habit."

"That's where you're wrong. One of these servants brashly told her employer, a woman I happen to know: 'You take me for a thief, Ma'am. I'm no more a thief than you are, Ma'am. It's the same with the lumps of sugar that you count every evening, Ma'am. Everything in this house is locked up as if I were a thief. . . .'"

"It's certainly true that the common people have been developing greater self-awareness over the last hundred years or so. Com-

2. Mrs. Lepic in Jules Renard's *Poil de Carotte* is another example of the unloved wife turned monster, venting her frustration, in carefully selected cruelties, on her "subjects": her maids, her children, her domestic animals. After having reduced her whole household to stony silence, Mrs. Lepic pours her laments into the patient ear of her dog.

pany managers realize this, but ladies out in the provinces have no inkling of it."

"And I'll tell you something more. I know servants who are nothing but drudges. You won't believe it when I tell you this, but my friends, the X family, have a maid who doesn't get a single day out all year long, except All-Souls Day. Mrs. X boasts about it! 'She'll never be able to leave me. When would she ever find time to hunt for another position?' In Mrs. Gagelin's house, the maid does not have the right to sit down in the kitchen, and her daily schedule is regulated to the minute.[3] When her timing is one minute off, an item of food is deleted from her next meal as punishment. The poor wretch ended up running away, abandoning her trunk and her wages, and making her escape down a ladder that some workmen had left behind."[4]

"Nothing like that happens in Paris any more!"

"I'm not so sure. Paris is to a large extent nothing but a big provincial town. A very elegant lady of fashion was saying to me recently: 'I always speak to my domestic servants with a pleasant smile. *My* system is to appear suddenly in the kitchen when I'm least expected, and woe betide those I catch doing something wrong!'"

"I don't really see what's so cruel about the system you describe."

"A hypocritical regime of that sort does not exactly make for good relations. The same lady also said this: 'A good housewife must go on the prudent assumption that every new servant is thievish, deceitful, and treacherous. A domestic servant is a Trojan horse that we have allowed inside the fortress gates . . .'"

"And yet that's not the picture you get of French society when you read our great Realist writers. Remember Marcel Proust and

3. Jacob immortalized his own mother as Mme Gagelin, a character whom we meet in many of his writings. The name Gagelin hints at Mme Jacob's habit of lending money and asking a *gage* as collateral. See also "We Are Each Alone," note 1. Max the prodigal son returned every summer to Quimper, hoping in vain for a word of praise from his family. When he displayed his latest work, his mother and the rest would maintain a heavy silence or start to discuss missing lumps of sugar.

4. How has the maid ended up running away, when the speaker has just been describing her woes as existing now? Presumably Jacob would have caught the discrepancy had he reworked this piece for publication. As it stands, it affords a glimpse of the transition from fact to fiction: the plight of Mrs. Gagelin's servant is real; her running away, perhaps a suitable invention.

his Françoise, the good, decent countrywoman who was so devoted to the family." [5]

"There was a Françoise in my family: she was what you might call a beast of burden, routinely subjected to every sort of humiliation. She grumbled in private, but how could she have walked out? She was very old and had no savings. Her employers were not unaware of this."

"My dear fellow, there are unions of private domestics . . ."

"Who knows they exist? Only the smartest Paris servants—"

"My dear boy, there's some truth in what you say, but you're considerably overstating the case. . . . Anyhow, if you were to go around saying these things, you'd be very apt to find yourself at odds with all the people who patronize music halls or read comic papers and are accustomed to the pert maidservants portrayed in the theater, the kind that force the family to give them a contract—"

"People think that's so funny only because it's very unusual. The female domestic is by definition an animal with no right to any human feelings. She can't have a daughter boarded out with a wet-nurse, and a desire to visit the child; nor may she have a boyfriend to kiss, or a day when she doesn't feel well, or a need to go out and have some fun now and then: 'A movie! She wants to go to a movie!' I've actually heard someone say that! Mrs. Gagelin says, in her maid's presence: 'Will you look at her! She dresses up like a princess, and here I've been wearing the same dress for the last year . . .'"

"That's no excuse for handing over all the middle-class housewives to all the Papin sisters to be killed off."

"Such is not my intention."

"Live and let live is what I always say."

5. Françoise, the family maid in Marcel Proust's *Remembrance of Things Past*, has considerable responsibility in running the household. She has a lifetime commitment to the family and they are bound through ties of mutual affection.

From *The Bouchaballe Property*

[*Max Jacob lovingly polished and repolished his favorite novel,* Le Terrain Bouchaballe, *for twenty years and upon submitting it to the publisher said he felt the pangs of a mother, deprived of a baby she has fed at her own breast.* Matorel in the Provinces, *published in 1921, contains material Jacob omitted from* The Bouchaballe Property *but even so, the novel itself, published in 1923, fills two hefty volumes.*

The setting is Guichen, Jacob's thinly disguised native Quimper, which the author declared was part of his very being. The plot, based on an actual event, serves as an excuse to study "bourgeoisism" in the portraiture of about a hundred "Shakespearian" characters who play out little games of universal hypocrisy. "I don't create types," claimed Jacob, "I impart life in a certain way." The characters, in whom, to its dismay, the local bourgeoisie recognized itself, gradually reveal their stupidity, ambition, meanness, greed, and sexual obsessions, through dialogue in the framework of an episodic plot revolving around a piece of land that Mr. Bouchaballe had left to the city many years before. Three factions advance their self-interest under the separate banners of culture, social progress, and municipal prosperity. The mayor, Thomas Lecourbe, wants to build a theater on the property— to favor his actress mistress, the opposition claims. The clerical faction, in a Machiavellian scheme, promotes an old people's home. Mr. Simonnot, a freelance geologist, on the other hand, wants to develop a coal mine on the site. This situation, with its inherent clash of interests, enables Jacob to illuminate, with the fireworks of his wit, the intrigues and manipulations of a provincial town at the turn of the century.

In the first excerpt, from the opening chapter, the author shows us Guichen (pronounced to rhyme with le guide Michelin) *on a Sunday. Along with the portrayal of the movement and atmosphere of the city itself, there are glimpses of all the main characters who will come into play in*

*his story, as in an orchestral prelude in which all the themes later to be
developed are presented in miniature.*

The titles of the last two excerpts were supplied by the editors.]

◆

Sunday in Guichen

Sunday! Whether Dame Week has earned it or not, she shall have
her Sunday! Her day in the Sun! Son-day! The day that belongs to
His Son! It's Sunday! The Guichentois leap from their beds, moved
by the same impulse as a passenger getting off at his destination
after sleeping all night in his railway coach: they feel an itch to
give themselves a thorough wash. In those heedless times, misfortune, or rather coal, was only at our doors, or rather at our city
toll-house. Everyone thought Simonnot the geologist, with his talk
of anthracite under the Bouchaballe orchard, was crazy; in those
days the Bouchaballe property yielded nothing but conversations
and lawsuits.

"Enough talk, my dear fellow! People might notice," said the
mayor to Plon the cabinet maker, who was his helper at election
time. Plon was standing in front of a small café (where men talked
politics) waiting for his wife and daughters to emerge from Mass.

"Is that understood, then? You're to write a petition asking that
at the very least a start be made on the bridge if not on the theater,
and you get them all to sign it."

"Not having gone to secondary school, Your Worship, I wouldn't
be able to draft the thing myself, but since I'll be spending my Sunday at Le Lesnard with Arsène Carent the butcher, I'll give it to
him to write up."

"I have every confidence in Carent; he's fully conversant with
the matter and he's a good alderman. Moreover your friend young
Daniel the clerk will probably be there: ask him to give you a hand.
I don't insist on your shouting it from the housetops that the idea
for the petition came from City Hall."

"Very well, Your Worship."

"You must admit it's strange, to say the least! A good thirty years
since the property was bequeathed to the city and so far nothing's

150

been done. We've won all the lawsuits and the Bouchaballe heirs know they have no complaint coming if we start exercising our rights to the use of this legacy, since approval by the Council of State is a mere formality. It's time something was done! I want a nice little building by the river's edge and a nice little bridge."

"Very well, Your Worship."

"Larche has a theater, and I'm determined to have a theater too. Drama is a delightful thing, I can tell you! By George, my dear Plon, I missed my calling: I should have been an actor!"

"When I was a pupil at the parochial school in Hautecôte, we used to put on plays there on Sundays, and for a while I intended to be. . . . just like you said, Your Worship."

"Fine! Fine! It's men like you that further the ideals of the Republic! If you don't have a carriage to go to Le Lesnard with your children, rent one from Cotté-Grelu's and tell them to charge it to me."

"I'll go to Le Lesnard in Arsène Carent's wagonette: it has a spare seat since he lost his little boy. My wife and daughters have just as good a time dancing on the lawn at The Pines in Le Fret as they would at the Lesnard Hotel."

Sunday! Sun-day! Sunday! His Son's day! It's Sunday! How unpleasant it is, even for the children, to be late for Mass! Entering the holy place in company with the rest of your family makes you blush, and the harder you try not to be shy the more embarrassed you become, for this blushing in the presence of others and in the presence of God results, we may be sure, from a Christian humility that is all the greater for our awareness of it. I shall not relate all the Devil's work being carried on at the very moment of the Elevation! I will grant that Mrs. Simonnot should have sat and prayed for the black charms of coal and Mrs. Lecourbe for the white arms of adultery to give them back their old husbands, while Miss Gaufre fervently requested that the angels intervene to offer her a brand-new one, but what about Mr. Hélary! Mr. Hélary who was studying law! He was simply counting on his wallet to supply enough pastries so that he could wait at Godivier's for Mrs. de Reversy and her young ladies. And Lucy Cadénat: right there in our cathedral she received and sent three love-letters in the course of a single Mass! Oh Heavenly Father, those weary, jaded prayers! Would you not have preferred the mystic utterances of the maidens there? Alas!

Those who suffer not, believe not. God has to beat us with a stick before we recognize His presence. The people of Guichen were late for Mass! If God gave us so little faith that when it's time for Mass we start thinking of our morning coffee, does that mean He had as much contempt for the Guichentois as they had for one another?

"If you don't get a move on," said a mother, twirling a new hat on her clenched fist, "we're going to be late."

The father was looking for his shaving brush, which young Amelia, with the help of a ribbon, had changed into a make-believe hand-bell. Octave couldn't find his red tie, and Jules, the lazybones, was on the verge of tears: he was wishing someone would help him divide 39,477 by 53.

"You can see we've all got things on our minds, Amelia, and you have to choose this moment to go getting your father upset!"

"Children, don't slide down the bannister. Amelia, not with your new dress! How many times have I told you you're not to do that? She's worse than a boy! If you would just look after your little sister. . . . Now look at her, acting the young lady!"

Till noon on Sundays, before Guichen was crushed by all that coal, people carrying packages prettily tied up with string used to say hello to each other on the sidewalk along Little River Street. The carriages of the nobility would wait beneath the chestnut trees and the nobles, attended by their lawyers and a few military officers, would exchange greetings. In general we preferred the old aristocrats to the young ones, and the ladies to the gentlemen. Old Mr. de Villequez was a cheerful conversationalist and one didn't dare to remind him about "that trifling unpaid account," but we did not like those sons of his. One of them had the bored look worn by fine gentlemen who have lost 500 francs playing baccarat, and the other seemed to be carrying the weight of the universe between his pretty moustache and his pretty hat. Why were we so fond of poor, stupid, ugly, grubby old Mr. de Ley? The "de" in his name was of uncertain authenticity; only his self-assurance and the stamp of nobility impressed us. What wouldn't we have given to possess his smile? The widely known hobbies of Mr. de la Tremblaie, Corresponding Member of the Institute, as well as the gout suffered by his overweight brother, were also to our liking, but the style of his daughter, who went about in an English dog-cart which she drove herself, did not suit the town at all.

After Mass, knots of people would assemble outside Godivier's pastry shop. A young officer might doff his cap in greeting to his betrothed:

"Why, how do you do, Mister Henry; do please put your hat back on, I thank you!"

"Good day to you, Lieutenant; pray don't keep your hat off on my account."

A Paris fashion designer and member of the Legion of Honor had, for weightier reasons that you can imagine, launched a new series of purple fabrics: zinzolin, and its matching materials zinzoleen, zinzolinet, and silk zinzolinet.[1] Mrs. Astic and Mrs. Lancret, who twice a year went to Paris to seek out the newest creations from the world of fashion, had brought these wonders back with them from the capital.

"It's a bit funereal," people said around their dining-room tables.

"To my mind it's unusual rather than pretty."

"It's just imperial purple, that's all."

"Yes, the same, but brighter."

"You may be sure that Mrs. Bidard will start using it. Remember when *petits-marquis* came out?[2] She fell upon them like a starving man upon a crust of bread!"

"My dear, Mrs. Bidard is not someone you would wish to take as your model."

"She's a woman of taste."

"Indeed she is! But you know what people say about her."

Mrs. Bidard looked like an armchair. She had married an attorney. She was a person for whom the people of Guichen had no respect: her manner was too bold, and had she been the first to wear zinzolin, that would have been reason enough for all the gentlemen to forbid their wives the use of it. Fortunately, it was not Mrs. Bidard who set the example. This came instead from a housewife and reliable shopkeeper, no less a person than Mrs. Lancret, and also from Mrs. Astic, a true lady of fashion and a decent woman besides.

"Show the dirt? Oh no, Ma'am, no more than black does!" Mrs.

1. The French word *zinzolin* means reddish violet. Taffeta, for instance, came in that color. Jacob's contribution is to imagine a fabric so named.

2. *Petits-marquis* were fashionable hats whose brims turned up to give a three-cornered hat effect.

Lancret would say, standing at her counter and taking her garment between two fingers at the knee. "Look at this skirt, for instance; I have it on from the time I get up till the time I go to bed."

Zinzolin can be worn everywhere and with anything! It's easy to work with, it's thick but light, never loses its luster, and doesn't fade in the sun. It suits brunettes as well as those who aspire to be fair-haired; it looks delightful on children and is the perfect material for middle-aged or older persons.

Shall I be completely frank with you? The ladies of Guichen weren't as staid as they appeared: the thing about zinzolin that caught their fancy was its name. No one had ever heard such a lovely word used as the name of a fabric! Zinzolin! Those three syllables, ladies, set your minds to dreaming about the perfumes that you sprinkled on your hair of a Sunday morning, about that liqueur you'd asked a traveling representative to get you twelve bottles of and which the children drank on the sly; about the notes that imitate chimes in certain piano compositions which you'd often enjoyed listening to or had yourselves played with such untroubled minds. It's a word that conjures up flowers, or exotic parrots in *Travel Magazine,* or the stylishness of *Femina* and *For the Record.* The same effect you get from almond candies with liqueur centers. Oh, Zinzolin, my Zinzolin, soon to delight an entire city and be the favorite color of the ladies of Guichen!

Today, Sunday, all the carriages were out at Le Lesnard. The only people in town were the shopkeepers who couldn't close up for the day and stood about in bare-headed converse, and the elderly women with their capes like priestly vestments.

In the afternoon there were ladies paying visits in the half-closed shops, and someone was playing a phonograph. Girls were gathered around a baby.

"Oh, Mummy, let me hold him! Oh, isn't he cute! Oh, what a cuddly bunny! Isn't he a pet, a petty-wetty! Ootchy-cootchy! What does-um say? What does-um say to um's little sugar-candy lady? D . . . dog! Look at the bow-wow! Oh, get away! Get away, you filthy dog! Filthy animal! Whose dog is that, anyway, Mrs. Astic?"

"Adrienne, my dear, do leave that child alone; you'll get him dizzy."

"You don't learn to cook by watching someone! I've seen it being made, indeed! What's the good of that? So have *I* seen other people making macaroni with tomatoes. That doesn't get me anywhere!

You have to do it yourself if you want to learn how."

"Aren't you giving him lessons?"

"He's taking piano, but what he wants to learn is the mandolin and his father doesn't want to buy a mandolin."

"But what if he has a natural gift for it?"

"Why would Father Domnère want to be concerned with Green Street?"[3]

Groups of farm women go by, and housemaids with umbrellas, and people from the working-class districts, with big shawls and white head-dresses. The sidewalk cafés are both deserted: everyone is out in the country; they've driven out to Le Lesnard.

In a big kitchen garden three ladies sit under an arbor, working for the poor. The good ladies are skinny and dressed in black. The good ladies are knitting with little iron hooks. The garden is in sunlight; the air is cool under the arbor; nearby the river is flowing; a metal ball hangs from the roof; and the clematis blossoms are like stars.

"I have a notion to embroider myself a zinzolin table-runner."

"A table-runner made of zinzolin! I must say, Angela, you certainly don't deny yourself luxuries!"

"Oh, it's no more expensive than any other fabric!"

"Zinzolin is such a nice shade!"

"Yes! You could line it with dapple-gray silk and then stitch all round the edges."

"Yes, and then in the middle you could embroider primroses! People do, you know."

"Primroses? You don't think that's a bit . . . vulgar? Wouldn't you rather do something in matching tones? Zinzolin on zinzolin?"

"Zinzolin on zinzolin! Or perhaps zinzoleen on zinzolin."

"You could edge it in white."

"Why not line it with silk zinzolinet and edge it with zinzoleen?"

"Goodness, how you do get carried away! Silk zinzolinet! No wonder they say that givers of advice don't pay the price."

. . . .

The universe with its wondrous harmonies. The presence of beauty causes thought to mature as sunlight does with fruit. Mr. Pancrasse, former sexton, simple building contractor, going by

3. Although Green Street, in this novel, is a red-light district, Father Domnère's interest is purely a matter of social welfare—he wants to build an old people's home there.

with his pipe between his teeth, was perhaps meditating on the Origin of Species and was stopped by Miss Lucy Cadénat:

"You're an architect, Mr. Pancrasse, so you can tell me: what's the difference between Romanesque and Gothic?"

"It's odd, isn't it, that a young lady like you should be thinking about such matters? Oh, ho, ho! Mr. Amédée will tell you what you want to know: he's studying fine arts . . . or something to do with fine arts! He's here on holiday, staying with his uncle Mr. Lecourbe."

Thus did Science reach out a hand to the Arts beneath thy chestnut-trees, O Guichen of my heart! Walking along the scorching-hot Customs House Embankment, where three ships were moored in a line, two ladies out for a stroll were discussing the serialized novel that each of them took to bed with her at night:

"If I had a husband like that . . . that . . . what's his name again? . . . I'd blow his brains out."

"He really is a special case, my dear, a real case!"

Across the river, two gentlemen were using the tips of their canes to prove the existence of God, at the foot of Salvat Hill, the hill that offers you a view of two churches, the seminary, the barracks, and the old folks home.

Meanwhile, the River Jet, accompanied by a towpath, wended its broadening way across the countryside and down to the Ocean. At the bend where, like a signal station, the Post Office encompasses in its gaze the villas on the Customs House Embankment and the shops on well-shaded Little River Street, a lieutenant was speaking to Mrs. de Snouff:

"*Infandum,*" he was saying, "*regina, jubes renovare dolorem!*[4] You have broken my heart, fairest Julia, and, so that you might revel in the sight of my blood, you would e'en have me display those very wounds yourself didst wantonly inflict!"

This is the place where the Jet receives the River Tille, which comes tumbling out of a granite archway as children come cascading out of school, its waves carrying along in their noisy train the sounds of the washerwomen and the ivy of the ancient walls. But I am forgetting this was Sunday; waves, ivy, and washerwomen were at rest! Two horses struck the pavement with the tips of their iron-

4. "You take delight, O Queen, in rekindling pain most horrible." Aeneas, when Queen Dido asks him to recount the sack of Troy, exclaims that he will find it painful to revive these bitter memories.

shod hooves; the setting sun gleamed on equine hindquarters and riders' boots, whilst the hair of the fair equestrienne, tied in a neat bun, moved among the chestnut-trees of the Embankment. "Do you have a taste for Spencer, Miss Emma?" "Have I not told you, my dear friend, how very much a Platonist I am?"

. . . .

And now the last act was about to be played out. A thing of the past now was your day in the country, good people of Guichen, and the carriages bringing you back to town while the shopkeepers dined behind closed shutters; deserted now were the sidewalk cafés where at seven o'clock the sunlight's warmth yet lingered. The table outside the Prosper Hotel was reduced to a last triangle of gaslight beneath the chestnut-trees. On all sides were the lights of Guichen's many inns and opposite the cathedral the glow of the big glass jar in a druggist's window. The blessed day was at its close; Sunday was no more. Sunday! Sun-day! It was no longer Sunday! Ah, yes—on the darkened parade square there was still a ring of torches and, surprisingly, the strains of military music. There was but one silence, the same for all the skies of prussian blue, and indeed for the plains as well. The dark is so uniquely uniform, so unifying in its uniformity! Every evening of the week the darkness bathes our cathedral, standing there too beautiful for words, as it has stood since the days when the night watchman heaved the shadows upward with his lantern; there it stands, looking out over the peaceful Welsbach lamps.[5] From afar its somber carvings make the dark night darker still, and at its amber feet the housetops are gathered in a heap. A time of day that had its special charm for those around the bandstand: the time for expressing Finer Feelings!

"Come, now, don't be petty. What's happened to your usual calm detachment?"

"If you want my opinion, Lucien Jollie, we should stop associating with that swaggering army type."

"And pray why should we, Philip Exaudy, if I happen to enjoy his company?"

"I don't like whys, nor do I like becauses: military men are not my cup of tea, that's all."

5. Carl Auer, Baron von Welsbach (1858–1929), invented the incandescent lamps which the French called *becs Auer* and the English and Americans Welsbach lamps.

"A man in uniform is a friend like any other, and this particular one keeps me amused with his amorous adventures."

"He'll have the eyes of the whole town on us."

"If anyone from the whole town—or any of my friends—wants to take offense, let them! Maxime Latour is a well-bred fellow, and that's good enough for me!"

"Then choose him as your constant companion, for *my* companionship you must henceforth do without. That blackguard can talk of nothing but womanizing."

"I'm beginning to think you're jealous because he has the kind of adventures you and I go looking for and have never managed to find."

After each musical number the throng of listeners rose like a cloud, broke up, disappeared, and reassembled its ranks. A rustling sound moved across this corner of the universal night in the silence of the unifying darkness.

"In the word *zinzolin*," said the seventh-grade schoolteacher, who dared to speak up when the river was being noisy, "we find the root *zol*, the prefix *sen* and the suffix *lin; sen, zol, lin*, a fabric woven with the sun, *sen*, with! A lovely word."

"But everyone keeps telling you that it's a color," said his wife.

"No, Mary, it's a fabric."

"To look at the word you would think it was of Circassian origin," said Mr. Goin the learned agriculturalist.[6]

"Isn't it the name of an animal, rather?" said Benazet the prefect's secretary. "Isn't the zinzolin a little animal in Siberia that lives on the shores of lakes?"

"You're confusing it with the sable, my dear Benazet; the sable, whose fur, as you know, is called zibeline."

PETITION

To the Mayor and Aldermen of Guichen
Your Worship and Members of City Council:
We the undersigned, reputable merchants and businessmen, respect-
fully present to you the following petition:

6. It is in fact of Arabic origin, from an Arab word for sesame, the source of *zinzolin* colorant. Dictionaries have it coming into French variously via Spanish or via Italian. Jacob delighted in odd words and their origins, and considered browsing in dictionaries essential for writers. He delighted equally in the half-baked learned discussions of provincial "scholars."

Whereas one Andrew Bouchaballe, esq., dealer in corks, born in Guichen in 1843, did, in the public interest, on the 20th day of July, 18–, bequeath to the Municipality of Guichen a plot of land known as the Bouchaballe Orchard, located between Green Street and the River and bearing numbers 21 and 22 in the registers of the Guichen Land Titles Office, as well as a capital of one hundred and fifty thousand francs invested in Government Bonds;

and whereas City Council did, on the 4th day of November, 18–, the Civil Court of Guichen having found in favor of the Mayor of Guichen, Mr. Lecourbe, and against the Bouchaballe heirs, and with the aforesaid Mayor acting as executor for the will of Andrew Bouchaballe, decide that the bequest would be accepted along with any obligations and encumbrances pertaining thereto, but, whereas this judgment was overturned by the Court of Appeal, the Mayor not having the right to act as a private citizen on behalf of a municipality;

and whereas the Court of Appeal declared the plot of land to be the property of the Municipality, the Mayor being executor in accordance with the will and testament of Mr. Bouchaballe;

and whereas on the 21st day of May, 18–, City Council did, at a special meeting, having heard the report of Mr. Pancrasse, building contractor—

Here Arsène Carent broke off to have a laugh as he considered the page that he was recopying.

"Ha! Pancrasse, you son-of-a-gun! You aren't going to like this, because you aren't referred to here as being an architect. We deliberately decided not to, this afternoon at Le Lesnard. Anyway, what business has he to be so proud?"

—as to the characteristics, resistance to erosion, and permeability of the aforesaid land, and having also heard the testimony of Mr. Orange, banking consultant to the Civil Court of Guichen, decide that a hall enabling a theatrical company to exist in the Municipality of Guichen and to be used for the performances of such a company at times and in circumstances to be determined at a future date;

therefore we, the aforementioned merchants and businessmen of Guichen, do respectfully present to Mr. Thomas Lecourbe, Mayor of Guichen and to the Members of City Council, this petition that work now be begun on construction of the bridge which is to connect the

Bouchaballe property to the city to accommodate carriages and other traffic.

We assure you, Mr. Mayor, of our firm adherence to the principles of the French Republic as well as the Aldermen, and in the hope that due account will be taken of our grievances we here convey to you our respectful greetings as well as the Aldermen.

A group of eligible voters.

◆

Pancrasse

Mister Pancrasse is not what you would call a sober-minded citizen.[1] When those poor dear aldermen in all those poor dear provinces of ours were ordered by a tyrannical government ministry to enlarge the living-quarters of the gendarmerie, our national police, and to install washrooms with bathtubs, all this at the expense of the municipalities, Mr. Pancrasse laughed. Now I ask you, was this a laughing matter? Why does the very word *gendarme* make people laugh, even so-called sober-minded people? A philosopher once said that we laugh only at unexpected contrasts. Mr. Gabriel de Lautrec was the discoverer of this remarkable law of psychology; not Mr. Ribot or Mr. Bergson or Mr. Louis Dugas; no, it was Mr. Gabriel de Lautrec. Hold on, I could be mistaken after all: it may have been Aristotle. The candid speech of our gendarmes is charmingly amusing as it issues from behind their leather straps, like the speech of a church verger girded up in his shoulder-harness. Pancrasse, who in his time has been a verger or at any rate a beadle, William-Henry-Athanasius-Victor Pancrasse, carrying the ceremonial mace and rod and wearing the cocked hat, once made others laugh the way he laughs today. We do not laugh at a liveried servant, because we assume he is shrewder than his master; we do laugh at a great stout royal coachman because we assume he is a fool 'neath all his proud

---

1. Just as the name Pangloss, in Voltaire's *Candide*, implies a man who comments on everything, so the name Pancrasse implies total crassness. Jacob confided to a friend that it was Guillaume Apollinaire or rather his looks, especially his pear-shaped head as represented in Picasso's famous drawing of him, and his amorous nature, that served as the inspiration for Henry Pancrasse.

array; we would laugh at his master could we but feel that he was as much of a fool as his coachman. When you were at university, studiously earning diplomas intended to deceive society as to your worth, I'm sure you laughed at those ushers who bear upon their breast the weight of Gallic academic dignity and who are called apparitors or bearers of the mace: rightly or not, you supposed them to be as foolish as their demeanor was grave.[2] Pancrasse is not foolish but he does look like a university apparitor. He also reminds you of the head waiter you saw once when you were celebrating by dining out in style (curious how we associate celebrating with dining in style): just as he was adjuring you, with all the majesty of the Great Kitchens of France, to make your choice from a list of wines, the sight of his shaven countenance caught you off guard. Pancrasse never walks into the washrooms that he built at the police barracks without humming a little ditty about the boots of the constabulary. It was not within your walls and as your beadle, revered Cathedral of Saint-Mathurin, that he learned the little ditty, but neither did you expunge it from his memory: human nature cannot be changed. It is permissible for a sober citizen to laugh when gendarmes are so much as mentioned or when walking into their washrooms complete with bathtubs, but he must not laugh if he was the one who built the washrooms on credit payments, for then he jeopardizes his status as sober citizen. Yes, yes, I know what you're going to say: the gendarmes have bathrooms whereas the Police Commissioner does not, and such a situation is comical. But you wouldn't say it to someone like me, with my democratic sympathies! You would also like to say: isn't it comical that the Minister of War is so insistent on a few gendarmes practicing cleanliness but does not seize every opportunity to inculcate such habits in the soldiers who are the nation's armed might?[3] Such a notion would have shaken Father Domnère to the core because Canon Domnère is a sober-minded man. He would have taken the attitude that since gendarmes are more fortunate than soldiers they must also be cleaner. But the source of Pancrasse's laughter is more immediate:

2. Jacob rarely missed an opportunity to ridicule academic degrees, convinced that the combination of three things smothers all spark of originality in his countrymen: the baccalaureate, military service, and the daily newspaper.

3. "It has been pointed out to me that the new army barracks in Toulouse are a model of Dutch cleanliness. The incident on which this book is based took

he made some thousands of francs building additions onto police barracks across the county; that's the action of a sober-minded citizen, but—this is the zany part—he spent the lot on fancy draperies and Gothic paneling for his house on River Street. It made Miss Gaufre weep: he owes her 10,000 francs.

As a pupil at the Teaching Brothers' school in Larche, he enjoyed successes in the plays that pupils stage to brighten up school festivals, and dreamed of becoming an actor. Born to an unwed female cook, he hesitated between the plough being offered him by Social Welfare and the priestly frock of his cousin Domnère; he became a bailiff's clerk and married one Miss Carent, whose father was a contractor for marble gravestones. In time Pancrasse became a beadle. In Paris when a priest collects the offerings he is accompanied by a verger in ceremonial dress; at Mass in Guichen, the beadle, robed in a red surplice, goes from chair to chair alone; the coins drop into a pewter plate; on Sundays they drop thick and fast; that day there are coins of different colors. O Pewter Plate, you led the beadle to commit a major sin which he durst not reveal even in the confessional, the bashful fellow! One Sunday, in short, he took a small coin and put it in his pocket. The following Sunday the pocket required two coins— Pancrasse stole three and thereafter stole regularly every Sunday! Pancrasse was robbing the Church, which at least can afford to be robbed! Pancrasse was likewise robbing the poor, who always get robbed more than the rich. One evening Mrs. Pancrasse picked up his trousers and a row of small coins came sliding out of the pocket. Pancrasse was in bed; he hid his face.

"Henry, are you asleep?"

Henry was not asleep. He is a man quickly moved to tears. Henry was crying.

The next Sunday Pancrasse threw at her feet enough copper coins to make a clock, if not to buy one ready-made. The truth was now plain to his wife:

place at the end of the last century. At that time the police barracks in Guichen were the opposite of the new army barracks in Toulouse. I grant you that the ministerial decree, concerning the washrooms of the gendarmerie, dates from 1912; I ask your indulgence for this little anachronism; after all, I am not a historian" (note by Max Jacob). Editor's note: The Gendarmerie nationale, though a police force, is under the Ministry of Defense.

"Pancrasse, what you're doing is wrong."

And every Sunday thereafter, Pancrasse would throw his plunder on the floor and go down on his knees beside it, praying Heaven to forgive him.

One Sunday Pancrasse said to his wife:

"Listen here a minute, Melanie! You know that darn fool Mrs. de la Chafrie put a hundred francs in the collection-plate to bring her husband back to the straight and narrow."

"A hundred francs, Pancrasse! . . . Well, but, Pancrasse—"

"Melanie, I want to stop being a beadle! I was tempted. It wouldn't be proper to take a hundred francs. It isn't right."

"You're a sinner, Pancrasse: you've got to go to confession and tell what you've done."

"To the good Lord I will, Melanie, but not to the little birdie! It's asking for trouble."

Melanie harangued him the whole night through. Next day, a wan and haggard Pancrasse sought out his cousin Canon Domnère.

"Cousin, I want to stop being a beadle."

"I'm sure you must have good and sufficient cause for such an irrational request. Explain the reasons for your decision if you want my consent, Henry Pancrasse."

"I want to go into the construction business."

"Surely the profession of building contractor is no more incompatible with the honorable duties of a beadle than your present profession as a wholesale wine merchant?"

"Please, Cousin, don't press the matter; I'm not a proper person to be a beadle; I can't in all decency be a beadle any more."

"The tragic pallor of your face betrays more emotion than your words express! And though in general you have your emotions under firm control, today you are unable to dissemble. I willingly receive the secrets that people bring me; others I occasionally guess, but none do I extort. Another beadle shall be found for the cathedral. Away you go, then!"

"You are not my confessor, Cousin."[4]

As a wine merchant, Pancrasse supplied liquid goods and accessories to suburban innkeepers: he became their sole creditor, and

4. To a confessor Pancrasse would have had to reveal his thefts from the collection plate, but to a cousin he need not.

when he had brought them to bankruptcy, he would buy them out and sell the same merchandise a second time to whoever took their place. He wanted to become a building contractor so he could build the inns himself and rent them to his customers. Were his business plans mingled with remorse for his behavior as a beadle? That I cannot say. Pancrasse as contractor and wine merchant would rapidly have made a fortune had not his cousin the priest threatened to hand him over to the public prosecutor.[5] Pancrasse took fright, had a falling-out with the Church and gave up the wine trade. This was a man at once uneasy and insolent, humble and overbearing, silent and noisy, cruel and easy-going, enjoying the pleasures of the bed, if not actually lecherous, and consumed by remorse. After he became a widower he slept with his housemaids, but then he would dismiss the young ones (out of repentance) and hire old ones in their place, only to dismiss the old ones and hire young ones again (out of need). And the years went by.

◆

The Amorous Adventures of Pancrasse

Since the day Mrs. Edmet told him that he had good taste, Pancrasse had bought a green vest with onyx buttons and begun putting scent on his handkerchief. For two weeks he wore a monocle with a flat lens, and at the same time avoided pronouncing his r's.[1] Then he didn't have the nerve not to pronounce his r's in the presence of certain people. When he was putting himself out to charm someone with this way of speaking, if a client or some other person of consequence came upon the scene he was placed in an awkward position, afraid of losing the good opinion of someone who mattered. What was he to do? Think of words with no r? Stop talking? Talk very fast? He finally decided to pronounce the r in some words and not in others. One day a citizen of Guichen laughed at him, and later Pancrasse was sorry he had not slapped the man's face, for he was sensitive to slights, but it is easier to be sorry later than to

5. Presumably not for Pancrasse's peccadilloes as a beadle but for his dishonesty as a wine merchant.

1. This was an affectation of the "jeunesse dorée" at the turn of the century.

be brave at the time. The thought of administering a slap and then possibly having to fight a duel led him to give up his exquisite pronunciation and his monocle. Held in contempt by the habitués of the Prosper Café, who thought he was crazy, he took to hobnobbing with the budding flower of the educated middle class. Negligently flexing a slender yellow cane against the sidewalk, the one-time beadle expounded his opinions on novels and their authors and styles, for the benefit of his new friends: Méry the dentist's apprentice, Lieutenant Maxime Latour and the law students who registered in Larche for their courses: Le Berre, Fortin, and Hélary the lady-killer. Upon discovering that these elegant scoffers were planning to stage a Guichentois Revue using the traveling theater that was home to the Carlton family, Pancrasse the architect offered to compose a couple of verses poking fun at the reinforced cement bridge he had built.

Oh, Lucy, Lucy Cadénat! Into what haunts am I, as your historiographer, obliged to follow you? Is it true that you and the Contortionist from the fair were having supper together in the Carltons' traveling-van at one o'clock in the morning? Complete with chaperon! And dignified father! And family of traveling actors! Mr. Carlton, a fair-haired man with a squint, wished to acquire the sort of knowledge city folk have. His wife, a frugal and distinguished lady, hoped to spend her old age fishing on a riverbank in Touraine. Their daughters were lazy; their sons liked to talk about Mr. de Max and Mr. Frédérick Lemaître.[2] Also present were four gentlemen of Guichen, Messrs. Fortin, Hélary, Le Berre, and Pancrasse. Mr. Carlton, in a spirit of friendliness, took some admission tickets out of a flower vase and handed them around; he would have been happy to invite them all to supper but there wasn't enough room; he would have offered them all a glass of beer at the Prosper Café but the café was closed. All these people were too tall for the inside of the van, and the oil lamps didn't give much light. The group had to consider breaking up.

"The great Plato," said Miss Cadénat, thrusting her bosom under the eyes of the ex-beadle and undismayed by the Contortionist's meaningful gaze, "would have no poets in his Republic, but he did admit architects. I think your bridge is rather nice!"

2. Edouard de Max (1869–1925) and Frédérick Lemaître (1800–1876) were famous actors.

These words, which Pancrasse took as a sign that he would soon be a happy man, were instead the signal for his discomfiture. Paolo Opi the Contortionist, whom Lucy was thus defying, and who knew women or at any rate his woman which is more to the point, went and roused his friend Jupiter, King of the Wrestlers, and Jupiter's employees.

"Okay you guys, let's go! I've got a little job I want attended to right now. There's this high-society jerk I want you to take and heave in the river!"

"Listen, Contusionist, I don't want no run-ins with the cops, see! You wanna get me in bad down at the Station, for godsake?"

"What the Hell's the matter with him, wakin' everybody up like a false-alarm clock?" inquired an athlete from where he lay in bed.

"Some high-society guy who's been getting Snake-Man's girl-friend all hot in the twat," answered Jupiter in his nightshirt. "Okay, Boa Constrictor, you can give my little army a franc apiece and consider it done! We'll give him the blanket treatment for you, a complete cleaning job from head to foot, reserved for our best customers."

"I hope it kills the bastard."

"You Wops are real sweeties, aincha?"

The carnival people who came to Guichen every year had made a careful study of its walls. The one around the Pancrasse building-supplies yard stood fairly low under its climbing vine; the front door to the house stood shielded from view in the arched walkway leading from the supply yard to the garden. Three wrestlers and Paolo waited for the rival lover; they were equipped with a horse-blanket and kitchen utensils—frying-pan, cooking-pot, roasting-spit—to be used for the military punishment known as blanketing.

When we are at the summit of our happiness, how can we go on living unless we go downhill? Pancrasse was at that very moment laughing his shy, coarse laugh at the thought that he would soon possess the voluptuous mistress of elegant young Maxime Latour. The downhill course I speak of is often very precipitous.

"The fact is, Miss Cadénat," he was saying, "that my character is something of a hybrid, and I can be a daydreamer on occasion. Those young gentlemen have taken a notion to work up a kind of satirical revue using the town as its theme. I've undertaken to see if I can't compose a few lines dealing with that little cement bridge of mine."

"Oh, I do like creative people, better than anything! Men who produce pretty things, things that are soft, round, pretty."

"So long as the work is properly done and sturdy, spacious and comfortable, Miss Cadénat, that's the main thing. The customer doesn't look for extravagance or fancy touches."

"Alas! Eheu! Eheu! as Homer says. You men are so dull! But I am sure none of you will betray the gracious traditions of gentlemanly behavior! Come, Mr. Pancrasse, escort me to the door of my father's house!"

When a man is famous, or about to be famous, he finds a woman to teach him how one behaves in real society, as though the gods did not wish us to sully the gold of public recognition with the mud of rustic manners. The constructor of the cement bridge, pleased to have mastered the techniques of courtesy, had now bowed the way Mrs. Edmet had taught him to; this one-time beadle had now kissed the hand of Miss Lucy Cadénat, the bookstore owner's buxom daughter, and she had said "That's right!" Oh, Tarpeian Rock! Oh, Capitol![3] The Capitol in this case was "Give me your arm! My, what firm muscles you have! . . ." The Tarpeian Rock I shall not describe! Read instead the adventure of Sancho Panza at the *venta*, in Cervantes' admirable *Don Quixote*, which is my bedside book.[4] Pancrasse was gagged, perhaps Italian-style, there in the passageway of his Guichentois home; what was said to him, I really do not know. When Paolo Opi was having a fit of anger he would speak Italian, like Napoleon in Sardou's play, and I don't understand Italian.[5]

3. In ancient Rome, a man might be at the summit of his glory one day, symbolically at the top of the Capitoline Hill, only to be overthrown the next and hurled to his doom from the Tarpeian Rock. Jacob used this comparison also in *The Story of King Kabul*, chapter 9.

4. "They placed Sancho in the middle of the blanket and began to toss him up in the air and make sport with him as they would with a dog at Shrovetide" (Cervantes, *Don Quixote*, translated by Walter Starkie. New American Library, 1957, pp. 71–72).

5. Victorien Sardou (1831–1908) was an enormously popular dramatist, the author of fifty comedies of manners and historical dramas. His best-known historical play is *Madame Sans-Gêne* (1893), the story of a former washerwoman whose husband became one of Napoleon's marshals.

Anyhow I wasn't there. I was told they called Pancrasse a "grease-ball," which was not inappropriate. A neighbor, standing at her window that night trying to soothe a toothache, had no notion why the city architect should repeatedly leap into view from the shadow of a wall, to rise beneath the moon. Her husband, joining her at the window in his comical apparel, and some half-dozen other on-lookers, had no more notion than she did, and the windows closed again without the victim achieving any more hope of succor than a "Hey, down there! What's going on?" indistinguishable from the sounds of waves where the Rivers Tille and Jet mingled their waters opposite the Post Office. After this adventure, the architect's re-nown spread—thanks to the newspapers—beyond the Guichen Customs house. As for refined social behavior, Pancrasse gave that up along with his monocle and the speech mannerisms of the *In-croyables*.[6] Nothing, but nothing, can survive corporal punishment! Lucy Cadénat, who disliked certain kinds of violence, although she would no longer allow the "grease-ball" to pay court to her, broke off with the Contortionist. To Sergeant Albert Perron of the Colo-nial Army, who was staying with his mother, Mrs. Assard, for the duration of his leave, were transferred Lucy's favors and her entire affection.

◆

The Social Welfare Bureau
[from the chapter "Further Grounds for Public Dissatisfaction with the Mayor's Administration"]

"The same with the Social Welfare Bureau: more negligence! There's a regulation dated the 24th of Vendémiaire, Year V of the Republican calendar, forbidding the giving of charity to vagrants who happen to be within the boundaries of this or that munici-pality. I realize Louisa comes from Guichen but the fact of the matter is that she chose thirty years ago to move away from the dis-trict; she's not entitled to Social Welfare, the law is quite explicit: '. . . who have resided in the municipality for at least one year!' City

---

6. "Les Incroyables" (the Unbelievables) were a set of people with affected manners of speech and dress, during the Directoire, 1795–99.

Hall may not know the law, but I do! Our dear friend the social aid director was her sweetheart once upon a time: is that an excuse for circumventing the law? It is not! The thing is, you see, gentlemen, when chaos prevails in high places it works its way down to the people at the bottom. The mayor is supposed to keep an eye on his staff, dammit! He's the one that chairs the Social Welfare Committee, he's the one that allocates the charitable funds! But our mayor is too busy with his love life to spare a thought for anything else; that's the real root of the problem! I'm as understanding and kindly as the next man, but I'm a café owner and at least I conscientiously discharge the duties of a café owner; every man is supposed to discharge his duties conscientiously! Wouldn't we have had our theater long since if the mayor were any sort of a man?"

The person who thus expressed himself was Mr. Prosper, the shining light who owned the Prosper Café.

The Social Welfare Bureau was an office with diamond-shaped windowpanes; it would have looked out onto the gardens of City Hall but for the fact that its venetian blinds were always closed. Simon Bloche, caretaker at City Hall, went there to read his copy of the *Western Cross* throughout the summer's day. Mr. Sanguinetti, the director, sojourned there for an hour. On Wednesdays, zealous, smartly dressed patronesses brought to the office the findings of their clever investigations. The director was invariably put out by their reports: as surely as one of his ladies recommended the giving of aid to some needy person, he at once became fearful lest the Social Welfare Fund be bilked by someone feigning poverty. To enrich the coffers of the Social Welfare Fund was his sole ambition. But as surely as the lady recommended such aid be denied, the director, a very kind man, became fearful lest the needy person be a victim of the patronesses. It pained him to give, for he was the miserly guardian of thy substance, O most excellent Social Welfare Bureau, but he was also afraid not to give! His countenance inspired terror; he trimmed his beard the way the late great Horace Vernet had trimmed his; but he was so tender-hearted that he could bear to gaze upon the poor only once a month, and then with distaste.[1] If, as everyone believed, he was a domestic tyrant,

1. Horace Vernet (1789–1863) was a painter, the son and grandson of famous painters. He did vast tableaux showing the battles of Napoleon Bonaparte.

how was it that his wife gave all the orders? If, as everyone knew, he was weak and painstaking at the office, why did the ladies of the Social Welfare Committee tremble in his presence?

"The director commands his little ship with great distinction," Mrs. de la Chafrie was saying to Bloche the caretaker as she waited to see Mr. Sanguinetti one Tuesday. "He is neither coarse nor unfeeling; but I do not sense the presence of God here in this office!"

"He is not a bad man," answered Simon Bloche, "but he is slowly and surely damning himself; I say that from the bottom of my heart. He does not practice his religion. Oh, well; the Bureau does its job and will go on doing it till we're all of us in our graves. No complaints about the Bureau!"

"There's going to be a complaint today, Simon Bloche: the director is no gentleman! Punctuality, they say, is the courtesy of kings: well it wouldn't do the civil servants of the Third Republic any harm either! It's two o'clock!"

"My son, whom God took unto Himself body and soul, used to say: 'When there's no faith in our Lord, you can expect nothing worthwhile.' Sanguinetti isn't courteous in his dealings with anyone, not even with me: he's a boor, that's a word people use; and yet he does have humility, which is a virtue to be commended."

"Not *even* with you! Not *even* with you! But you're not a woman! All that's asked of you is to do your appointed tasks! You don't have to know . . . to know mathematics in order to open doors for other people in a . . . a seemly manner!"

"My dear good Mrs. de la Chafrie, your mind should be set on higher things! We were talking religion! We all know you have the piety and charity of a saint! But of course, I realize, your charitable thoughts don't extend to me! Life is short; life is just a short sleep and when we're all in the graveyard, bishop though you may be, Judgment Day will have rung for you just the same as for everyone else."

"Simon Bloche, your visit to the Social Welfare Bureau is, I'm sure, timely and helpful . . . now, why don't you just take yourself off somewheres, and that will do nicely."

"No infringement, Mrs. de la Chafrie, no infringement!" said the director as he came strolling in. "I pay homage to merit and nobility of spirit whenever I have the pleasure of furthering my acquaintance with those qualities, but I make so bold as to state, here in this

office—for a man's office is his castle, after all—that there has been
no infringement of the rules! It's no pleasant thing to uproot a bad
habit once it has dug itself in. We must bear in mind, Ma'am, that
this is not a Wednesday; the calendar is right there on the wall!"

"Sir, your very obedient servant! Sir, my compliments! Far be it
from me to criticize you, Sir, but you are late, Sir, and with a lady
waiting to see you, what's more . . . Sir!"

"Allow me to point out—"

"Yes, very well, this is a Tuesday. Merely a little device on my part,
for in short let us simply say that a conversation with a man as much
in demand as you are is no easy thing to achieve, on a Wednesday."

"Be reasonable, Ma'am! Let us assume that I will always have
some half-dozen lady advocates in my little courtroom; it will be
physically impossible for me to hear each of them present her brief;
there just isn't time. Any case can be convincingly argued in five or
ten well-chosen words. It may not be as elegant, but it's certainly
more practical. If, on the other hand, I have only one advocate that
day, what a torrent of verbiage! What long, involved stories—like
the plot of a Fenimore Cooper novel! But I, Ma'am, I am the judge
responsible for the funds of the Social Welfare program. That's an
awesome responsibility, Ma'am! Do be seated!"

"You are most gracious! Thank you! It happens that I *am* seated,
not very comfortably, to be sure. . . . In short let us simply say that
I am seated."

The director slid some keys into a lock and at once withdrew
them again to hold them in front of his belly. He was a short, fat,
pink-complexioned old man with a full head of hair.

"I am sure that if you are appearing before my little court, it can
only be in a noble, delicate, and practical cause. I shall therefore
endeavor to help you in any way I can."

"In the year 18–, an unwed mother . . . (it was September the
second) . . . in short let us simply say an unwed mother since
that is in fact what she was! set off on a journey to the City of
Lights which draws to itself all those innocent moths—innocent,
Sir, rather than wicked—in short let us simply say that she set off
for Paris. On September the second, 18–, she was at the railroad
station accompanied by her swain, some sort of butcher's boy from
Mr. David's establishment. He was carrying the trunk . . . I must say
the trunk can't have been very heavy, but there was a trunk, that

fact has been established! . . . At the time, Mr. David had a butcher shop on Saint-Mathurin Square, at the spot where Carent's is now. The Carents bought the business on January seventeenth, 18–, for 12,000 francs, in short let us simply say they bought it for a song. They haven't exactly made a howling success of it, not what one might have expected. Mrs. Carent was fond of elaborate meals, fine china, and naturally that sort of thing costs money. She'd bought a table service of rock crystal, a magnificent set. Moreover they lost a child, and everything has gone all topsy-turvy for that poor, unfortunate family! But to return to my unwed mother. Her name is Jean Maréchal and she must be fifty-eight. Jean Maréchal was on her way to Paris, in short let us simply say she was going off to have her baby in secret. For in Paris one can well and truly hide! What numberless horrors, Mr. Sanguinetti, what innumerable sorrows, in a city of such magnificence, such opulence! Now listen most carefully. That unwed mother was the actual niece of some sort of gardener, since deceased, who worked for the de Chantrels."

"What did I tell you! Fenimore Cooper! I knew it; I knew you were going to construct a whole Fenimore Cooper novel for my benefit! How well I know you good ladies, all of you! Let's come to the point, Ma'am! And the point, Ma'am, is that I am a philanthropist, not a confessor. And philanthropy, Ma'am, is a finer thing than all the English novels ever written. Pardon me if I take the liberty of interrupting you: the public service is the public service and cannot grind to a halt."

"Very well! I shall say no more! You'll have to manage the affair as best you can! These matters are your concern, not mine, upon my word! You have interrupted me, Sir! I shall say not another thing! She came all the way here from Paris on foot! Three hundred and twenty-two kilometers! How do you like *that*, my dear Sir!"

"Statute dated the twenty-fourth of Vendémiaire, Year V of the Republican calendar. Has she been domiciled in the municipality for one year? No! I have no obligation to her! Her case is sad but clear-cut! Good day, Ma'am!"

"Oh, is that so? Is that so?"

"*Dura lex sed lex*. The law is harsh but it's the law. It would be illegal for the Social Welfare Fund to fatten up all the indigents on land and sea who come here from the Lord knows where and get my patronesses to make fine speeches to me."

"But you must have known her! You were business manager at the old people's home when she was a waitress at the Paris Bar here in Guichen: her name at that time was Louisa! She was a very good waitress. Gentlemen of your age may well have known the poor woman."

"Louisa? Louisa, you say? A butcher's boy from David's! Really? No . . . I don't seem to recall any Louisa; mind you, it's been a great many years! Poor Louisa, 322 kilometers on foot! But there's still the statute dated twenty-fourth of Vendémiaire."

"The poor woman has nothing to eat other than what my cook brings her."

"I'm not an archangel, you know, Ma'am! But neither am I as dead to human feeling as you might think. I'm thankful to say that I have friends of thirty years' standing who will come forward to help someone they used to know. The Paris Bar, however, was patronized only by the lower classes, and I doubt whether—"

"Come now, Mr. Sanguinetti, don't take that attitude."

"H'mmm. Louisa. Louisa. . . . If this Louisa, before she walked highways, used to walk streets, it seems to me our chief of police will have to step in. Tell this creature you've befriended to come and see us."

"She's waiting outside. I'll leave you now. Good day to you, Sir!"

"Are you sure Mr. Sanguinetti isn't in his cups occasionally?" said Mrs. de la Chafrie to Simon Bloche; "He seems to me to be highly excited today and a little out of his senses."

"Drunk or sober, he's a good man," said Simon Bloche, "but a religious man he is not."

Mr. Sanguinetti was in an emotional state. However slight may have been the stimulus for our greatest loves, consisting sometimes of no more than the hope of sensual pleasure on a day when we are a prey to gloom, and however unworthy the object of those loves, they always leave enough traces to stir us when we think of them again. A man may forget all about the women he has merely possessed, but not the ones he has loved. Mr. Sanguinetti was in a fix: he had no hesitation in helping this unfortunate woman whom he once had loved, and he had set the monetary value of his great-heartedness at five francs; the problem was that neither Sanguinetti private citizen nor Sanguinetti director of the Social Welfare Bureau could lay his hands on five francs: the one was accountable to his wife for his own funds, the other to the mayor and prefect for the funds of the Social Welfare program and its Bureau. What was to be done? He thought of borrowing five francs from Curot, or Simon Bloche, or Mr. Debout the chief of police. But how was he to pay it back without asking Mrs. Sanguinetti for the money? He decided to borrow five francs from the Social Welfare Fund and repay it ten centimes at a time by going without tobacco for fifty days. He said quite distinctly:

"There are chasms in the human heart where God Himself would see nothing but shadows!"

"Madam," he said, addressing Louisa with downcast eyes, "the authorities are unable to help you, but I believe I can of my own free will show a personal concern for your plight. Take this modest sum, use it well, mention it to no one and please go. I . . . I am not at ease in your presence."

"Is that all you have to say to me, Joseph?" answered Louisa.

"You've put on weight, Louisa!"

She smelled of drink; she had a child in her arms; she told her story, and the director listened as a man may listen to the judge who is sentencing him. She explained that the child belonged to a woman friend who had entrusted the child to Louisa one day and who had not been in touch with her since.

He proposed that she take a job shelling peas and beans in a canning factory; she replied that she was expecting a letter from Paris. On emerging from City Hall, she told Simon Bloche how clever she was to have got charitable aid from Mr. Sanguinetti, who at that moment was thinking:

"She was deceiving a business manager at the old people's home so she could sleep with a butcher! That's women for you!"

The next month and the next, Louisa came again and, the statute of Vendémiaire in the Year V of the Republican calendar notwithstanding, Joseph added her name to the public assistance roles. Meanwhile, Simon Bloche, who was a frequent caller at the Seminary, propagated amongst the clergy the news that the director had taken to giving needy people money from his own wallet, and the canon's housemaid Eliza had extolled this generosity on a visit to Carent's butchershop. The members of City Council instructed their mayor to convey to the director their congratulations; whereupon the director, much moved, humbly confessed his infraction of the rules. Our good Mr. Lecourbe the mayor, in order to court favor with the aldermen, demanded Mr. Sanguinetti's resignation. The entire city now rose up in one concerted cry of Down with the Mayor! The prefect requested that the Social Welfare employee be retained in his position. At the Prosper Café, some condemned the tyrannical harshness with which the mayor had reacted to the ex-lover's human frailties, while others deplored the behavior of the mayor's staff. Mrs. Sanguinetti spoke tearfully of divorce.

◆

The Story of the Comb
and the Saga of the Peaches
[from the chapter "The Love-Life
of Thomas Lecourbe"]

There was no doubt in the minds of the townspeople that whenever Mr. Lecourbe, wine merchant and mayor of Guichen, went to the spa at Vichy, his sole purpose was to meet his current mistress there. True, there was no doubt in their minds about his liver ailment, either: you had only to look at his complexion! But although they might meet the wine merchant once or twice a day standing in front of his wine cellars bemoaning his yellow complexion, they also had, lying in plain view all day long on the bars at which they drank, Busby's newspaper disseminating the notion that for Lecourbe "Vichy" meant "mistresses." This may have been a lie, but after all what difference is there between truth, and a lie restated as often as required? Just ask the Press! Busby kept repeating that Lecourbe's mistress was "from the theatrical world" and that Lecourbe wanted a theater built on the Bouchaballe property so she would have a place to perform. The lies most successful at passing for truths are not always, when the press is involved, the lies that are most far-fetched. When Mr. Lecourbe was a law student in Paris, he had gone to the Opéra Comique almost every evening, and each time he emerged he would write a love letter to one or another of our great prima donnas offering to marry her. He worked his way down to the singers with bit parts! His prose style finally earned him the favors of an usherette, but it also earned him a number of satirical gibes on stage. Busby did not know these details: thus his slanders contained an element of inspired guess-work, which was not surprising coming from a poet. Moreover, "news items," as everyone knows, are the stuff of which works of fiction are made.[1] And if Busby's newspaper articles were so many works of fiction, Lecourbe's life was one long news item. Thus—for instance!—a woman's ornamental comb was found at City Hall!

Although Simon Bloche's father had outlived his usefulness at the Canvas and Linen Goods Store, Mr. Mouzot kept him on, for he stood in awe of the old man and his elephantine manner.

"Blaise," Mr. Mouzot said to him one day, "I have a piece of news that will really delight you; just sit there and savor it a moment! I've had a letter sent to the War Department asking that you be granted a little allowance of 200 francs as a veteran of the War of 1870 . . . h'mm, yes, quite!"

"That's nonsense! I earn a humble but honest living working for you. I want no part of any allowance; you can keep your allowance. My name is Blaise Bloche, and I don't beg for a living."

"Enough of your sage utterances, Blaise, and no wails and moans! You should be pleased at the benefits your military valor has brought you. Do make an effort to understand that you aren't as spry as you used to be and that a young man would be extremely helpful to me here in the store, h'mm, yes, quite. Two hundred francs! It's not a fortune, no reason to dance in the streets for joy, but your present salary isn't that much higher, and I was certainly not expecting such a sour reaction."

"I'm being dismissed! Me, Blaise Bloche! After all these years! Me, a veteran of 1870! I knew you when you were knee-high to a grasshopper, and you of all people are dismissing me? Now you listen to me, Augustus! I speak for your father when I tell you that what you are doing is not very nice! No, not very nice, and if the good Lord is looking at you at this moment I'm sure he's turning his eyes the other way!"

"Now, let's be practical, Blaise! My position in Guichen is good, but also threatened because of Ferval who is my business rival and

1. Ironic reference to Flaubert's *Madame Bovary*, based on a real-life news-paper story. Jacob particularly disliked Flaubert for his pessimism. See *Letters from Max Jacob to Marcel Béalu*, letter dated June 10, 1937.

my political enemy. He's got young fellows who aren't veterans of
1870 but who are alert and bright-eyed and have the very quickness
which. . . . I have to hold my own!"

"Bunch of baloney . . . phooey!"

"But this is nonsensical, Blaise! You'll have your veteran's allowance and some help from the city as regular polling clerk at elec-
tions. That's nothing to be sneezed at, you know, Blaise."

"Mutual aid stuff! My children will never let me fall so low!"

"Exactly! You have your children, too, don't you, Blaise?"

"Enough! *Sufficit!* Me, Blaise Bloche, veteran of the Franco-
Prussian War, wounded in action at Le Mans, father of the caretaker at City Hall, old retainer of the firm of Mouzot, seventy-seven
years old! I thought I knew what life was about, but I still hadn't
emptied the, er, . . . drunk my cup of bitterness to the bottom. I tell
you, this house is fallen upon evil days, days of ruin, captivity, and
devastation. Flood, too!"

"What a note of doom, Blaise! You amaze me! Come now, buck
up! I'll waylay the mayor and wring some concession out of him for
your benefit. Let's shake hands like the good friends we are! Here
is your month's pay and a month's advance on salary."

Said Blaise to his son Simon Bloche:

"The law may be on his side, but the good Lord is on mine! My
boy won't allow a Bloche to go to the public authorities asking for
handouts."

"The duty of a Christian is to think of the living as well as the
dead. I say that from the bottom of my heart and in the name of
my pure, innocent son whose funeral procession carried him away
from this earth, taking along my broken heart. Stop and think for
a minute, you old humbug, you'll be living like a bishop! The city
will be paying you for doing nothing, the government will be paying you for doing nothing! And still you come to a poor Christian
like me, saying: it's up to you to support me!"

"Simon, I know the capital of France is the city where everything
costs twice as much; otherwise I would have said to your brother,
who is a draughtsman in a factory there: 'Are you going to let a
Bloche go to the public authorities asking for handouts?' You're a
widower, Simon, and you've lost your son, and it's you I'm saying
it to: Simon, your father will not go to the authorities asking for
handouts."

"They're bound and determined to force your retirement. Resign yourself to being sensible about it, that's all! And think about the life hereafter, which is the best thing to do in the circumstances."

"The War of 1870! The Siege of Paris! The Commune! That wasn't enough devastation for Blaise Bloche! I thought I'd known the woes of human kind, all my sad life long! But it wasn't enough, Blaise Bloche! There was more to come!"

Meanwhile, since Mouzot was opposed to the plan for a theater, his putting in a word to the mayor on behalf of Blaise was unproductive. He tried to see the regional prefect, but was unable to obtain an interview. City Hall did, however, look into the matter, and decided that Bloche (Blaise), since he had nondependent children with jobs, and an allowance from the War Department, was not entitled to a further allowance. The War Ministry, having been approached by Mouzot and by Darimon, the local member of the National Assembly, decided upon inquiry that Bloche (Blaise), since he had nondependent children with jobs, and an allowance from his native city, was not entitled to a further allowance. Batted back and forth from City Hall to the Regional National Office and from the Regional National Office to City Hall, Bloche (Blaise) was constrained from an official viewpoint to go without eating for a year.

The caretaker from City Hall found it hard to put up with his father's solemn speeches, and the father was reciprocally unappreciative of the pious speeches made by his son. Simon had spoken about his father to Mr. Lecourbe, but with no success. One day, however, when he went to put the mail on Mr. Lecourbe's desk, Simon Bloche found a woman's ornamental comb there in the mayor's office. He turned it over to Father Davant. Father Davant mentioned it to Canon Domnère. The canon unleashed a terrible burst of anger against Davant and Bloche, calling them a couple of blackmailers, and against the mayor, the city, and the times they were living in. Father Davant gave the comb back to Bloche, saying that the only advice he could give him was to put the comb back in the mayor's office.

"Mr. Mayor, I found a woman's comb in your office after you'd gone home. I thought of taking it to Mrs. Lecourbe, but Mrs. Lecourbe is away in the country."

"Hand me that comb this instant, Simon, or I'll fire you here and now. I've been too easy-going with you."

"You can't fire me without consulting City Council!"

"Hand me that comb! My office is like a goldfish bowl! This is outrageous!"

"It's in my lodge downstairs. There's no use you giving me Hell about it, you old humbug!"

The comb could not be found.

A month later, the City Council voted an annual allowance to Blaise Bloche, "a particularly deserving veteran of 1870." Moreover, with the mayor's sponsorship, he was chosen to be inspector of the women who shelled peas and beans at the canning factory. The comb turned up in the caretaker's lodge.

"Knowing your way around at City Hall, you old humbug," said Simon Bloche to his father, "is as simple as saying Mass, but first you have to be at City Hall! Once you are, then you've got more elbowroom than in a double casket at the cemetery, for sure! The good Lord hasn't done badly by us, Dad!"

The story of the comb became known via the canon's housemaid Eliza, and Carent's butchershop. Busby wrote an article that reduced Mrs. Lecourbe to tears.

"The comb belonged to that woman who runs the Normal School, didn't it? Swear to me that it isn't so, Thomas! Swear it isn't so!"

This light-skinned little lady, who had a crabby disposition though she didn't look it, had lived her life in worshipful admiration of her husband, the gentle Thomas Lecourbe. Busby made her jealous and submissive. The jealousy was for Miss Lenoble, principal of the Normal School for Girls, and this is why:

"Angela, my chaste one," the history teacher was saying to the literature teacher in the garden of the Normal School, "there are fewer peaches on the trees against the wall than there were at this time yesterday! Angela, my chaste one, we must be on our guard against the boss-lady!"

"Noélie, my dearest, I had already noted the fact but had thought it prudent not to breathe a word. I beg you, Noélie, do, do be prudent as I!"

"The wrath of the Republic must I shun. Think of *Nicomède*![2]

2. In Corneille's tragedy *Nicomède*, King Prusias of Bithynia is fearful of

Besides, why should that sourpuss get all the peaches? This garden isn't reserved for the principal, after all. Let her eat the peaches from her own garden, and if it has none, let her do without!"

"Let us pick peaches in our own garden, a piece of Oriental wisdom, my fairest one! Come let me kiss you for so exquisite an utterance."

"My own true sage. . . . All the same I intend to have speech—"

"S . . . peach!"

"—to have speech in this matter, Angela, my chaste one, with the divisional school inspector, who gazes with Rodrigue's eyes upon his fair Chimène . . . Chimène, in this instance, is me!"[3]

"Because of your—peaches-and-cream!—complexion. Here he is; make haste to accost him and impeach the headmistress! Peaches, speeches, impeaches! Just like conjugating a verb, my pretty Noélie; how I do love thee!"

The divisional inspector came daily to the school. He had the sort of face that indulgent popular memory is still apt to associate with Francisque Sarcey, and so Angela and Noélie had nicknamed him Francis.[4] When he had listened to these ladies air their grievances about the peaches, Francis went back to the principal's rooms to raise the matter with her. After a lecture, during which the lady heard him out with downcast eyes, Francis, returning to the garden, encountered there a student clad in black, and she said to him:

"We have much more courage in your presence than we ever did with your predecessor, Inspector. You're such a kind man!"

"Indeed, child, I am neither a Cronus nor a Ugolino; you may speak freely."

"I think you mean Saturn, Inspector.[5] Please, Sir, have you just been seeing our principal about the peaches?"

---

alienating the Roman Republic. The peaches in Jacob's story, being on the grounds of a state school, are the property of the French Republic. Like their colleague Miss Tripier, whom we have met, Angela and Noélie enjoy making classical allusions.

3. Reference to Corneille's very popular *Le Cid* (1637), a drama of the conflict between honor and passionate love in the hearts of Rodrigue and Chimène. "To gaze at something as Rodrigue gazed at Chimène" remains a much-used expression in French.

4. Francisque Sarcey (1827–99) was a drama critic whose judgments guided the theatre-going middle class for forty years.

5. Cronus and Ugolino are the inspector's pedantic way of saying "an eater

"Aha! Piercing vision and keen hearing, that's what you young people have! You are quite right, I have just been seeing that good principal of yours about the peaches in this very garden."

"Please, Inspector, to be perfectly fair, now, wouldn't you say that this isn't just the garden of the teaching staff, but also the garden of the senior girls and that consequently the peaches in the staff garden are also the peaches in the senior girls' garden?"

"Very neatly put, child! So that what we have here is a Garden of Plenty, a Garden of Milk and Honey! And honey not just from the trees along the wall; honey also from the lips of the Naiads."

"I think you mean the Dryads, or Nymphs, Inspector. Isn't it only fair that if the teachers' dining table is to feature the produce of their espaliered fruit trees, the senior girls' table should do so too?"

"I greatly fear we may not have enough peaches for all those charming, eager lips," said the inspector, and back he went a second time to the principal's rooms.

When Francis had finished what he had to say, the principal, extremely annoyed, said to him:

"Every morning I shall send you a basket filled with this fruit, this litigious fruit, as they say in the courts. I trust you will allow me to do that, my dear Inspector, for your rank sets you above us all: principal, teachers, and girls alike, and who should have a better right to these peaches than you!"

"Miss Lenoble, I appreciate your kind gesture, which, I may say, comes as no surprise to one who knows what a refined and gracious person you are. But would the world not be apt to interpret your offer, should it become known, as an attempt to diminish the impartiality in my day-to-day evaluations of your establishment. . . . Who knows? as our good Rabelais used to say."

"I think you mean Montaigne, Inspector."[6]

"Montaigne . . . Rabelais! Rabelais . . . Montaigne! Yes . . . yes, of course! Montaigne. You're quite right; it was Montaigne that used to say: 'Who knows?' Ah, he was quite a man, that Montaigne! Yes, indeed!"

---

of children." Since Cronus came to be identified with the Roman harvest god Saturn, the inspector and the equally pedantic student are both right.

6. Although Montaigne is indeed known for the quotation, this is an absurd correction of an absurd reference, for it was certainly not Montaigne who first said: "Who knows?"

"Would you like to offer our peaches to the regional prefect, Inspector?"

"The prefect appreciates tokens of esteem. I'll have a word with him. I'll . . . HAVE . . . a . . . WORD . . . with . . . HIM, tra, la! Ha, ha, ha!"

Francis did mention the incident of the peaches to him, and proposed to turn the problem to the prefect's profit. The prefect asked for time to consider the matter: he had a reply sent round to the inspector, to the effect that the prefect's wife found herself unable to accept courtesies she would not be in a position to return, the prefect's wife having decided not to entertain in her home that winter.

Miss Lenoble was still determined that if she was to be denied the right to eat the fruit, her staff should not be allowed to enjoy it either. She took a basket, filled it with peaches, and sent it to Mrs. Edmet, whom she admired as a woman of fine feelings and good taste.

Mrs. Edmet, with that impetuousness for which she was known, said to the gardener who had brought her the basket:

"Oh, yes, I know: the peaches. They fed them to the pigs and the pigs have had all they want! . . ."

And she laughed.

Miss Lenoble sent the same basket to poor Mrs. Carent, who had been so depressed ever since one of her children died.

"There's been a mistake," said Mrs. Carent to the gardener. "These peaches are meant for Mrs. Edmet."

"You're being foolish, Mimi!" said Arsène Carent as he cut up a roast of lamb. "You don't look a gift horse in the mouth."

"She's sending me peaches because Mrs. Edmet doesn't want them."

"Come on, now, Mimi, be honest! If you weren't on a diet for your diabetes you'd have been quite happy to eat peaches from the staff garden up at the school. And anyway, you could have kept them to give me! That's not very nice of you!"

"Hush, Arsène! You just have no sensitivity! But what can you expect? . . . Men! . . ."

Miss Lenoble was eating her heart out. Sitting in a red armchair, surrounded by the bare walls of her parlor, she was gazing through the open window at the peaches, which had ripened for the first time in eleven years. At about half past three she came to a decision.

"Mary," she said to the housemaid, "take the basket of peaches to Mr. Lecourbe! 4 Courthouse Street."

The maid came back with no basket and no fruit, and Miss Lenoble, who was awaiting her return, smiled.

"Mr. Lecourbe said he'd come by and talk to you, Ma'am."

The mayor appeared: he was wearing a frock coat because he had a sense of occasion and a round hat because this was not an official call. He was carrying the basket of peaches.

"Miss Lenoble, courtesy is a delightful quality which, it sorely grieves me to say, is steadily vanishing. Gallant behavior these days is nowhere to be seen! Society has ceased to exist, and we live among savages. This being so, I am extremely touched at the charming impulse which led you to offer me this delicious fruit! I appreciate it firstly as an administrator and then, I make bold to say, as an admirer of the fair sex. Madam, I thank you! And please give my compliments to your business manager for keeping gardens that yield such agreeable produce. Unfortunately (it hurts me to say this, for I am a fine trencherman and fond of good food), I was obliged to decline accepting this gift: I am not entitled to eat fruit belonging to the Administrative Region: the Normal School is Regional Property. . . . What's the matter, Miss Lenoble; are you ill? and even National Property. I, you realize, am a municipal official, eminently municipal—are those tears, Miss Lenoble?"

From behind her handkerchief, the spinster nodded an affirmative; then she apologized, with a vague reference to her nerves. Lecourbe's emotions were stirred. She was a bit heavy, but still a fine-looking woman. He took her hand. The principal sat up straight. The mayor ceremoniously took his leave. He was sure she was in love with him.

The principal went and got a big kitchen hamper, filled it with the ripest peaches and told the maid to take it to the Joint Public and Military Hospital and Nursing home. The principal received from the chief housekeeper at that establishment a somewhat sharply worded letter. The writer expressed her astonishment that the most highly educated persons should be ignorant of the rules of hygiene: the code of rules governing the Hospital and Nursing

Home did not allow whimsical gestures of this sort. The patients were well enough fed not to need "help from outside." Moreover, the Nursing Home's own gardens supplied, if not peaches, at any rate a great deal of fruit. The housekeeper expressed her thanks and was returning the basket herewith. The basket, with its contents, spent the night out in the garden of the Normal School.

Next morning after sunup, Mr. Oscar came to the school to give the young ladies their gym class. Always to be seen astride a bicycle, father of seven, fisherman, hunter, manicurist, pedicurist, one-time watch repairman, athletics supervisor, former drill sergeant, in short a kind of Guichentois Figaro, Mr. Oscar was tall, gaunt, red-faced, and khaki-clad. He spied the basket and learned from George the gardener the facts that lay behind this unlikely sight. By eight-thirty he was repeating the story to Canon Domnère, whose feet he regularly tended. The canon's feet were things of perfect beauty; he was vain about their appearance, and his noble dimensions prevented him massaging them himself.

"Just stop for a moment till I've had my laugh out! Otherwise you may damage my lower extremities, which would be a great pity, for I am, God forgive me, very proud of their perfect proportions. By gad, I think I can predict the crowning episode in the Saga of the Peaches! You, Oscar, shall be the one to eat and savor them, you lucky fellow! You and Mrs. Oscar's seven bambinos, how does that strike you? Why should you not, after all? The revered boss-lady over at the diploma-mill is less concerned with enjoying the peaches than with preventing her subordinates from having them. Sentiments worthy of young ladies studying philosophy, I must say! Considering that when you get your hands on those peaches, you will not only be embellishing your table but also 'helping thy neighbor,' I'm sure that your confessor, if any, will grant you absolution. I want you to negotiate this remarkable transaction, and I predict a favorable outcome! Your mighty brain will spawn some adroit little lie, and when next you visit me I shall hail the conquering hero!"

"Oh, Canon Domnère, that would really be something! By God, I swear on my army boots, if this little deal comes off right, I'll split the loot with you!"

"Don't swear any such thing, Oscar! I love peaches, but you're forgetting, as the heroes of this tragedy would say, that Regional Property is not Church Property. Let me shake your hand, for this morning, thanks to you, I've enjoyed myself hugely and laughed to my heart's content. Don't come tempting me with your peaches, because if you did they'd be rejected by the Church authorities with as much pomp and dignity as they were by the authorities ending in -al, whose glorious names hide their spiritual nudity."[7]

"Miss Lenoble," said Oscar to the principal of the Normal School for Girls, "it takes a lot of nerve to go knocking at the captain's door when you're nothing but an orderly. You'll have to excuse me! I'm just an old soldier and a pretty peculiar fellow. I know about flying jumps on the high bar, but when it comes to correct manners, well there I'm kind of rusty, as they say."

"Speak freely, Mr. Oscar."

"Miss Lenoble, even if a man was made of iron it wouldn't help, once the surgeon's gone in with his chisel and carved you in pieces and chopped you up till he's good and finished; when they've hollowed you out here and screwed you back together there, and then anemia nails you one fine day too . . . or else a man would have to be vulcanized. My wife has had seven children! Tuesday she had a miscarriage; her back is still bothering her!"

"Oh, poor woman!"

"Doctor Breach, the doctor for the Mothers' Association, told her what she should take: 'Give her lots of fruit!' he says, 'That'll thin out her blood!' I tried to sweet-talk the man that runs your garden, that George fellow, so's I could get a few pears that are lying on the ground, y'know, just the crumbs, like! He told me he doesn't move one stick of wood without he has your permission."

"Pears that were lying on the ground, my dear Mr. Oscar! Oh, my dear man, how little you know me! Come with me right now! I'm going to send your wife a big basket of peaches as a gift, and when she's emptied that basket I'll fill her another one. I say here's to the mothers of large families, Mr. Oscar! We can never do too much for them. Motherhood is the key to our country's future!"

"Noélie, my fairest," said the literature teacher to the history teacher, "we've been a pair of fools!"

"Speak for me, wisest Angela, for fool I am indeed, but not for yourself, for you have genius!"

"Dear Noélie! If those peaches had but stayed upon the trees,

---

7. The canon refers to -al as in regional or municipal authorities.

where we could feast our eyes on them if not our mouths, there would have been some chance of our swiping one or two of them each day! Are we now to go and petition Mr. Oscar for them?"

"Angela, my chaste one, what you didn't know was that the principal was counting them twice each morning!"

The Name

To Gabriel Bounoure

[*The painter René Rimbert mentioned in a letter to Jacob that if his expected child were to be a girl, he would name her Saskia after Rembrandt's young wife. In his answer, Jacob pointed out that Saskia is not a Christian name and that it is important not to subject a child to lifelong ridicule. This exchange of letters gave him the impetus to write the charming story,* Le Nom *(1923) whose opening chapter we have here. Strangely enough, not only the fictional character, but Max Jacob himself suffered on account of the name Saskia: in a letter to Kahnweiler, the art dealer, he bitterly complained about a critic who refused to read and write about this story because he was put off by the Russian name.*]

◆

It must indeed be painful for any pious mother to know that her daughter's name is that of a mare, but how much more so when the mother numbers among her ancestors Saint Rose of Lima, for the baroness was Peruvian, fair-haired but Peruvian. Like her native city, her family had been founded by Pizarro in 1535, on the banks of the Rimac. At the mansion in the rue de la Chaussée-d'Antin, as also in the castle keep of the family Morfeuil in Lower Poitou, the feast day of Saint Rose of Lima was observed each year on the thirtieth of August: would it henceforth be necessary to observe little Saskia's feast day on the date of the Grand Prix?[1] Was there anyone that year who did not know? Was there anyone who did not know that the winning mare in the Grand Prix that spring was out of the

1. The street Chaussée-d'Antin, and the district of Paris named for it, were highly fashionable during the Restoration, 1814–30.

187

Morfeuil stables and was called Saskia? And yet the cruel baron, for his personal glory, was immolating every religious scruple and a number of others besides: he was endowing his daughter with a name which the Bollandist fathers do not mention, a name which instead perpetuated the memory of his ephemeral triumph for the lifetime of her whose story we propose to tell.[2] Poor Baroness! How could you foresee that the name of a mare was to weigh heavily upon the child you were bringing into the world?

Slow tears which she could not hold back welled up in the baroness's eyes when she had heard the baron's horrible pronouncement.

"Madam," said he, with that courtesy which never deserted him, "your daughter's name will be Saskia." The fair-haired mother of the newborn babe turned as white as her bed which was as white as her soul. The baron had boots, short black side-whiskers, a riding crop, a top hat, and a thick moustache. The most obtuse observer, seeing this outwardly happy couple, would have said: "The executioner and his victim!" and for once the observer would not have been mistaken.

"That's a Russian name!" said Amelia-the-Red, the aunt who did stiletto-work embroidery. This nickname served to distinguish her from another Aunt Amelia, Amelia-of-les-Tournelles, who read the novels of George Sand. Amelia-of-les-Tournelles lived on the street of that name in one of those ancient dwellings which the pickaxe of the demolition contractor had thus far spared.

"Saskia is the feminine of Sachacha," said Amelia-of-les-Tournelles. "It is reported in Scripture that Sachacha housed Our Lord in his own home: the Bollandist fathers are wrong, that's all!"

"She was a Russian saint," said Amelia-the-Red as her stiletto darted back and forth through her embroidery, on oilcloth that was green behind and black in front.

And you, readers, friends, can any of you tell me the true facts about this name "Saskia"? Is Saskia really a Russian name? In the *History of Dutch Painters*, reference is made to a Saskia who is supposed to have had no less a person than Rembrandt for a husband! A seventeenth-century Dutch painter went and found himself a wife in Russia? What an extraordinary notion for a Dutch painter to take into his head in the seventeenth century! Later on, my heroine will want to clear up once and for all this matter of her name

2. The Bollandist fathers wrote the *Acta Sanctorum* (*Lives of the Saints*).

and its exotic origins: on that account she will, I fear, be mixing socially with any Russians fit to be mixed with, in Paris as it was before the disasters of 1870. Poor child! There, there, you poor child, let me . . . let me tell your woeful story! The fact is that around the year 1850, Saskia was thought to be a Russian name, unusual but Russian. Indeed, this opinion still prevails in certain areas of the Parisian hellhole (where may God preserve you from ever setting foot!) and those who hold to this opinion may be right. But then . . . that leaves us with the "Rembrandt" business . . . oh, pooh! Let's not be so sticky where other people's names are concerned, and besides, I ask you, now, which of us would ever want to call his "nearest and dearest" Saskia anyway? In short, let us simply take it that the mare of the wicked baron had a Russian name, and his daughter had one also!

When it was decided that Saskia's education would be entrusted to Birds of the Field Convent, the nun in charge of public relations checked the Bollandist publication to see whether the name "Saskia" had ever been consecrated by belonging to a saint, discovered that it had not, and pointed out that a well-regulated establishment could scarcely accept a boarding student who did not come under the umbrella of the Calendar. The reverend superior took into account the wealth of the Morfeuils, their position in society, the mansion in the rue de la Chaussée-d'Antin and the castle keep in Lower Poitou, and found a compromise.

"We'll name her Mary of Angels to avoid causing a scandal," she said, "You'd like that, wouldn't you, child? Do you agree to being called Mary of Angels by your schoolfellows?"

"I am Saskia de Morfeuil!" replied the descendant of the Pizarros. "I will not have my name changed as though I were a domestic servant."

"Now, there's a tough little spirit that will have to be brought into line!" the reverend superior said to herself; but to the two Amelias, who had accompanied the schoolgirl, she directed a glance that read: "Hark how the noble blood of the Pizarros speaks out!"

Let us draw the veil of mystery and discretion over ten years of convent school which were ten years of suffering! How could anyone control the malicious behavior of those dear little schoolmates?

> Saskia was her Daddy's mare
> Jockey's colors pink and pear

Saskia was your Daddy's horse
You were named for her, of course!

sang the nice little classmates as they danced around the hapless
girl. And the blood of the Pizarros was helpless against the mob.
What could the blood of the indomitable Pizarros do against the
nastiness of little girls? Suffer in silence.

"She really has a face like a Saskia!" Amelia-the-Red would say
on Sundays. She said it every Sunday, this idle spinster, as her stiletto darted back and forth through her white embroidery. "No
one has ever been able to discover why the child really has a face
like a Saskia," Amelia-of-les-Tournelles would say. And the author,
moved to pity, asks in turn: Do all Saskias have a great, high forehead and a lower profile like a rabbit's? Do Saskias always have
red hair like Amelia-the-Red and her niece? According to the baroness, who was permanently ill, there was not a shred of sense in
Amelia's remark. Just between you and me, I agree with the poor
baroness and I shall undertake Saskia's defense! Would that I, like
a guardian angel, might always have been there to wipe away your
tears, child, your tears of rage! That remark of Amelia's had no
more claim to common sense than a phrase of poetry does when
it expresses the confluence of a number of disparate sensations.
Amelia's remark simply voiced, in a teasing, family sort of way, a
connection between the strange appellation and the no less strange
facial characteristics of the last of the Pizarros. You really had a face
like a Saskia, poor child, and—who knows?—perhaps you had a
fate like a Saskia as well. You may not have married a seventeenth-
century Dutch painter, but you did marry a nineteenth-century
anarchist. I leave my readers to reflect on the parallel.

The baroness died. It was the Amelias who brought Saskia out
into the world when she left the convent. And that is how, because
she was named for a horse, a girl raised on the purest principles
of good Christian upbringing, around the year 1850, became an
intellectual, a republican, and even something more.

"Gluttony Is a
Many-Splendored Thing"

[*This piece first appeared as part of* Les Sept péchés capitaux, *1926.
Each contributor was assigned one of the seven deadly sins to write about.
Max's, fittingly enough, was gluttony. For his sketch, he momentarily
brought back to life characters from* The Bouchaballe Property, *some
encountered in our extracts, others not.*]

◆

"It's the Ministry calling, Mr. Prefect," said the private secretary to his distinguished superior, who was solemnly consuming his
Olympian repast. "Tell them I'm going around the Region inspect-
ing horses." "The minister is on the line, Sir." "Doesn't that man
ever eat?" muttered the Prefect, but he gave a slight formal bow
all the same. "I assure you, Mr. Prefect, that the repasts enjoyed by
the minister of the interior are as Olympian as your own; they just
don't coincide with yours."

* * *

"People could really choose some other time to come and see
me," said that most devoted cleric Father Davant, who was having
his dinner. "It's for someone who's dying, Father." Father Davant,
godly man that he was, rose from the table. Only death is a greater
god than the ritual of our daily lives.

* * *

Two old vagabonds were rubbing their backs against the rough
wooden wall of the covered market, and from somewhere between
their beards and their hats came these words: "A leg of lamb, now!
There's nothing like a leg of lamb!" "Yeah! They serve them at
weddings."

Thus the two ancients gave voice to their Olympian dreams, while three children stood watching. The children had their own Olympus clutched firmly in their hands: sticks of licorice-root, on which they were chewing away to the detriment of their appetites.

"A couple of drunks!" said Mr. Goin the learned agriculturalist, as he accompanied Mrs. Lecourbe (the former Miss Lecointre) and Mr. Lecourbe, better known to his municipal constituents as "the old gray Mayor who ain't what he used to be." "When Mr. Debout throws them in the clink, I hope he keeps them there a good long time. They're a disgrace to our fair city."

"When your table's not set, you drink to forget," said Mrs. Lecourbe, the former Miss Lecointre. "Be fair, now, they're no different from us."

"Don't be too hard on the poor fellows, Goin! Agatha, why do we never have prawns? And I'd really enjoy a slice of nice fresh Swiss cheese. So, are we agreed on buying Vermouth? Vermouth it is, then!" . . . and, with a smile on her lips, Mrs. Lecourbe, the former Miss Lecointre, moved on into the covered market.

A Traveler's Notebook

[*Reality was always only a springboard for Jacob's fertile imagination. Thus when the friend he is staying with at Naples goes to fetch letters, Jacob comes up with the fantastic image of Robinson Crusoe carrying on a secret correspondence with Andromeda, the connecting link being, apparently, nothing more than a rock by the seashore where letters were kept. This characteristic of Jacob the conversationalist: transmuting topics and words of daily reality into something more, is well conveyed in* Carnet de voyage *(written in 1925; first published in 1953). The work also brings out Jacob's distancing, or, as he variously called it, "Saturn's ring," "aura," or "margin"; that is, he does not describe from a personal point of view, despite his highly individual images, but as if the landscape and the people in it were floating in space the way figured landscapes do in Chinese paintings.*

In Jacob's Notebook *we do not find the exact chronological rendering of his journey, but rather an artistic rearrangement, based on his first impressions. In his many letters of 1925, he reiterated his love for Italy, more impressed by its people and by the atmosphere of the country than by the picturesque sights. One evening, when crossing Tuscany, in a golden twilight, he felt as if he were in Paradise. From that moment on he would recall throughout his life, pastoral, creative, tuneful Italy, a country bubbling with the vitality of affectionate people who are not afraid of displaying emotion.*

With Spain, however—despite an earlier enthusiasm for the dances of Catalonia, when he was there as Picasso's guest—he had no affinity. He found the Spanish withdrawn and as unsociable as their forbidding rocky landscapes. In Spain, he liked only the treasury of the Toledo Cathedral and the Prado, especially its collection of Bosch and Breughel the elder.]

Naples.

Arrival via a cable car that smelled of circus stable and was littered with paper. Red plush like in theaters.

The Vomero is a mixture of buildings and fallen rock the way Montmartre Hill used to be.[1] Only here the people in the bars are eating ice cream. Your typical café-bar is the same everywhere.

Italian gardens: more trees than flowers, and occasionally flowers in profusion. Italian streets: paving-stones; sometimes no sidewalk; shops, often in under carriage entrances. The other Italian cities: on the Parisian model. Naples, more on the model of Nice, and what a big city it is! A million inhabitants, and endless, featureless suburbs. I look around for the abject poverty you hear about; I find it, briefly, along the road to Pompeii, which is just a suburb. Naples: a dirty, tedious version of Nice! Needless to say, spacious house plus refreshments.

Pompeii seen in the flesh is quite like what we learned at school. The paintings come as a revelation. In the Naples Museum are the ancient equivalents of the finest sculptures, already showing Christian feeling, Christian emotion. All that's lacking is Christian fervor. I wished very much to see the Naples you read about in books, and I almost saw it: opening a door, I found a man getting into bed: "You've come to the wrong room; you're in the maid's room. And we're engaged to be married, you know." In this household, an honorable one I might add, you don't close your door, you put a chair in front of it. And there's a horrid German man-servant who asks whether you sleep by yourself.

Heat and commotion.

More about Naples.

J.G. goes and fetches letters from the hollow of a rock: you step through a little storybook door.[2] This "Cassetta," or hiding place, always makes me think of Robinson Crusoe carrying on a secret correspondence with Andromeda.

1. Vomero: a hilly district on the west side of Naples facing the sea.
2. J. G., Jacob's philosopher friend Jean Grenier (1898–1972), invited him to Naples where Grenier was teaching at the French Institute.

I'm not sending any letters. In Naples I don't have the peace and quiet [. . .]. On my table, the mysticism of Father Surin, as revealed to me by Father Bremond's book.[3] O Salutary Table! I take advantage of the fact that Jean Grenier is off at an old Neapolitan palace lecturing to young people who want to have a degree from the French Institute in Naples. All these young people, with their warm complexions, their luxuriant hair! These young people, filling entire trains and only this morning a whole huge church for a Fascist funeral—Fascists wherever you go—Fascist action programs on every Italian wall, Fascist celebrations, special Fascist offices in every government agency. I take advantage of the fact that Grenier is out lecturing, to get my hands on some writing paper and settle down in the Gambrinus. I could have used the Post Office, where they have a writing room for twenty centimes; the force of French habit: you write in cafés in France, not in Italy if I may judge from the reply, in French, of a *cameriere* who had generously given me a sheet of paper and an envelope: "You write them too long!" Today, the only person who might decide that the *cameriere* was right is the reader; my publisher didn't comment.

A city with almost no sidewalks, like Pompeii. In this climate they don't like sidewalks. The streets are no wider than the ones Vesuvius so easily filled. Walking through them, you're ready to swoon with dizziness from the cars reflecting sunlight in your eyes all day, the smells, the shouts, the hairy chests emerging from half-unbuttoned shirts. Naturally, all you people who stay in Naples's Boche-run hotels, complaining that the city is eluding you when you're making no effort to look for it, are secretly delighted to find yourselves with the same room attendants you remember from Cannes, and being unacquainted with Montmartre, you clap enthusiastically for the strolling singers doing "Santa Lucia"! Mont-

3. Max Jacob's mysticism is very like that of the Jesuit J.J. Surin (1600–1665), author of *A Spiritual Catechism*. Both believed an individual can be sometimes possessed by the devil, sometimes favored by grace. Both stress the concept of inner life, in which love and charity are goals and existence a chance to progress toward those goals. (Jacob's *Advice to a Young Poet* begins: "I shall open a school of inner life and write on the door: Art School.") Each thinker felt that he had achieved spiritual union with God, partly through nonverbal prayer called by Surin "ordinary contemplation" and by Jacob "orison." Henri Bremond (1865–1933) was the author of the *Histoire littéraire du sentiment religieux en France*, in eleven volumes. He describes Father Surin's mysticism in 5:148–310.

martre, too, can offer you Neapolitan melodies and the sea represented by the street lamps of Paris.

I note in passing the phosphorescent moths in the garden of a Sorrento hotel. Also the arrival in Sorrento, at ten o'clock, of a cardinal archbishop: the streets crowded with people under archways of electric lights, set up at ten-meter intervals. The procession, led by the municipal band; the Fascist children; hotel staff abandoning their posts to go see the cardinal. Next day, celebrations for the cardinal. In Italy, let it be said, everything is an occasion for a celebration. But to come back to Naples, or rather to Pompeii and the vast, inescapable dullness of the guide at Pompeii who speaks French the way you would speak Chinese if you had studied the ideographic alphabet. A visitor would enjoy the beauty of the wall paintings if he could just be spared the vast dreariness of everything else at Pompeii. I remember sitting comfortably at home reading Boissier's archaeological walks: I should have brought his book along and settled for the hovels of Ostia that you can see for 5 liras, out in the middle of a moor, past a turnstile which the casual visitor is surprised to find set up there, instead of spending 280 on lunch and on absurd handouts to beggars who are obviously filthy rich, to some Sisters of Charity, and to a crazy guide who never stopped talking and was so weary of repeating his line of patter that he stammered over it. "I show you! I show you Amalfi!" Let's admit it: better the train than a car with all those unending, flat, sickening residential areas where an occasional gap reveals only a milky-looking Bay. Better, too, in my opinion, the Castellamare end of the Bay, even with its factory workers and its crowded tram, than the vines of Posilipo and the Vomero where Lamartine's Graziella took refuge, which gives you the impression of a Paris suburb when the Paris suburb tries to look like a watering resort.

Incidentally, Virgil's tomb is impossible to locate, unknown to the local inhabitants with the exception of a scholar who informs you that the tomb is apocryphal. But if it doesn't exist, how can it be apocryphal? There's also Vesuvius, like a policeman's hat, no different from just any hill in the Apennines and not nearly as nice as all the mountains I've seen in the past month. "Vesuvius smoking his pipe," Cocteau said. That's right: an old reprobate who occasionally spits his contempt down onto the stupidity of Naples. Devoid of interest. I will not go up for a look. I've had enough disappointments. You mean to say you didn't go to see Vesuvius? —No. I was afraid it would be like everything else: it's beauties worn thin by constant admiration. —Yet you uttered ecstatic cries as you walked along up there, 400 meters above a lapis-lazuli bay. —There is no connection between cries forced out of you by those great heights, cries that are like the nauseous expression of your unutterable vertigo, and lasting admiration. Amalfi is definitely blue. Yes, there is enough vertigo going from Sorrento to Vetteri. The straight line produces quite a different sort of vertigo from that induced by the curved line.

I will admit that if what you're looking for is mountain-village-beside-the-sea, or above-the-sea, or halfway-up-from-the-sea, you couldn't hope for better than the region around Naples. And especially in my case, I didn't see the Naples region first, before I'd had time to become saturated with that particular kind of natural beauty. You get to Naples having already seen the lakes in the North, where villages have come tumbling down onto the shore to stand mirrored by the water in a peaceful atmosphere that has a charm of its own. "You prefer that Swiss type of thing, do you?" — No, I don't prefer anything. I'm just afraid that nature's more dramatic spectacles may have dried up the love I have for her humbler ones. I wonder if we can admire anything except what our hearts grew up with, and whether anything other than Brittany is capable of moving me. If anything can, it certainly won't be Naples, which is a copy of Nice; not Naples, and not its milky bay. If I really stop to think about it, I discover that the only thing that moved me was the faded frescoes I was shown under the scaffolding inside a church. The church is in the courtyard of the city hall, and since 1923 they have been tearing down the Renaissance walls that are just a stage setting over a Gothic church. Now it so happens that on this Gothic church are old frescoes, including at least one by Giotto: a strikingly rendered head of Saint Francis. You may also picture me as being stirred by mementos of Saint Thomas Aquinas. Here is the monastery where he lived, a building all aglow with sunlight. They show you the bell that used to summon him, and a portrait of Aquinas: stiff, sallow, cold, solemn, with the lackluster eyes of great contemplatives, and the antique crucifix that Christ told him about. Of course the whole chapel is cluttered; they've put famous paintings in it, and marble steps. But in this semidarkness, something of him remains. It's very moving: Giotto here and there beneath scaffolding! Especially after the bustle of the boat crossing.

—Like the justice of the peace being in the same house with the brothel.

Assisi.

No theater or movie house, no shops, and yet no feeling of being in "Bruges, City of the Dead." A few scattered photographers' shops, a few beggars, a few monks, and houses that somehow suggest fortresses. And the boulevard three meters off the ground. And the tunnels serving as vaulting, at the church decorated throughout with work by Giotto and Simone di Martini.

No Germans, few cars, and English people at mealtime only. One, a woman, has a domed forehead, hair coiled round her head and a liver ailment. I think she's the only person who has come here for the sake of the art. The others are here as pilgrims. She has a husband whom I mark down as a fool because he looks at me [. . . lacuna in text].

Criticalitaly.

How would you like to go for a car ride through some real countryside?

How would you like to sit outside at the Borgo and eat a *gelati*?

How would you like to have your picture taken standing in front of the Coleone dressed up as a tourist?

How would you like me to buy you a complete set of dishes in Siena earthenware?

How would you like to go up to Saint Peter's Cathedral again so you can exclaim "Bella vista! Bella vista!"

How would you like to hug the whole universe to your bosom so you can kiss it on the neck?

I would like nothing, nothing, I tell you! Just some frescoes on the ceiling, frescoes, freshly decorated frescoes entirely renovated and skillfully repainted!

Men differ from one another only in the things that separate them from God. Anything that brings them back to Him makes them alike. Love, piety, charity, are everywhere the same. Hatred, the ways of killing, stealing, doing wrong, these differ.

Siena.

To be sure, if what you want is ravines, shops in an old fortress, squares paved with flagstones, streets with no sidewalk, and a crowd of hatless young people, Italy offers nothing finer than Siena. From one slope of the ravine you can gaze across at the other. At the edges of the roofs, those chicken coops that I like, and, set in from the street under the houses, archways with staircases. All this, disposed amphitheater-fashion or some other way, with the black and white marble church on this side and the dark red brick one on the opposite side. Near the church, that town hall like the one in Bruges, with its Venetian windows that I saw on the hospital in Milan. In the town hall (Sweet Lord, these civil servants are lavishly housed! All that carpeted marble floor for His Worship the Mayor!), the mayor has a photo of Mussolini looking magnificent. The attendant waits to see how I will react: I say "Napoleone!" and he smiles, much pleased.

Around this fortress broader than it is high, a delightful public square, oval along its width, with irregularly shaped houses, the lower ones dominated by the taller ones behind, window-awnings, porticoes part way up the facades, and not a shop to be seen. Not a café, nothing! The streets running off the square are higher than the square itself, and have sudden turns making shadowy corners. Slopes lead down to this amphitheater which is so colorful, so aglitter with sunlight and at the same time so graceful.

Within all this, somber frescoes are hidden. The art of this region is sad; the figures don't have much character. Also to be seen here are many works by Il Sodoma, an overly ornate painter, literary like Botticelli and often distorted. Il Bronzino is quite successful at overcoming whatever tendency he may have had toward this same sort of bad taste. Many painters whose names I don't remember. One that does stick in my mind is San Pietro, with a fresco depicting Mercy, at the town hall.[4]

Siena is a more successful Florence, minus the masterpieces.

You don't really know what an Italian city is if you haven't seen Siena, or the Italian countryside if you haven't seen the plain lying between Siena and Pisa, with its flat-roofed, scattered farmhouses marked off by the commas of cypress trees in the distance, alternating with umbrella pines.

4. Sano di Pietro, properly Ansano di Pietro di Mencio (1406–81), was the head of the largest artists' workshop in Siena during the fifteenth century. The workshop produced altar pieces in a popular style.

[SPAIN]

[Madrid.][5]

Madrid, at night, is delightful, with all sorts of "Lapin-Agile's" and other Les Halles wine-cellar nightclubs. Conversation—here you're living in history, you're part of the story. People stay in the streets till late at night. They dine late, the theaters play till late, and you linger talking late after the play. The story goes on, and you're part of History!! There's a square like Place des Vosges but not as nice.

The Prado Museum, with a tiny little room full of sublime El Grecos. And Velasquez everywhere, that outwardly realist painter who makes you think he invented our French romanticism and V. H.[6] I prefer my naïve Titian, so naïvely amorous, and Tintoretto the Magnificent. The Prado really boils down to that: El Greco and Tintoretto. Goya is too nasty to be great, and too much a product of his period, when painters read Lavater and discovered how ridiculous the human face is.[7] Roubandson and Hogarth are from that period as well.

What a dreadful thing art criticism is. Painting is to be seen, not written about.

The houses are vast; they tend to be low and broad with big, low, rounded windows. Luxurious inside; bare walls and heavy, dark furniture; pictures few in number and of good quality.

Lunch with a gent who knows H. de Régnier and looks like him. He tries to write like Anatole France.

Today's big event is a visit to a laboratory: young doctors as fresh-faced as children, their egg-shaped heads bald or clean-shaven.

I discover that poor old Saint Anthony's Church is decorated with frescoes by Goya and that I hadn't noticed. To think that I was such a rotten *sulpicien*![8]

5. In 1926 Jacob was invited to Madrid to give a lecture at the Student Residence on his favorite topic, the symbolic representation of the Scriptures.

6. Victor Hugo.

7. Johann Kaspar Lavater (1741–1801), Swiss philosopher, poet, and Protestant theologian, was the founder of "physiognomy," a study of the correlation between facial characteristics and character traits.

8. Goya's frescoes in the Church of San Antonio de la Florida in Madrid deal, of course, with "the miracles of Saint Anthony." A *sulpicien* is a person capable

The Prado Museum.

Patinir the visionary. The best Breughels and Bosches. Collections amassed by the kings of Spain not out of a desire to instruct the multitudes as in the Louvre, but out of the love they had which was a sure guide. Berruguete, one of the best primitives who ever lived and whose name is virtually unknown; with some of the gifts of a humanist and all the gifts of a painter.

Italy, mother of all our accepted notions: all our notions about Roman antiquity, about Christianity, about art; Italy shaped our minds, and we apprehend Beauty through her and according to her canons; Spain is much further removed from us. To understand all this desolate grandeur, what was required was a century of romanticism when artists grow right up out of the boulders.

Madrid, city of mud, rain, and cold. These Spaniards know, as is said of them in France, that they are a nation of sun-people, so that they perish with cold beside their *braseros* or put horse-blankets around their heads. —The city of mud.

Definition of an express train: one that grinds to a halt at every stop, station, or resting place and also, if necessary, whenever people wave at it from a road, so that nothing could be more boring than these luxury coaches built for speed, painfully inching their way through the mountains; the contrast between these comfortable armchair seats and the mountain wilderness is just ridiculous. You're too much like a spectator.

Some of the mountains are square at the top; others have a fortress. At Burgos the church is down in the valley; what you see are square or pointed towers, more like elongated prawns than lobsters. The rivers don't flow between clearly defined banks; they're narrow and not very deep. My sleeping-car companion washes and dresses with great care: at Burgos, a woman boards the train—fair-haired, very mild-mannered, apparently a relative. They launch into explanations of letters that never arrived, and telegrams, and their whole life story.

[. . .] Sheep and low walls on russet hills, as in Brittany. Forests of umbrella pines, with their disproportions. Along the road,

---

of appreciating religious art that is in bad taste, such as is sold in shops around Saint-Sulpice Church in Paris. Jacob ironically reproaches himself for not having noticed the Goyas which, for him, are likewise in bad taste.

people on horseback wrapped in blankets, mules laden with baskets. Madrid and its Beggars are far away; here, mountain folk, things picturesque.

[Toledo.]

Toledo is essential Gothic, the ochre rushes that come right down into the valley, the buildings with their monastery look— that's the feel of the place. Rockery style! The inner streets are those of southern France, and how snugly the houses are fitted one to the next; the pavement is like what you find in the small towns of Provence rather than the handsome pavement of Italy. The gutter running down the middle of the smaller streets, and the peaceful public squares. A winding promenade on the slope of the mountain at the place where Toledo is. The market square is an assemblage of little painted houses, each with a balcony and all pressed against one another. The windows are squarer than in France, with white paneling round them, and the ochre begs to be rendered by a painter.

The pastry is excellent. Let us not talk about painting, but instead remember Toledo for its cathedral and for the diamonds on the priestly chasubles. Wrought-iron reliquaries that are genuine masterpieces, painted chasubles, such laces as I have never seen. Apparently none of this has been catalogued, so that things can be either stolen or sold. But it's well guarded: you can't move an inch without the room being full of priests, policemen, etc. They have entire rooms just for their reliquaries.

Every foot of the church is sculpted and carved; French altar screens, the like of which we don't have in France or in Flanders. After the miniatures come huge heavy sculptures on the walls, for example the one of Saint James on horseback surrounded by immense scallop shells.

Spain is a succession of mountains and endless plains. In the eye of the beholder, the two exist without reference to one another.

Four Meditations

[*From Saint-Benoît-sur-Loire, Max Jacob dispatched a meditation every day to his friends. He usually meditated at 6:00 a.m. in an unheated room, on an empty stomach, before serving Mass in the icy basilica. Although this regimen was not good for his lungs, it is typical of those seeking a mystic vision. North American Indians, too, fasted and subjected themselves to cold in the hope of attaining a mystic vision. Sometimes Jacob wrote his meditation after Mass or during the day. Meditating was an integral part of his way of life and his daily schedule. After Mass, he wrote eight or more letters to friends, worked on his poems and gouaches, and in the afternoon he meditated in the basilica at the Stations of the Cross and participated in evening common prayers. All these activities of his waking day served one purpose: to enrich and intensify his inner life, a goal toward which steady progress could be observed daily.*

The main model for his meditations was the Introduction to the Devout Life *by Saint Francis of Sales and to a lesser degree Loyola's* Spiritual Exercises. *However, he deviated from the pattern of Saint Francis of Sales which was rather impersonal and from his own sets of rules which followed the saint's model, because he was unable to be impersonal. He threw himself, body and soul, into everything he did and also felt that any set pattern intended to govern writing quickly becomes a straitjacket.*

When Max Jacob was meditating, he felt himself in touch with God; so much so, that we often have the feeling he is chatting with an old acquaintance. He kept in mind also the edification, conversion, or individual needs of the person who was to receive each day's meditation. Sometimes he wanted to strengthen the morale of a soldier friend at the front; sometimes a friend needed a pledge of affection or consolation in sickness. René Plantier, who wrote an enlightening introduction to sixty-two of the meditations (Gallimard, 1972), states that Jacob wanted to open a school for inner life and offered his meditations as correspondence courses.

He wrote thousands of meditations. The four included here are from Méditations religieuses *(1947),* Méditations *(1972), and* Max Jacob l'universel *(by J. Pérard, Editions Alsatia, 1974). Collectively, the meditations deal with great questions of life and death: Paradise and Hell and the choice between them, human solitude, virtue and sin, pagans and Christians, the Last Judgment, the excellence of the spirit, the blessings of God. Sometimes he meditated on the Scripture or the Epistle of the day.*

In spite of the conventional topics, the many clichés, and his effort to avoid poetic invention or literary embellishments in his meditations, the poet's hand, the painter's eye, the outpouring of his inner thoughts, his joy and love of life, his preoccupations of the moment and the daily events of his life endow these texts with the warmth of Max Jacob's unique presence.]

◆

Blessings of God   7:15 A.M.
(a Meditation)

Come out from among them.—2 Corinthians 7.17

Come out from among them if you want God's blessings for God does not go among the devils and He does not hear the prayers of the devils but He hears the prayer of the person who is in a state of grace.[1] Was it when you were with the Devil that He came to seek you out, or because you had in mind a noble purpose?[2] And did not that noble purpose enable you to achieve the selflessness and compassion of the life you lived in those days? Is it not true that His abandoning you dates from the day when you were overcome by the desire for riches? Isn't the successful man the one He has abandoned to every sort of temptation? And alas, see what a sanctimonious hypocrite, what a Tartufe you have become where once you had been a poor child in search of truths and beauties![3] The

1. The biblical references in the first two paragraphs are all based on 2 Corinthians: (1) "Come out ..." is from 6.17, not 7.17 as Jacob indicates; (2) "I will live in them ..." is from 6.16; (3) "I have great confidence ..." is from 7.4 but the Bible reads "our affliction," not "your"; (4) "God who comforts ..." is from 7.6; (5) "The grief that he leaves ..." is inspired by 7.10 "For godly grief produces a repentance that leads to salvation and brings no regret."

2. This is a reference to Jacob's mystical experience: see the five consecutive pieces of the "Revelation" cycle (*In Defense of Tartufe*).

3. See *In Defense of Tartufe*.

only good elements in your productions are what remains from your days of innocence. As soon as you were sold to the publishers and art dealers your soul began to decay.[4] So I repeat with Saint Paul to the Corinthians, come out from among them. "I will live in them and move among them, and I will be their God, and they shall be my people." God is among us and in us if we want Him to be, and we do want Him to be. So let us seek grace for it is with grace that our prayers shall be granted.

God is among us and in us! He is in us in the Host and in our stomachs.[5] He is in our ears and our inward eyes. He speaks to us and we try to answer Him in spite of our dumb stupidity. "I have great confidence in you; I have great pride in you; I am filled with comfort. With all your affliction, I am overjoyed." It is a fact that God is a comfort to me. I arrive at church full of black bile, rheumatism, heartburn, and instantly I am restored to health, cheerfulness, self-control. "God who comforts the downcast," says Saint Paul. He does not comfort them with false assurances, vague hopes, encouraging words—but he cures them of their physical ills, their anxieties, their needless worries. The grief that He leaves us does not lead to death, says Saint Paul. I have known that other grief, the grief of despondency, of discouragement: the eagerness, the apologies, the indignation, fear, desire, zeal, punishment, the grief left by God leads to repentance, to salvation; this is repentance which we never repent.

God's blessings! It would take a dictionary, for everything you

4. After his first stay at Saint-Benoît, 1921–28, the poet returned to Paris where he stayed till 1936, after which time he returned permanently to Saint-Benoît. These eight years were the most successful of his life. His books were published, his drawings and gouaches exhibited and sold, and he held a "court" in his Nollet Street hotel, where admiring young poets, artists, and musicians crowded around him. From his retreat in Saint-Benoît, he considered these years as the most "criminal" of his life, because he yielded both to the homosexual temptations of his nature and the lure of money and fame.

5. In prose and verse, Max Jacob extolled the miraculous healing power of the "cake of love" without which his lips were "starving." "The Host listens to our desires," he claimed, "it watches over us." When he had a quarrel with the Princess Ghika, he excused himself by saying he had warned the princess that if he missed his daily Communion the Devil had the upper hand with him. He needed the Host not only as the promise of eternal life, but also to feel morally and physically fit. When Cocteau complained that he prescribed the Host as an aspirin, Jacob answered that "the Host must be taken like an aspirin" (Jean Cocteau, *Professional Secrets*, Farrar, Strauss & Giroux, 1970, p. 109).

have comes from Him: that sun rising over the houses in the morning and casting its rays through that window is the Creator's ingenious contrivance. The trees I see from my window, that foun-
tain with its water rising up, the water itself!—everything is the
work of the Creator. That friend who comes to make sure I'm all
right and looks out for my interests, that other friend I'm expecting tomorrow.[6] All these, God, are your work! What ingratitude
is mine! Ought I not to spend my time thanking so bountiful and
generous a God? Especially when I consider my past and see His
hand at every turning point in my life. You have suffered a great
deal, I hear someone say.

Have I not learned the usefulness of pain and suffering? Do I
not know from experience that only suffering makes us tractable
and humane? A little while ago I wrote to a poet who complains of
the demands made by a particular profession, to say that my painful professions are what equipped me for living and that I owe what
little I have done to my painful contacts with other people. Was it
not illness that taught me compassion, for we understand only that
which we have experienced? Praise be to God for the painful times
in my life! I have learned nothing from my joys and on the contrary have retained everything derived from my sufferings. That is
why God said to Adam as one who bestows not a punishment but a
gift: "In the sweat of your face shall you eat bread; in pain you shall
bring forth children!" The serpent (that is, matter, earthly force)
shall bruise your heel, shall bruise your soul (your wife) in its foot
(that is, in your divine religious instincts) and your wife, your soul,
shall crush it (that is, she shall triumph over nature. The spirit tri-
umphs over suffering).[7] Suffering is the most excellent gift of God
for it is in suffering that we rediscover ourselves. If we want to seek
God, the place to find Him is in the inmost depths, the remotest
crevices of our own selves. I thank you, God, for your presence in
my life and even more for giving me a way to find you when I have
lost you. Grace is a most excellent blessing; it uplifts me, purifies

6. This is a reference to the young painter from Orleans, Roger Toulouse,
and the young poet from Montargis, Marcel Béalu, both of whom lived just a
few kilometers away and who were Jacob's most faithful friends during his last
years at Saint-Benoît. See *Letters from Max Jacob to Marcel Béalu*, introduction and
note 17. (Another Montargis friend, Dr. Robert Szigeti, died in 1990.)

7. Fascinated by hidden meanings, Jacob loved to offer symbolic inter-

me, makes me worthy to be a man. What folly to throw it away in a moment of giddiness.

◆

Paradise 7:10 A.M.
(a Meditation)

Dying doesn't mean death, it means life. Let us take ourselves firmly in hand! Let us know ourselves, so that being known to ourselves we may amend ourselves and, being perfect, we may come at last through faith to Paradise. There is no lack of models to guide us; men of charitable heart abound, compared to whom I am but a base and spineless creature. Paradise is grace revealed, grace indelible: grace is compatible with earthly life, but merely colors it. Here on earth grace passes back and forth like the dice with which the soldiers mock the Lord whom they have fleeced by stripping Him of His tunic. Grace in Paradise spreads outward and cannot be taken away again: grace hovers and is transmitted from one to the next. Even as from ancient holy relics grace yet emanates, so it emanates from the wondrous objects in Paradise and no doubt from the animals there; then imagine how it must be with the chosen! The saints on earth cause those who visit them to weep, so truly does life flow outward from one to the other. Grace in Paradise abounds, you breathe it in; a buxom thing, no longer the skinny creature we see amongst us here. In my Father's house are many mansions, saith the Scripture; are there levels of grace still in Paradise? Grace is regal in direct encounters with God who raises up the great saints in a melodious act of levitation! Grace is unassuming with the others and is in proportion to the deserving we have acquired during our wretched earthly existence.

---

pretations of Scripture, though not often, as here, in the *Meditations*: these were intended rather to bring Christ into the writer's daily experience.

The serpent (matter) stands in many religions for the obscure forces of life; Jacob added a dynamic "mechanism" in which the coiled serpent is a diagram of the universe's primeval centrifugal whirling. The foot in Jacob's "religious anatomy" is associated with the zodiacal sign of the Fish, and symbolizes divine intelligence. The presentation of woman as the soul of man, in this context, turns God's malediction of His creature into a prophecy that the Christian shall subdue matter.

What we desired in our youth, we have in our mature years, says Goethe. What we desired in our mature years, we have after death. If we have desired orisons, we shall have ecstasy. If we have desired understanding we shall have it for the least of beings in Paradise is greater than John the Baptist, greatest of men. I have plenty of examples of this, having received intimations in my dreams as I lie asleep at night. With the angel, in the vision I had, was a landscape which I lovingly drew![1] And my sister in a Breton setting with the music that she loved and my aunt beneath the trees at one of those country feasts she used to love. I have enjoyed the company of great minds, and been inspired to achieve beauty. So perhaps in Paradise I would be able to paint masterpieces and write paradisiacal poems. That is how I imagine Paradise. Perhaps I would definitely get life into the landscapes of my native Brittany of bygone days or into my Piranesi buildings.[2] Perhaps, with the new senses born of new light and celestial flesh, I would see other colors, hear other sounds, smell other fragrances. In any case, since death does not exist in Paradise, there will be neither waste nor dust nor rubbish, but order, cleanliness, harmony: thought shall be unhampered, for tiredness is a lesser form of death. Paradise is untiring.

I long for Paradise. That longing is what caused me to come here in 1936, renouncing the worldly pleasures I was lost in, and no doubt renouncing life's vanities as well (am I being quite honest?). That longing is what impels me to acts of kindness, patience, charity, impels me to resist temptations as best I can, to get up in the cold instead of waiting for morning to bring me restorative sleep after my wakeful nights, impels me to try and bring peace to my surroundings.

1. Jacob was convinced he had seen Christ himself on the wall of his wretched room, and his book *In Defense of Tartufe* describes this vision; but when theologians pointed out to him that he could not possibly have seen Him, as no mortal had seen Christ since His Ascension, he referred to the apparition as an "angel."

2. Subjects treated by Jacob in his paintings. Piranesi (1720–78) established a classical style of architecture.

◆

We Are Each Alone
(a Meditation)

a quarter of an hour

We talk to each other! We do business together! We love each other! We hate each other! We fear each other! We show trust! We share our joys, our sorrows! We sympathize! We sit next to each other, eating and drinking! We call each other friends, enemies, wife and spouse, father and children, but we don't really know each other. We have all had the experience of seeing someone we know behave in a way that surprised us. Someone who was generally held to be a heartless brute, suddenly in a particular situation reveals greatness of heart and perfection of soul, and conversely behold yon hypocrite unmasked. Just before she died, my mother said something that showed she considered me a hard-hearted man, when in fact my whole life has consisted of feelings and affections. Either that, or the person who doesn't know what I am really like is *me*. "I would never have thought you could be so nice!" was what the dying woman said.[1] But even supposing I am hard-hearted, being nice is the very essence of my nature. Perhaps the word itself was ill-chosen and was meant to include kindness of heart? Kind I am not, but nice in the social sense I very basically am: in all probability the poor dead woman didn't know me, and I am convinced that divorces—marriages, too, for that matter—result from people not knowing one another's true nature. When children are badly brought up, it's because their parents don't really know them: what is going on in those young minds, so intimidated by their teachers that they dare not confess what they are thinking? Especially at the

1. We know from Jacob's letters that on her deathbed his mother felt very bitter about the widow Gagelin, in whom she recognized herself. The ficticious character had a birthdate identical to hers and appeared in her son's *Mirror of Astrology* as a self-centered, superficial, ruthless, stubborn, avaricious, cold, haughty woman of an earthbound nature. Her son tried to explain to her the difference between fiction and reality in the creative process, but she seems to have been unable to forgive him and thus left him with a legacy of remorse. See also "The Maid," note 3.

age of puberty. But after all, isn't it a fact that we don't know our-selves, let alone know others? Our conscious minds are not even subject to supervision; our unconscious and our conscious selves live in unhappy cohabitation and we are left more than alone. Man acts without even knowing how or why he acts. This is more than solitude, since it can even be claimed that there is no personality. There is no "I." There is a composite that knows not itself nor yet others. I seek in vain for a word that might denote this more-than-solitude which is not nonexistence but rather total absence of knowledge and which is not total indifference either. Chasm? Dark-ness? No, for we have words to denote this chasm, that darkness. What do we know, other than these words? Man is not alone, he is *more* than alone, he is a world that doesn't know itself and does not even realize it doesn't know itself, or realizes it but doesn't know itself any the better for that. He tries to shed light on his past and the past escapes him: I cannot reconstruct what happened yester-day and here I am trying to reconstruct whole centuries, using the imaginings, legends, or reports of falsified memoirs, police reports that are altered, inaccurate, or forged; we gather up old bricks and we know that on this spot there was a palace, a city, a civilization; we hear an old expression from the previous generation, an old joke, and we become aware that the words don't have the same meaning any more and that today we wouldn't understand our grandfather or even our father. What hope have we of understanding the past? Let us by all means be grateful to those men of genius who render unto man the eternal truth about himself, but let us have no illu-sions about how eternal it is: our notions about the masterpieces of yesterday are mighty ridiculous; three-quarters of Homer is apoc-ryphal. Shakespeare is translated with shades of meaning that vary with the changing eras. Jouve and Pitoëff make him speak one way, François V. Hugo or Bitaubé another.[2] An unknown, that's what man is! An unknown!

But whereas everything involving memory, imagination, or meaning eludes the grasp of certainty, anything connected with

2. Pierre-Jean Jouve (1887–1976), poet and novelist, translated Shakespeare and Hölderlin into French. Georges Pitoëff (1884–1939), actor and producer of Russian origin, gave a memorable performance of Hamlet. J. F.V. Hugo, son of Victor Hugo, translated Shakespeare. Paul Bitaubé (1732–1808) was known for his translations of Homer, Goethe, and, assuming Jacob is right, Shakespeare.

faith is, on the contrary, sure and certain. I am not sure of my own personality, but I am sure of God's. I am not sure of my own mind and spirit, but I am sure of the existence of the Spirit and the existence of Spirits. I think, therefore I am. Wrong! I think, therefore thought exists and that's all! The "I" might well be a "we." The "I" is a hypothesis. Thus it may well be that there are a number of us engaged in thinking, in fact it's a certainty. The spirits and I think, or the spirits think and we are affected by it. "We, I." I think, therefore God exists. Because I am certain of this, my faith is sure. If the only thing I'm sure of is God, I should concern myself solely with Him and care little for the opinions of men, not aspiring to please them nor fearing to displease them; nothing will happen except what God allows. So work with a view to pleasing God, lead your life not for money or the gratification of your vanity, but for God and the love of God. Pray more, and pray harder. I give thanks!

◆

Simon of Cyrene
(a Meditation)

Another man carrying a wooden beam bigger than himself.[1] Another man putting his trust in something other than himself. God came for those unready to carry the wooden beam. You can see I am carrying it as I follow behind you along the road of life. It was for people like me that you came down on earth. I am Simon of Cyrene. I know I have displeased the Lord in every way: He put me under the wooden beam and I don't know what is going to happen to me. I am the dead wood and I am carrying the dead wood and where is the wood being taken? I have looked at myself from every angle and seen nothing but weakness, illness, helplessness, foolishness, and sin. In theory humility is quite straightforward; in daily

---

1. Simon of Cyrene appears as a symbol in numerous meditations of Max Jacob, in his "Stations of the Cross," in poems and letters, whenever he deals with the concept and purpose of suffering. He finds endless interlocking answers to the question of why Simon is chosen to take over the burden of the cross: Simon *is* humankind, at once earth and sun, essence of compassion, reluctant humanity prodded into the "Imitation of Christ."

practice it is terribly difficult. What must I do to carry the cross of the Lord as it should be carried? See how I carry the cross and give way beneath the abuse and collapse into the mud of my life. No strength! No strength in me any more, and the strength to weep has been taken from me too and the strength to complain. Here beneath the beam I have nothing to say; I can only hold my tongue because I deserve even worse. We are moving along toward Judgment Day, that's where we're headed, and I shall get there eaten away by worms like this wood. I entreat you to deliver me from temptations and from everything that is oppressing me including human malice, my own and that which I endure. I am susceptible, preyed upon, perhaps because I have strayed from you.

I offer you, God, the weight of what I am enduring; in offering it I rend myself asunder, and humbly I submit.

Humanity, in the person of Simon, follows along behind the Lord. If we do not follow the Lord when we are suffering, do our sufferings count toward salvation?[2] We ought not to complain but rather offer Him our sorrows, and yet we see that the sons of Simon were rewarded by Him, for Alexander and Rufus received the glory of being martyred. So our sufferings count even when not offered up, for Simon did not want to suffer or to help the Lord. Who can say what he might have become had he offered these things up? A great saint. Let us try to offer up our sufferings for our salvation. Lord, I offer you those few cares which I have: my money problems and what remains of my uncertain health. Give me as well the strength to resist the many temptations and to hate whatever is not chaste or sober, mild or meek. In the name of Simon of Cyrene, I ask to be allowed to suffer as I follow the Lord. Give me back the vigor of my striving toward you, which marked the first days following my conversion. Suffering, we follow you. How I should like all those people out there to follow after you as I do, suffering along the way! Oh, had I but the strength of an apostle!

2. See *The Artist Introduces Himself*, note 2.

Letters from Max Jacob
to Marcel Béalu

[*The correspondence with Marcel Béalu (1908–) is a typical example of how Max Jacob, a born teacher, encouraged young poets and taught them not only his poetic art, but also how to be themselves. Béalu, who later became famous for his poems of dreams and the subconscious, claims it was Jacob who revealed to him that poetry is inconceivable without a grain of folly. Their friendship started when Béalu, a young hatter from Montargis, sent his poems to Jacob who responded warmly as he had to many other aspiring poets seeking his advice. Béalu traced an excellent physical portrait and character analysis of his friend in the book* Dernier visage de Max Jacob *(Fanlac, 1946). Béalu's prose portrait was republished with 212 letters from Jacob to Béalu in the volume* Max Jacob—Lettres à Marcel Béalu—précédées de Dernier visage de Max Jacob *(Vitte, 1959). The letters given here are from Béalu's book and were written by Jacob between 1937 and 1942.*

One fragment, dated July 8, 1937, has been included because of its reference to the Kabala, a subject that intrigued Jacob all his life, comes up repeatedly in his correspondence, and influenced his poetry. Kabbalah in Hebrew means "the received lore," referring to the mystic origin of this esoteric doctrine about God and the universe, disclosed as revelation in a remote past to a select group of the initiated. Neoplatonic, Neopythagorean, and Stoic philosophy added a speculative turn to the ancient oral tradition of Kabala when it was described in the sacred book of the Zohar *in Spain in the thirteenth century. It attempted to reconcile universal reason with mysticism, giving a symbolic interpretation to the letters, words, and contents of the Bible. The* Zohar *represents the universe as consisting of interlinked concentric spheres, enveloping one another, the lower world*]

213

having its model in the next higher world, forming an onionlike, unified, overlapping whole. The Kabalistic universe consisted of a gradation of both positive and negative emanations in which human beings could turn to evil by plunging into the finite, material world, and to good by uniting with the divine, primal source. Intense meditation, prayer, and a vivid imagination placed the Kabalist in direct contact with the divine, not with the help of intelligence, but through the Kabalist's spiritual, moral nature thus purified.

The reading of the Zohar, *in French translation, had an immediate and lasting impact on Jacob. (1) It appealed to his Faustian nature and desire to unravel the secrets of the universe by illumination. (2) The metaphysical dimension satisfied his speculative side. Was he not called the Jewish Pascal? (3) As a poet and creator of myths he found inspiration in its rich symbolism. (4) The twenty-two letters of the Hebrew alphabet, constituting the form of God's creation in the Kabala, struck a chord in his soul. He believed that the word has a magic power to express the inexpressible in poetry. (5) He strove to grasp the hidden meaning of the Scriptures, believing like the Kabalists that all visible, exoteric phenomena contain a mystical, esoteric reality, enlightening human beings concerning the invisible. (6) The* Zohar *assigns the first place in religion to the imagination and the emotion of faith. This choice harmonized both with Jacob's religious feelings and his poetic practice. (7) The Kabalistic doctrine of the heavenly alphabet legitimized astrology, so dear to Jacob's heart. (8) Both the Kabalists and Jacob saw intelligence and ideas in terms of a creative process. His ambition was to reconcile the Kabala with his religion. This is not as far-fetched as it sounds because the Kabala contains several Christian ideas, among others the Fall and Redemption of humankind and the doctrine of the Trinity.*

In spite of this multiple appeal, Kabalistic mysticism was just one *source of Jacob's inspiratin, serving merely as a springboard to his own poetic imagination.*]

◆

My dear Marcel,

I would like to see you again . . . the sooner the better.

Your poetry has such conviction, such depth of emotion, that it makes me weep. But rather than send you four pages filled with compliments, sincere though these would be, I wonder if I don't have a duty to perform here.

You have the gift. The most precious gift of all—believe me, it's

almost the only gift that matters, and quite rare: *amplitude of diction.*
This can take a poet a long way, a very long way. It was the gift that
Victor Hugo had. A gift, the most precious of gifts; the question is,
how are you going to use it?

Are you going to go on admiring our traditional French poetry
of the nineteenth century, as you have every right to do? Or will
you join me in thinking that the only way you can win fame and
glory is by bringing to art a totally new voice, a new personality
and approach? According to me, there are two ways to go about it.
Either you ponder aesthetics and decide what is beautiful for all
people or at any rate for you, and how one achieves Beauty—and
indeed it would be most unusual if having chosen an ideal you did
not come upon a shortcut by which to reach it, the short-cut being
your own personality of which I was just speaking . . .

Either that, or you set out to find "your pearl," by going down
even further into the deepest depths of your own personal "Well
of Truth." This true self of yours is what the readers want. They're
a bunch of cannibals, and just as God wants your *true self* and not
the obstructions that hide it, so your readers are hungry for the
real *you* and not for things that remind them of other poets. The
readers do not want—*and it is the readers who decide which are the
real poets*—do not want little everyday jolts and yelps, they want
the genuine cry wrenched from the entrails of the genuine you.
They want a pearl of unique luster and that pearl is down inside
you. We're talking about emotion, and that is the essential thing, but
emotion deeper than the next man's, the kind that comes not from
your senses or your nerve-endings but from the ultimate discovery
of what is uniquely human in you. And oddly enough, this human
quality, this pearl that has to be uncovered, is the very image of
Our Lord Jesus Christ. When you have understood this, you'll have
taken a great step forward. Ideally you should never write anything
without using "the stuff of God's Heaven which I explained to you
when we were out driving yesterday," even if your subject is a vulgar chamber-pot. But you'll tell me that in the same breath I talk
of going down deep inside yourself and the stuff of Heaven, and
what's the connection? I won't explain! It's a fact based on experience, and when you've grasped it you'll have succeeded where I
have not. And what a beautiful voice the Spirit will find in you that
day, with which to speak to all men!

Lyricism! If it were just a case of love or sorrow, there would be no difference between one poet and the next: obviously feeling is the basic component of all art, but so is style the "basic component." Style is the molding of word and sentence to fit the emotion—the more perfect the fit, the more nakedly the emotion stands out and the more moving will be your poem. The word has to bear directly on the emotion! Syntax (or sentence structure) has to be direct as well. So we must somehow fashion lyrical man if we want to achieve lyrical expression. *Lyricism is a convergent flow or surge;* the passages you admire in Rimbaud or Verlaine, who are lyrical writers, are the ones marking such a flow or surge. Apollinaire had lines that surge, stanzas that surge; people try to ape them by being stupidly or deliberately obscure, and it doesn't come off. A surge of emotion producing harmonious verse is a very rare thing; you have to have been born with the ability. A lifetime spent in pursuit of a "lyrical sense" will get you nowhere.

If you want to be the great poet it is in you to become, think about what is entailed, suffer much and on many counts, reflect on all things, be as an aeolian harp and be wary of trivial, skin-deep sensations. Send everything deep down inside to search out that secret little inner pearl which is at once Our Lord Jesus Christ and your self.[1]

poor Max
Saint-Benoît, April 13, 1937

I expect you already know all this, but I cannot guess how far your knowledge extends or where it stops; forgive me my commonplace utterances if by any chance some word of mine has made you pause and reflect!

*　*　*

Don't expect a point-by-point critical analysis of your poems; I'm not a good critic. As for my aesthetic theory (if, as I humbly believe, I am an aesthetic theorist), it has varied with the varying ages and stages of my life and I've lost the nerve to make positive statements. I think you have *fully* understood what form modern poetry must take, but I would like you to go one better: I would like you to create YOUR form of modern poetry. I told you in my letter what my ideas are on that score: (l) scraping away at yourself until you get

1. The Kabala expresses the same idea when it places the pearl, symbolizing God, in the luminous center of the celestial spheres.

down to the basic you; (2) thinking about what constitutes beauty, and the implications of this for the poet. On these matters I still haven't had your response.

Almost the only thing I still like nowadays is this process of scraping away. No more stylistic gewgaws. Tear yourself in half or else take the finished poem and tear that in half. [. . .]

When I write and tell you something, you can assume it's the fruit of much reflection, so stop and think about what I've said. I can't turn it into a hundred-page essay. Read my letters carefully.

If you don't understand what I'm getting at, say so, and I'll explain; that's my job.

                                                        April 15, 1937
                        *   *   *

It's always been said of me that I don't take life seriously, whereas in fact there's not one of them who is capable of cutting himself off from his past, as I have done three times in the course of my life, and accepting martyrdom and poverty the way I have done, THE WAY I AM DOING! Yes, they treat life seriously, all of them, but not in the same sense.

. . . I shall talk to you SERIOUSLY about your poetry!

                                                        April 16, 1937
                        *   *   *

Everyone or each one is alone.[2] I was hoping that you felt you were just a bit less alone than others because I was there trying to understand you. On Sundays it's impossible "not to be alone," because there are always people, which is why I'd been asking you to come after you'd closed up for the night. But we're too poor, you and I, to invite each other over: I live on a tiny income of 700 francs and budget-balancing expedients which perhaps you have some notion of. I don't suppose you're rolling in money either. [. . .]

                                                        April 20, 1937
                        *   *   *

I think I can safely tell you to avoid facile satire: satire blinds the way pride blinds. You don't get very far on the strength of having said: "Those idiots! Those middle-class philistines!" and so on, with variations. Take it for granted that everyone is quite perfect; it's very salutary to start from that lofty general assumption and

---

2. See the meditation "We Are Each Alone."

then gradually lower the *individual sphere* by finding little blemishes in it. This in contrast to what writers have been doing for the last hundred years, which is to start from the assumption that everyone is bad. Great works of literature are premised on optimism. Since the nineteenth century there have been no great works, because of Flaubert and his stupid pessimism. Balzac was inclined to see genius everywhere, and so he was optimistic: although he is not an artist, his work is great on account of its optimism. Think about that.

You must realize that everything in art comes down to a question of accenting and relief. Repeat this, believe it, put it into practice, get those around you to say it back to you. Express yourself to others. [. . .]

Quimper, June 10, 1937

* * *

Seek out every opportunity, my dear Marcel, to listen to your fellow writers, answer them and so on. . . . Rub shoulders with other writers as much as you can. I don't think the Closerie des Lilas still exists as a gathering place, but Paul Fort is one poet who knows what he's doing.[3] He's a decent, kindly man, who will be good for you in every way: what I mean is, he will steady you, sweeten your disposition, give you the optimism without which there can be no great works of literature, no all-encompassing works. In his orbit you will hear other people and what they have to say; admittedly, you'll hear a certain amount of foolishness, but some kinds of foolishness are good for you: you'll hear discussions about art, and art is what you stand most in need of. Probably people will tell you a lot of bad things about me, but I don't matter; what matters is you. You can't continue living on the essence of what constitutes your own character, particularly as that essence is as yet incomplete. And that's the whole point! In order to complete it, you need to come up against other people, young people. The Café de Flore, Lipp's, Les Deux-Magots across from Saint-Germain-des-Prés, are cafés frequented by literary people. If you're prepared to follow this advice, I could find you the entrée; I'll send you to Mr. This, That or

3. Paul Fort (1872–1960), Symbolist playwright and author of fifty volumes of poetry, was called the "Prince of Poets." A native of Champagne, he celebrated, in the forty volumes of his *French Ballads* and *Chronicle of France*, the natural beauties, folklore, legends, and traditions of central France. Max Jacob appreciated the simplicity and clarity of his poetry.

the Other, who will show you off to the crowd. For I do consider it necessary that other people should see your face and you theirs— though the process were to cost me your good opinion and, beyond that, your friendship (yes, yes, I know what your answer to that will be—but I also know what I know . . .). —If the seed die not—Perhaps I may be (in your case) the seed, as I have been for others, etc. . . .

The great thing is to be yourself.[4] If only you could find a way to be yourself and not something else! The *great danger* for you in life will consist of being too clever, whereas art is guileless. When you are able to put aside whatever is not guileless, you will be a great writer. Think about that! To become as one without guile is the ultimate feat of skill, but you haven't yet reached the stage where you can understand that. The ultimate feat of skill is an unbroken expanse of white with no taint of falsehood. [. . .]

M.J.

Quimper, June 13, 1937

*   *   *

No, I shall not leave Saint-Benoît! I will have you know that this town is a harsh penance for me, apart from the dear, delightful proximity of Montargis, but it is only right that I should do harsh penance on account of the sins that weigh so heavily upon my life.[5] Here, by a sea sparkling in the sun, with children's faces visible here and there on the stretches of lawn, in this very orderly, very Catholic, very intelligent environment, the harshness of my usual routine is brought home to me. I am not entitled to great Happiness, having filched too many bits and pieces of lesser happiness. My great Happiness will be the one my death brings me, provided that before then—by deepening my sensitivity, which means getting my brain to go down into my solar plexus—I manage to become worthy of the fate of humankind. I'm just a sheepskin, that is to say, a diploma. (They're on parchment.)

Lorient, at Dr Benoiste's, June 1937

4. From the beginning to the end of his career, Jacob consistently taught the art of being oneself. He categorically refused to make other, younger poets into little Max Jacobs and tirelessly encouraged and helped his young friends to find their own voices and the means of expressing their inner lives.

5. Saint-Benoît and Montargis. See *Meditations*, "Blessings of God," note 6.

* * *

I have devoted vast amounts of time to the study of Kabala, from which I stood to learn a great deal. It's a system of metaphysics, the only metaphysic and, so I believe, the basis of all religions. We'll speak of it again. [. . .]

Kerpape, July 8, 1937

* * *

The joy of reading your letter. Each new poem marks further progress. Consider "words." I hope you haven't forgotten what Tauler wrote: "Live the present minute and not the previous one or the next one."[6] If you apply this method you will deepen your awareness; thus will you acquire *the word*, which is simply a deepened awareness. Try to establish the atmosphere of the poem, that's the key thing; try to convey an impression: for example the impression of velvet, or of damp, or of the supernatural, or whatever it may be . . . , all this by means of words, by means of the word. Very important.

I'll be in Saint-Benoît early in the week. I'll phone immediately upon my arrival.

M.J.

Quimper, July 21, 1937

* * *

Every biography has its particular adventure. Verlaine has the horns of the faun, Bloy the whip of Christ driving the Pharisees and others out of the temple, Ronsard has King Francis, Villon the gallows and prison, Racine his conversion, Descartes has his tile-heated room, and Rousseau his kitchen stove.[7] If you achieve celebrity, they'll find you a badge without you ever having given

6. In his meditations, the mystic Johann Tauler (1297–1361) endeavored to strip the mind of all forms, images, and ideas. Jacob applied Tauler's method in both the spiritual and aesthetic realms, to him inseparable. Spiritual progress is integrating God into oneself through contemplation so as to become as naught in God's infinity; artistic progress is integrating ordinary experience through objectivization and distancing so as to take one's place humbly in the immensity of Art.

7. Léon-Marie Bloy (1846–1917), writer and Christian thinker, attacked contemporary society in his pamphlets and books. In his novels, *Salvation by the*

the matter any thought. [. . .] Being yourself is the hardest task of all but also the most rewarding because in being yourself you are bound to be original. They'll create a legend around you as they did in my case with no help from me.[8] No need to go looking for adventures, they come to the reader's minds even if you'd never stirred from your table. (I haven't stirred from my table a single day in my life.) If we dig deep into our hearts, into our bodies, we find feelings there, and these feelings, when we have laid them bare, emerge, go far and wide and give rise to the legendary adventures we have never had. [. . .]

There is no one I love more than I do you. I shall strive to be worthy of your friendship.

M.J.

Saint-Benoît, August 6, 1937

* * *

Devoured with remorse—at having discouraged you by my bored indifference. [. . .] The mark of literature is that it bears no resemblance to Literature: we write a masterpiece only with that part of us which is distinct from Literature, creating by that very distinctiveness a *new* literature. Think a page; set it down in writing when you've examined it fore and aft. Many are called but there are few chosen to be found in Paradise. That sentence from Scripture means that you have to be exceptional to earn your way into Paradise. Literature bears ample witness to this truth. Only the monsters get into Paradise. So make your brain an abscess: when the abscess is ready, you'll be operated on. But if you don't put yourself through this process of cerebral congestion at your age, when will you? So use your mind unflaggingly, every minute, every hour, every second, and dive deep! Dive deep into the present, into situation and character. Only the diver can rise triumphantly from the depths, clutching the magic ring.

M.J.

Toul, April 26, 1938

Jews, The Pilgrim of the Absolute, At the Threshold of Apocalypse, writing in a biblical style, he pleads urgently for change in our hypocritical society. Jacob disliked his preachy tone.

8. This is not entirely true in Jacob's case. On occasion, Jacob said to his friends: "Let's lead the researcher astray and cultivate our own legend."

* * *

I am not in the least blasé. It's just that I have a capacity for boredom, and once I'm bored, not many things in the realm of art can rekindle my interest.

What do I care that your poems were deeply felt, if they give me the impression that they aren't? I'd rather have a stirring lie than a truth not clearly brought out. Strive to be a good liar, or to state your truth forcefully. . . . Sincerity, eh? . . . I remember a priest who used to weep in the pulpit . . . everybody laughed. Instead he should have looked for better ways to communicate his sincerity.[9]

You are utterly mistaken in thinking I am not aware how much you have improved. A totally blind person couldn't fail to see how much you've improved. Nor do I in the least consider that you and your poetry are of no further concern; otherwise why would I be striving to make you improve? Which does not mean that when you do, I take the credit.

I have to poke you in order to keep you moving along. If I handed you compliments, you would think you had reached your goal, whereas in fact you've got to demand more of yourself.

The right poetic image is the one found after long, deep contemplation of the object to be depicted.

To be sure, I know nothing about your love-life any more than you do about mine. Make yours known to the world; the public would like nothing better.

I thank you for your respect. I much prefer your friendship. In return, receive my unchanging devotion.

* * *   July 15, 1938

My Dears, yesterday there was a young donkey ready to go, in watercolor and gouache. You're to come and get it. Plus donkeys

---

9. Definition after definition tumbles forth in Jacob's correspondence, revealing his preoccupation with sincerity. "Art is a lie, but a great artist never lies." "Sincerity means having your topic in your blood." "A sincere work is forceful enough to endow an illusion with life." "A work can be based on a lie, but the way in which the author expresses it makes it sincere, as he can express only what is in himself." The multiple definitions all boil down to his conviction that only the "pearl" (which Federico Fellini called the autobiography of the oyster) is sincere and moving. The rest is merely "déjà vu," the development of dictionaries, inkwells, and the books of others.

various. . . . Roger Lannes will be here this evening and I think tomorrow the 3rd.[10] Take heed.

On Sunday I sold a drawing, *The Dipsomaniac Lady*, to an American for 500 francs, through Maratier the dealer from Toulouse; in addition, there's another sale in the works: the view of Paris facing my bed, but this one won't go through. He considers 2,000 francs too expensive. . . . Anyhow, we'll see.

Messiaen wants someone to get him a job sweeping streets in Montargis.[11]

I've done a little view of the donkey road, near Germiny. The little preliminary sketch is yours. The painting is very elaborate.

I think, Marcel my dear, that it might be indispensable for you *to learn to write prose*. The language in your poems would develop into something as a result. I know the truth is unpleasant. My duty is to tell you these things; yours will consist of not holding it against me.

August 2, 1938

* * *

In literature, until you have learned to write high-quality, erasure-based prose, you have learned nothing, you are nothing. This high-quality prose can exist only through knowledge of the exact word. The exact word can be assessed only against the marble touchstone of coarse, everyday language such as is spoken by a farmer or a caretaker. In that context, a word emerges and takes on its full connotation: that is what I would or could have explained to you, were I but permitted to speak in your "inhibiting" presence.

[August 1938]

* * *

My dear B . . . s, how many drawings (1920 or 1938 vintage), how very many drawings I owe you for all your kindness and all your kindnesses![12] The paintbrushes are the right sort; they were im-

10. Writer, poet, publisher, Roger Lannes (born 1909) was a friend of Cocteau who influenced his poetry. He came to visit Jacob in Saint-Benoît and described Jacob's first retreat there in his novel *La Peine capitale* (Denoël, 1942).

11. Alain Messiaen (born 1911), a Catholic poet, is the son of the poet Cécile Sauvage and brother of the celebrated composer Olivier Messiaen. He submitted his first poems to Jacob, who promptly told him: "Your poetry is so awful that you can't help but become a great poet." Besides poetry, Messiaen also wrote a *History of Music*, in which he gives lyrical interpretations of his favorite musical works. In their letters to one another, he and Jacob often discussed the German mystic Anne-Catherine Emmerich whom they both admired.

12. The plural B . . . s refers to Marcel Béalu and his first wife Marguerite.

mediately put to use and, seized with renewed fervor, I have made a fresh start on the hideous 1900-model landau, to which I have added a red velvet veranda.[13] Since I don't know which of you to thank, thank you both! I've also written a note to Mr. Gayon. I turn toward God, who has provided so many remedies for my afflictions and my loneliness by sending friendly angels who shower me with paintbrushes, not to mention the beret I am wearing and everything I touch that has come to me directly or indirectly from you. May He repay you a hundredfold!

* * *   August 31, 1938

For a long time I signed my letters "Poor Max"; now it's friend Max.

I won't be going to Montargis any more: my mission to you is completed: your latest poem shows that you have found your feet, through your own agency and not through me.

* * *   October 20, 1938

Think your sentences before you write them; otherwise they are like the continuous humps of bubbly soap that used to be left in the bowl instead of becoming the iridescent globes desired by the pipes of our childhood. A line of poetry is an iridescent soap-bubble.

* * *   March 1, 1940

The way *to write* dialogue is to put, into a mouth, only words chosen after long deliberation and which that particular mouth is bound to utter. A miserly woman in *The Bouchaballe Property* says: "You can sit down if you want: in this house seats don't have to be paid for the way they are in church." An authoritarian person says: "Sit down!" From another person, who prides himself on his courtesy: "Do please have a seat." These are the little details that give life to your writings . . .

Using dirty words is no way to please the reader. People are supersaturated with Céline, Zola, and even Sartre. You'll attract your reader if you present individuals who stand out, which means individuals conceived and thought about by you over a long period

13. Marcel Béalu told Maria Green that Jacob is describing a gouache he was working on, depicting a carriage with a red velvet top. Landaus had fold-down tops. Béalu later owned the gouache.

of time; and the more thoroughly you have understood them the more sharply they will stand out. Collect the vocabulary of that gentleman you mean to create; when you're alone, imitate his gestures and his little habits; puff out your cheeks if he's stout; make yourself obese if that's how he looks. The time for writing is not when you're staring at a sheet of paper but when you're lying in bed unable to sleep, when you're out walking or when you're selling hats. You have to believe in the existence of these heroes; in that way you will find the right words for them to say. Dirty words don't contribute anything. The reader is quite capable of putting in "shit" at the point where your hero must have said that, without your having written it: "shit" never made a story come alive.

Happy the day that brings you! I enjoy your visits and I enjoy your being here. I have no new poems: in the way of literary production I have my regular morning meditation.

Nov. 19, 1940

* * *

I'm having or rather I've just had a lengthy bout of asthma and bronchitis. I'm ashamed of myself, wretch that I am! Not the tiniest little poem! And on the other hand scarcely any painting. I'm living in something like a state of dread: the Jewish shopkeepers in Paris are being forced out of their stores. I have a brother sixty years old who is out of work; he's trying to find a job as a laborer or caretaker. Here in Saint-Benoît there is still prosperity of sorts, except for soap, and wool for darning socks!!! My occasional visitors like what I'm doing or what I've done: the place in Nantes has *The Jolly Ploughman* and is requesting gouaches, which I can't send for lack of stiff enough cardboard: the situation is ludicrous and outrageous.

January 23, 1941

* * *

Cadou has sent me a splendid poem and insists that you show me "The Crusades."[14] That's not the reason I'm writing. I want to ask you not to tell anyone where it was we met. To you it seems perfectly natural, but it could be dangerous for the people in that house. I'm

14. The friendship with René Guy Cadou (1920–51) started when, at the age of seventeen, Cadou sent his first volume of poetry to Max Jacob, who immediately recognized Cadou's great talent. Cadou based his poetry on the Jacobian aesthetic principles of "inner life" and "suffering." His *Esthétique de Max Jacob*

sure you find it all very funny, but any day I may have to deal with the police a second time and be obliged to account for my movements. The Jews aren't the only ones being watched and harassed. Just think for a moment! After all, they've unsealed my letters and noted the addresses of my friends; they can just as easily take down the addresses of people who've had me in their home. You are right when you say that I have influential people protecting me and I now know from a reliable source that such is the case. . . . [15] It could very well cease to be the case when Mr. This, Mr. That, or Mr. So-and-So cease to enjoy the power they presently have. You have no notion what is meant by "police" and "living in constant danger." Surely you would not use terms such as "dramatizing" or "fanciful imaginings" to describe facts that have reduced my family to despair, to illness brought on by grief, and the like. Did I tell you *Paul Petit is under arrest* and being held *in Fresnes?* [16] I'm in touch with various people by mail, to see what can be done. So . . . mum's the word, and be careful what you say or what you write. Don't mention the painter in connection with me, so as to avoid making trouble for *him*.[17] I shall urge Cadou to be similarly discreet. . . . It may be too late.

February 1942

(Seghers, 1956) is a succession of excerpts from letters in which the older poet imparts the secrets of poetic creation to the younger one.

15. Max Jacob placed so much faith in his influential protectors that he refused his friends' urgings to hide at the home of their relatives. He is referring, most likely, to Roger Toulouse's friend, the German officer Albert Buesche, an art critic who knew and appreciated Jacob's work and had an important position at the German newspaper *Parizer Zeitung* during the Occupation of France.

16. Paul Petit, the career diplomat, scholar, and translator of Kierkegaard, invited Jacob to Rome in 1925. It was through him that the poet became acquainted with the Danish thinker. Paul Petit edited the only anthology of Jacob before the present one. (It was in French.) Arrested for his participation in the French Underground in 1942, Petit was first held in Fresnes, a town near Paris, where the Germans detained political prisoners during the Occupation, and he died in Buchenwald.

17. Jacob discovered the "great eighteen-year-old painter" Roger Toulouse of Orleans in 1936. Gertrude Stein, who loved Toulouse's paintings, claimed that Jacob discovered young talent before anybody else. Painter, sculptor, and poet, Toulouse exhibited in more than twenty French cities and in a dozen countries. He also published three volumes of poetry. His works are sought after in the United States today. Toulouse's articles on Max Jacob as poet and painter and his portraits of him enhanced Jacob's fame.

—I still have wood and heat, not for very long. I'm getting enough to eat.

*   *   *

Yesterday I had a visit from a farming gentleman: an agriculturist, a Catholic, with a wife and family I think, at any rate a man in his forties.[18] He confided that he wrote poetry and had come to show it to me. He then proceded to parade past my eyes five pages of insipid verse like color-prints for nice young ladies. . . . I wouldn't have mentioned the incident to you, were it not for the fact that all of a sudden I experienced a magnificent burst of light. In a bland poem about the ploughman, suddenly this phrase = the *faithful* horses! This phrase and its adjective struck me as so poignant, so realistic, so evocative, so pale and intense the way Chateaubriand is pale and intense, that I began to talk to him as one talks to a man.

"Let's see, now," I said to him, "suppose you had to describe that fire there, what would you say?"

Whereupon the man thought deeply for a time, and then came out with: "*hesitant* fire!" It was exactly the word that fitted. I advised him always to write like that, that is, to put down on paper only what had been deeply thought and felt.

February 27 [1942], Saint Antigone,
Patron saint of Jean Cocteau

18. The farming gentleman was Gaston Girard, later mayor of Jacob's adopted town of Saint-Benoît-sur-Loire, and member of the National Assembly. When Girard died in 1990 at the age of ninety-one, a newspaper referred to the "hesitant fire" episode described here.